The Dandy Book 1971

A riddle, a riddle, tell me, please,
What's red and round and sails the seas?
My drawing's a clue to give you a guide,
And if you don't know, the answer's inside.

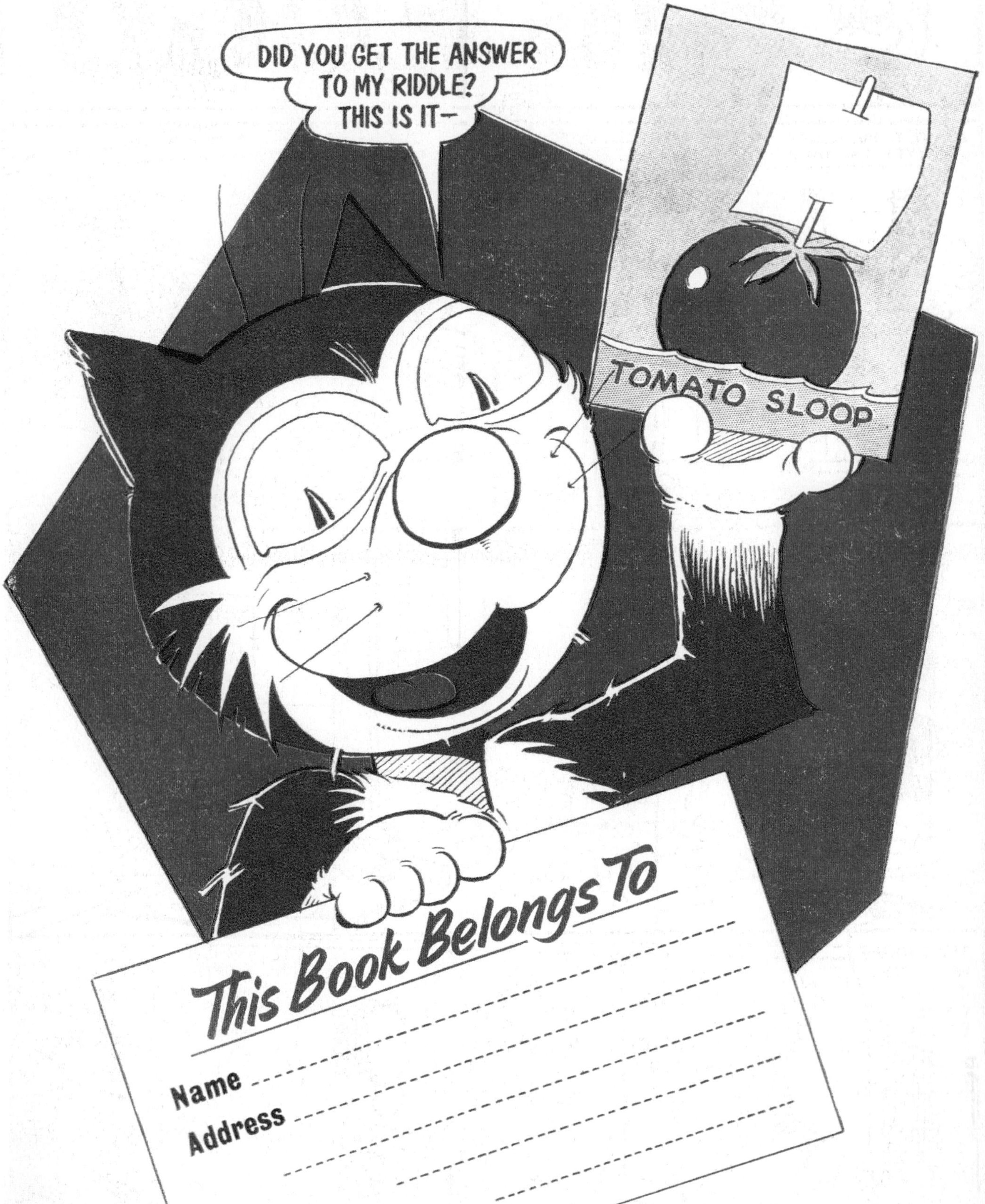
DID YOU GET THE ANSWER TO MY RIDDLE? THIS IS IT—
TOMATO SLOOP
This Book Belongs To
Name
Address

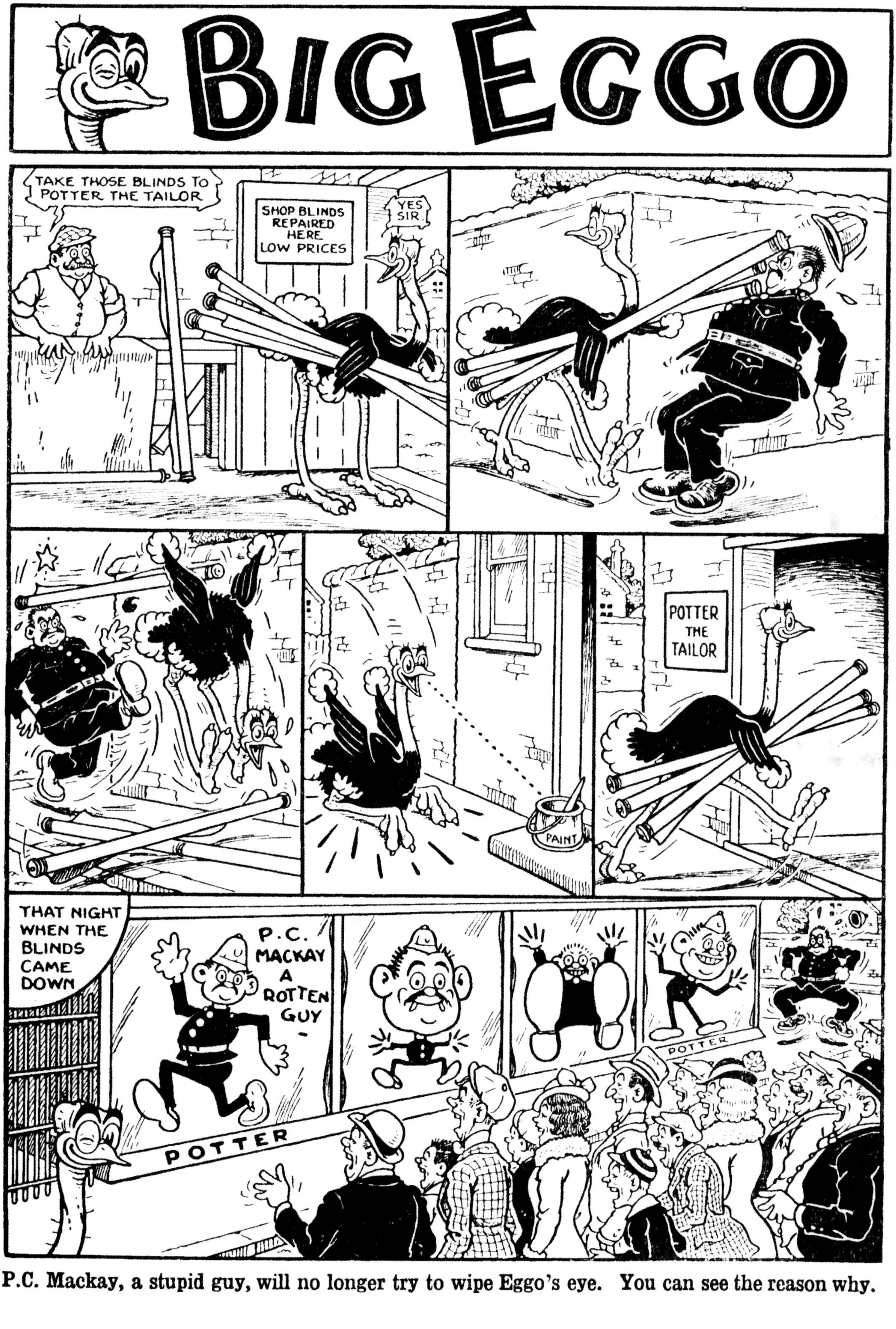
BIG EGGO
TAKE THOSE BLINDS TO POTTER THE TAILOR
SHOP BLINDS REPAIRED HERE LOW PRICES
YES SIR.
POTTER THE TAILOR
PAINT
THAT NIGHT WHEN THE BLINDS CAME DOWN
P.C. MACKAY A ROTTEN GUY
POTTER
POTTER

P.C. Mackay, a stupid guy, will no longer try to wipe Eggo's eye. You can see the reason why.

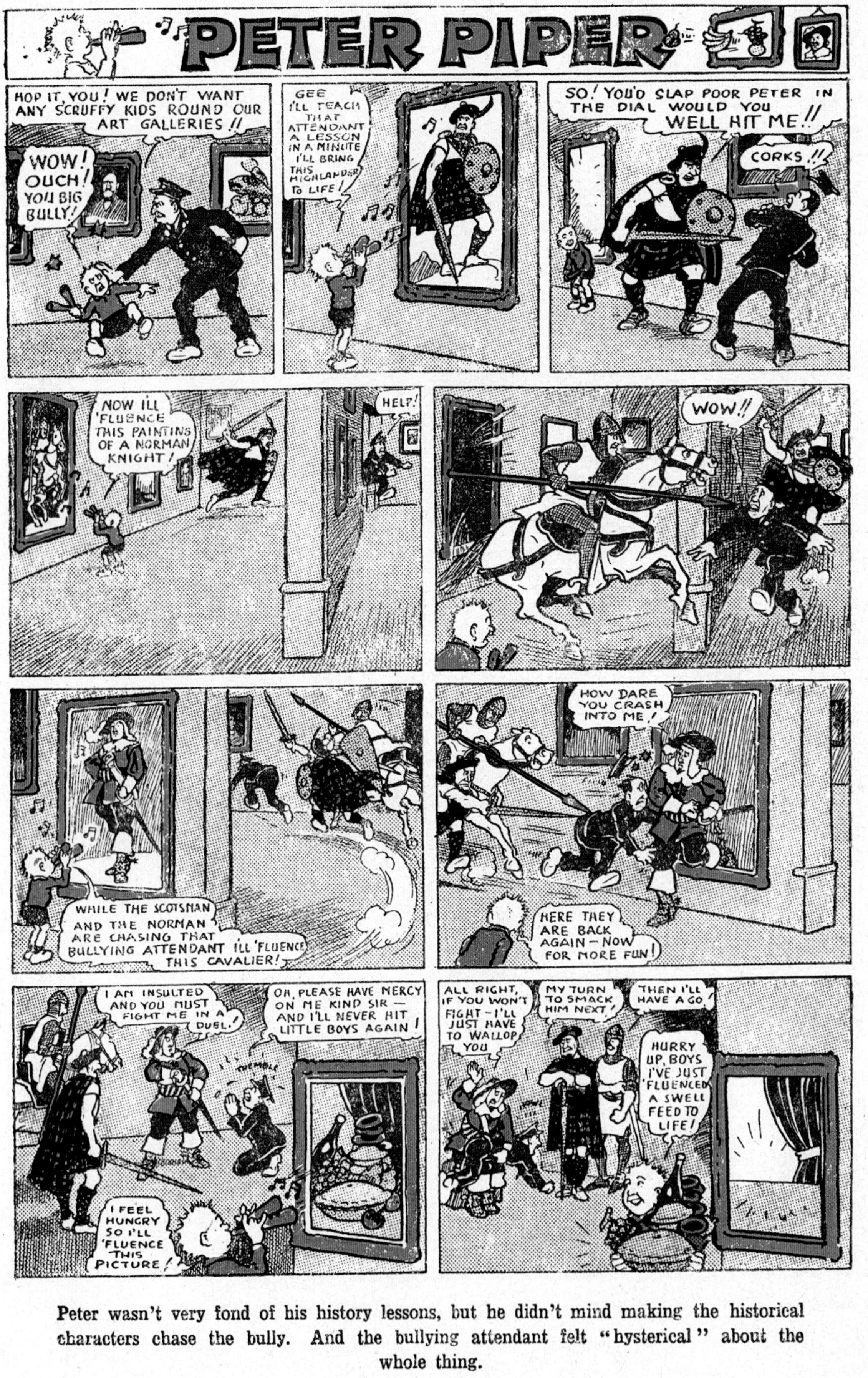
PETER PIPER
HOP IT, YOU! WE DON'T WANT ANY SCRUFFY KIDS ROUND OUR ART GALLERIES !!
WOW! OUCH! YOU BIG BULLY!
GEE I'LL TEACH THAT ATTENDANT A LESSON IN A MINUTE I'LL BRING THIS HIGHLANDER TO LIFE!
SO! YOU'D SLAP POOR PETER IN THE DIAL WOULD YOU WELL HIT ME!!
CORKS!!
NOW I'LL 'FLUENCE THIS PAINTING OF A NORMAN KNIGHT!
HELP!
WOW!!
WHILE THE SCOTSMAN AND THE NORMAN ARE CHASING THAT BULLYING ATTENDANT I'LL 'FLUENCE THIS CAVALIER!
HOW DARE YOU CRASH INTO ME!
HERE THEY ARE BACK AGAIN—NOW FOR MORE FUN!
I AM INSULTED AND YOU MUST FIGHT ME IN A DUEL!
OH, PLEASE HAVE MERCY ON ME KIND SIR—AND I'LL NEVER HIT LITTLE BOYS AGAIN!
I FEEL HUNGRY SO I'LL 'FLUENCE THIS PICTURE!
ALL RIGHT, IF YOU WON'T FIGHT—I'LL JUST HAVE TO WALLOP YOU
MY TURN TO SMACK HIM NEXT!
THEN I'LL HAVE A GO!
HURRY UP, BOYS I'VE JUST 'FLUENCED A SWELL FEED TO LIFE!

Peter wasn't very fond of his history lessons, but he didn't mind making the historical characters chase the bully. And the bullying attendant felt "hysterical" about the whole thing.

GOOD KING COKE
HE'S STONEY BROKE

COKE the FIRST
COKE the SECOND
COKE the THIRD
THIS SPACE IS RESERVED FOR A PORTRAIT OF GOOD KING COKE
OH DEAR, MY PICTURE WON'T LOOK VERY NOBLE HANGING ON THE WALL WITH MY ANCESTORS. THEY WERE ALL SUCH BRAVE MEN AND I'VE NEVER DONE ANY DARING DEEDS

Our Good King Coke went out one day
To see the Royal Gallery,
Where, placed in state all down the hall,
Portraits of kings hung on the wall.

Pictures of Coke Kings, One, Two, and Three,
Portrayed great feats of gallantry,
But Coke was not too glad to know
A space was left for him to go.

I WANT YOU TO PAINT SOMETHING ON THE WALL FOR ME
ANYTHING YOU SAY, SIRE
THAT'S FINE - IT LOOKS JUST LIKE A REAL MOUNTAIN TOP

King Coke had done no daring feat
Which could with these brave men compete,
And so he knew he'd have to fake
A scene, for reputation's sake !

His artist pal was keen to do
Whatever King Coke asked him to,
And so he painted on the wall
A mountain peak, snow-capped and tall.

I WANT YOU TO MAKE AN ELARGEMENT OF THIS
SMILE, PLEASE
LEDGE
A KING TO BE PROUD OF!
WHAT A MOUNTAINEER!
WHAT A NERVE!
GOOD KING COKE

Now Good King Coke (the wise old man),
Told the photographer his plan,
" I'll stand here on a ledge, you see,
And you must take a snap of me."

The photograph was duly framed,
And Good King Coke was then proclaimed,
By all his loyal country folks,
" The Noblest One of all the Cokes !"

DOLLY DIMPLE
NOT SO SIMPLE

LOOK UNCLE I'VE PAINTED A PICTURE OF A HORSE!
HA! HA! VERY FUNNY MY DEAR!
— BUT NOT VERY LIKE A REAL HORSE!
IDEA

A horse young Dolly Dimple drew,
With her new coloured paint.
She showed it to her uncle who
Thought it was very quaint.

So poor wee Dolly got no praise.
(She thought it very cruel.)
She said, " I'll make sure that he pays.
I'll make him feel a fool."

OH DEAR! SOME-ONE MUST HAVE THROWN A SNOW-BALL THROUGH THE WINDOW!

When Uncle went off for a stroll,
Out came her paints again.
She painted what looked like a hole
Upon the window pane.

When uncle came back home and found
The broken pane of glass,
He looked at it, and then he frowned,
" We cannot let this pass ! "

I MUST GET A MAN TO MEND THE BROKEN WINDOW!
NOW I'LL WIPE IT OFF!
WELL! WHERE'S THE BROKEN WINDOW?

So off he went to get a man
To mend the damage done.
Young Dolly laughed and knew her plan
Was working—Oh, what fun !

Then Dolly wiped the paint mark off,
And when the pair came back,
The man, of course, began to scoff
And said, " Well, where's the crack ? "

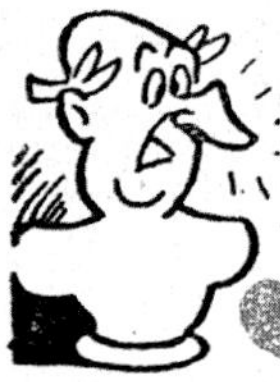

JULIUS SNEEZER

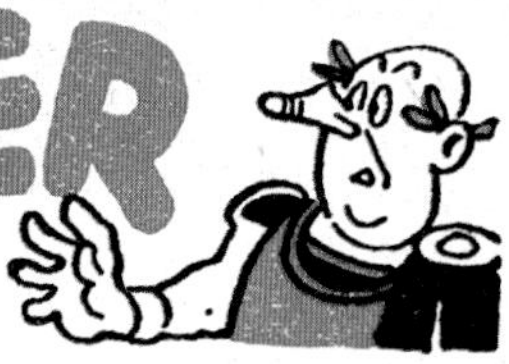

THE SNEEZING CAESAR

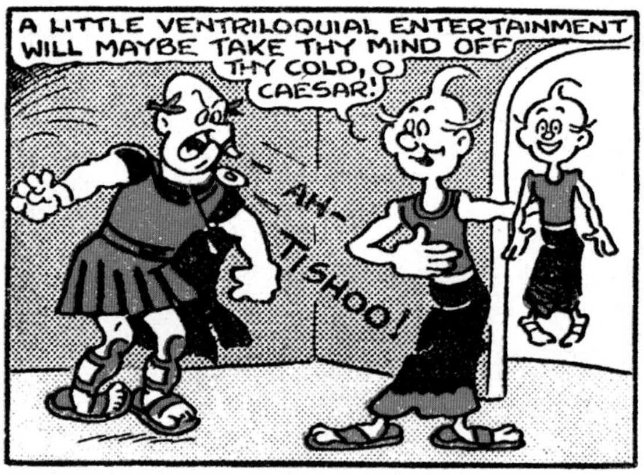
A LITTLE VENTRILOQUIAL ENTERTAINMENT WILL MAYBE TAKE THY MIND OFF THY COLD, O CAESAR!
AH-TISHOO!

A great ventriloquist one day
Said, " Sire, I'll charm your cold away.
Now just stand there and I will do
An entertainment all for you."

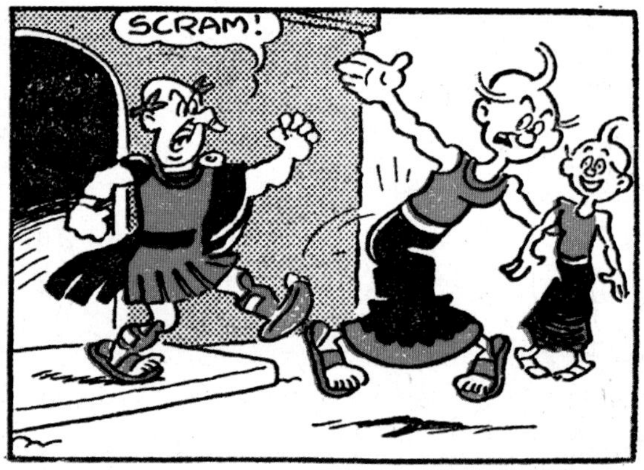
SCRAM!

The King was in an angry mood.
He yelled, " Get out, you'd be no good.
No one can cure my sneeze I know.
Now leave my presence. Out you go."

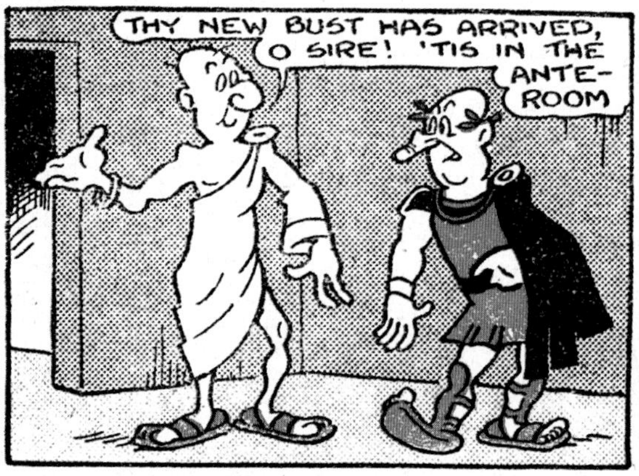
THY NEW BUST HAS ARRIVED, O SIRE! 'TIS IN THE ANTE-ROOM

Then Julius met a sculptor who
Said, " I have made that bust of you.
It's in the ante-room right now.
Your living image, sire, I vow."

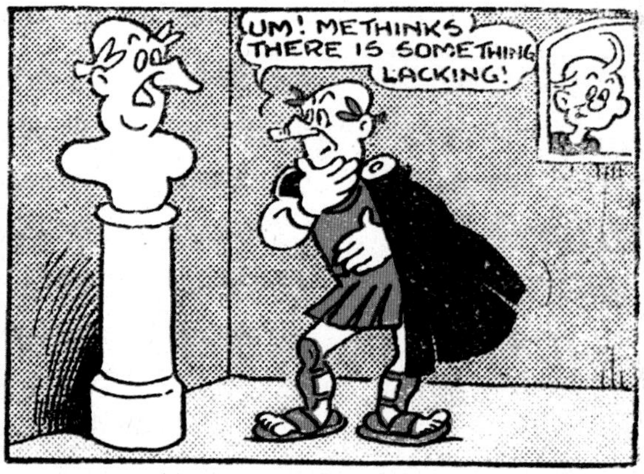
UM! METHINKS THERE IS SOMETHING LACKING!

" Me thinks there's something lacking there "
Said Sneezer. " That bust looks so bare."
He rubbed his chin in sore dismay.
Said he, " I look cold made of clay."

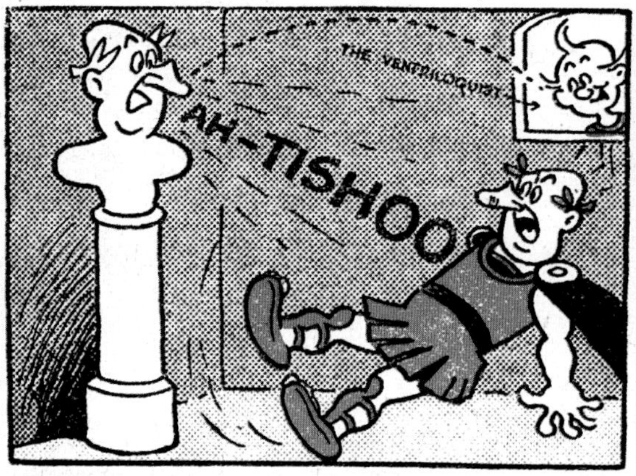
THE VENTRILOQUIST
AH-TISHOO

Then the ventriloquist passed by,
And stopped when he heard Sneezer's sigh.
" I'll add the something. He'll be pleased,"
Said he, and then the clay bust sneezed.

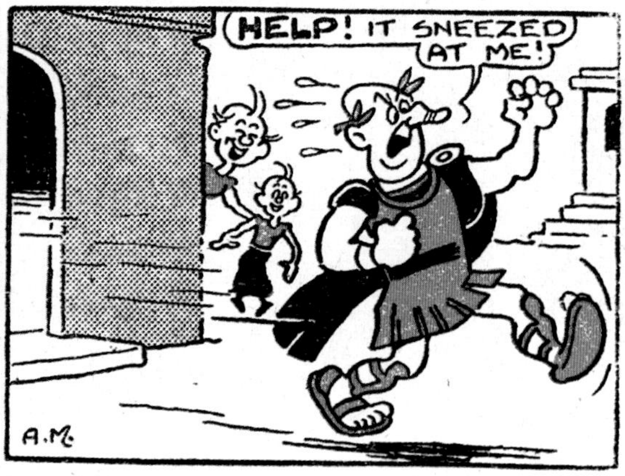
HELP! IT SNEEZED AT ME!
A.M.

" Oh, help !" cried Sneezer as he fled.
" It sneezed at me," poor Julius said.
The young ventriloquist in glee
Just laughed to see old Sneezer flee.

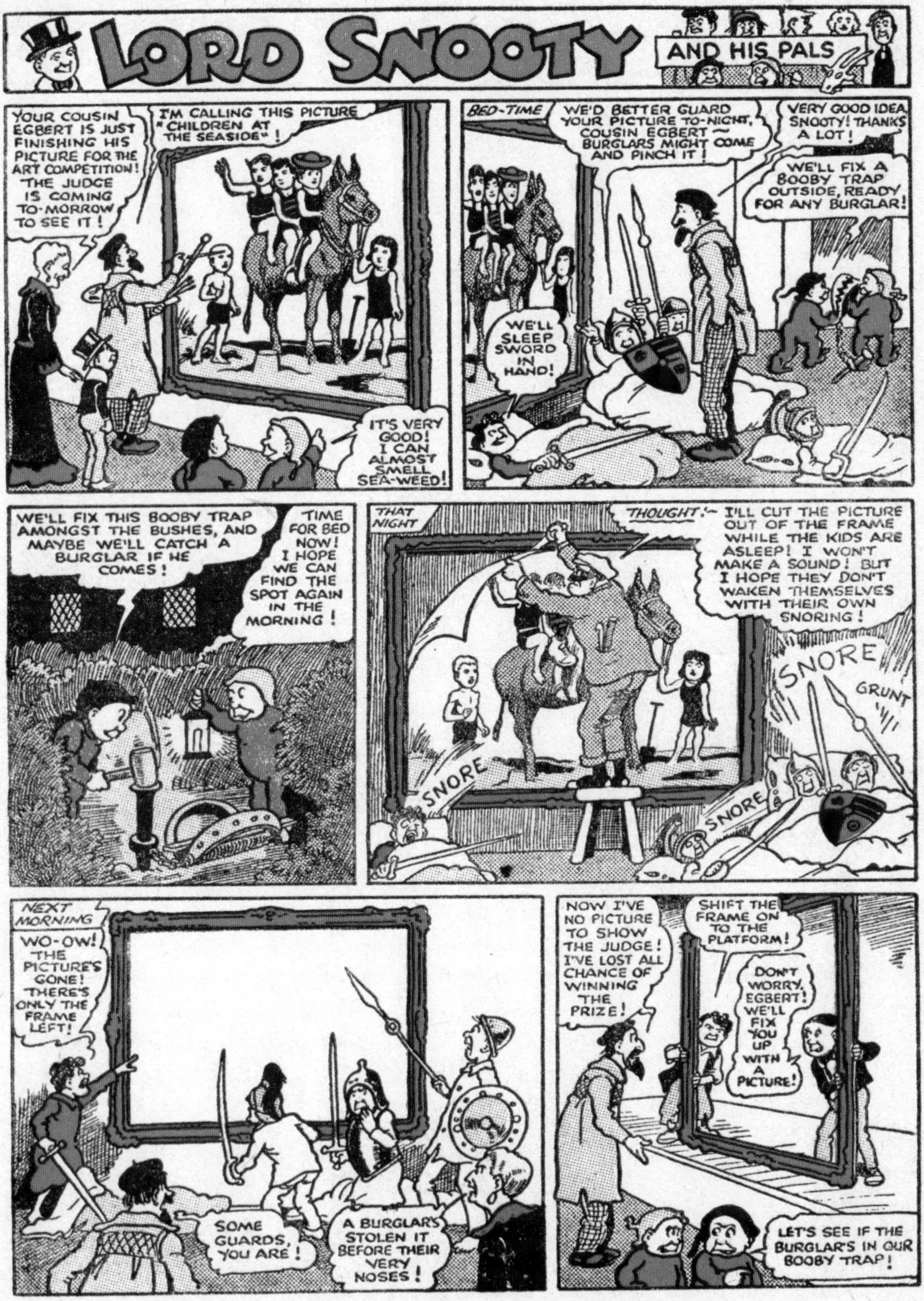
LORD SNOOTY
AND HIS PALS
YOUR COUSIN EGBERT IS JUST FINISHING HIS PICTURE FOR THE ART COMPETITION! THE JUDGE IS COMING TO-MORROW TO SEE IT!
I'M CALLING THIS PICTURE "CHILDREN AT THE SEASIDE"!
IT'S VERY GOOD! I CAN ALMOST SMELL SEA-WEED!
BED-TIME
WE'D BETTER GUARD YOUR PICTURE TO-NIGHT, COUSIN EGBERT — BURGLARS MIGHT COME AND PINCH IT!
VERY GOOD IDEA, SNOOTY! THANKS A LOT!
WE'LL FIX A BOOBY TRAP OUTSIDE, READY FOR ANY BURGLAR!
WE'LL SLEEP SWORD IN HAND!
WE'LL FIX THIS BOOBY TRAP AMONGST THE BUSHES, AND MAYBE WE'LL CATCH A BURGLAR IF HE COMES!
TIME FOR BED NOW! I HOPE WE CAN FIND THE SPOT AGAIN IN THE MORNING!
THAT NIGHT
THOUGHT:— I'LL CUT THE PICTURE OUT OF THE FRAME WHILE THE KIDS ARE ASLEEP! I WON'T MAKE A SOUND! BUT I HOPE THEY DON'T WAKEN THEMSELVES WITH THEIR OWN SNORING!
SNORE
GRUNT
SNORE
SNORE
NEXT MORNING
WO-OW! THE PICTURE'S GONE! THERE'S ONLY THE FRAME LEFT!
SOME GUARDS, YOU ARE!
A BURGLAR'S STOLEN IT BEFORE THEIR VERY NOSES!
NOW I'VE NO PICTURE TO SHOW THE JUDGE! I'VE LOST ALL CHANCE OF WINNING THE PRIZE!
SHIFT THE FRAME ON TO THE PLATFORM!
DON'T WORRY, EGBERT! WE'LL FIX YOU UP WITH A PICTURE!
LET'S SEE IF THE BURGLAR'S IN OUR BOOBY TRAP!

The judge didn't know that the picture was just a frame-up, with Lord Snooty behind it all!

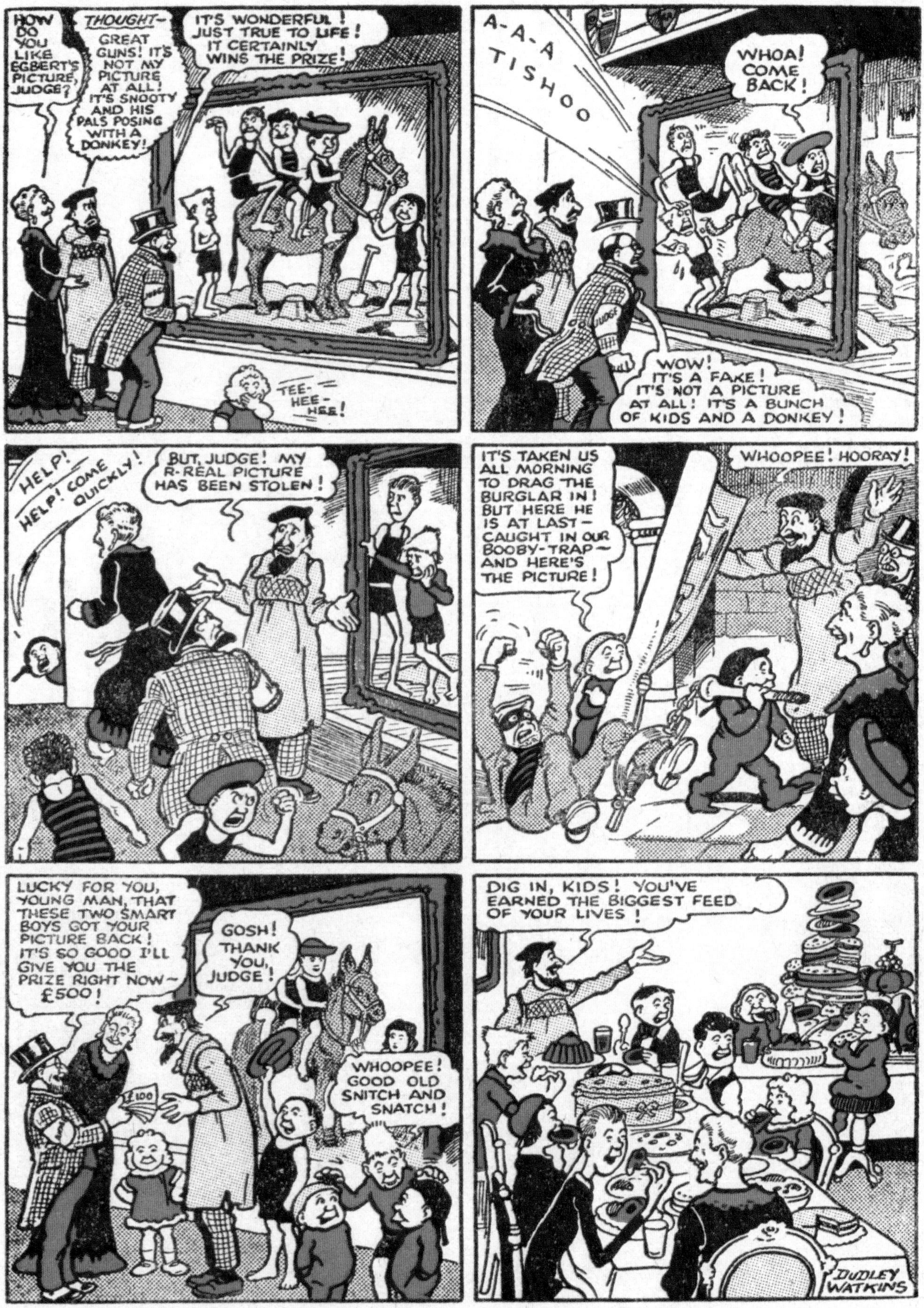
HOW DO YOU LIKE EGBERT'S PICTURE, JUDGE?
THOUGHT— GREAT GUNS! IT'S NOT MY PICTURE AT ALL! IT'S SNOOTY AND HIS PALS POSING WITH A DONKEY!
IT'S WONDERFUL! JUST TRUE TO LIFE! IT CERTAINLY WINS THE PRIZE!
TEE-HEE-HEE!
A-A-A TISHOO
WHOA! COME BACK!
WOW! IT'S A FAKE! IT'S NOT A PICTURE AT ALL! IT'S A BUNCH OF KIDS AND A DONKEY!
HELP! HELP! COME QUICKLY!
BUT, JUDGE! MY R-REAL PICTURE HAS BEEN STOLEN!
IT'S TAKEN US ALL MORNING TO DRAG THE BURGLAR IN! BUT HERE HE IS AT LAST— CAUGHT IN OUR BOOBY-TRAP— AND HERE'S THE PICTURE!
WHOOPEE! HOORAY!
LUCKY FOR YOU, YOUNG MAN, THAT THESE TWO SMART BOYS GOT YOUR PICTURE BACK! IT'S SO GOOD I'LL GIVE YOU THE PRIZE RIGHT NOW— £500!
GOSH! THANK YOU, JUDGE!
WHOOPEE! GOOD OLD SNITCH AND SNATCH!
DIG IN, KIDS! YOU'VE EARNED THE BIGGEST FEED OF YOUR LIVES!
DUDLEY WATKINS

However, that picture soon faded when the real one returned, and everyone was pleased with the results.

Without a doubt — the finest rubber out!

SAMMY'S SUPER RUBBER

I CAN REMOVE THAT POST FOR YOU WITH MY MAGIC RUBBER!
THAT'S FINE—!

OUR Sammy's here. He's feeling grand!
He'll always lend a helping hand.
Now here's a workman chap to-day
Who has a post to take away.

That job gives Sammy lots of fun.
His rubber is a magic one—
It rubs the post right out of sight,
Much faster than a streak of light.

NOW YOU CAN REMOVE YOURSELF!
NASTY FELLOW! JUST FOR THAT I'LL PAINT IT IN AGAIN!

But our pal gets no thanks at all.
Instead, the workman makes Sam bawl,
By giving him a nasty clout
That nearly lays our young pal out.

But Sammy's not a boy to fret.
Just watch! He'll get his own back yet!
He quickly brings some paint, and then
He makes the post appear again!

I TOLD YOU TO REMOVE THIS POST, NOT PAINT IT!
?
SERVES HIM RIGHT!
YOU'RE FIRED!
A M.

Then Phil, the foreman, comes along.
He's red with rage, for something's wrong.
His orders have been disobeyed
By Jake, the fellow with the spade.

The foreman kicks out with his foot,
And gives that nasty lad the boot.
While Sammy chuckles, Jake feels sore.
He won't hurt Sammy any more.

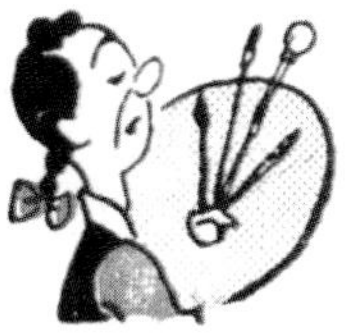

Swanky Lanky Liz

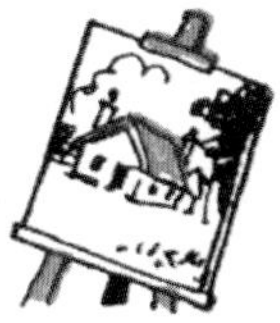

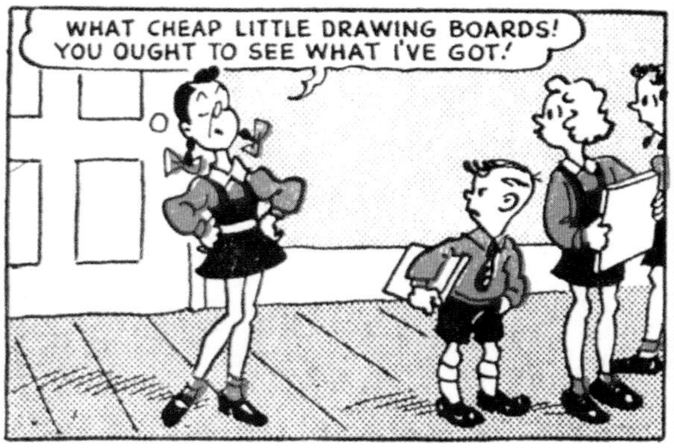
WHAT CHEAP LITTLE DRAWING BOARDS! YOU OUGHT TO SEE WHAT I'VE GOT!

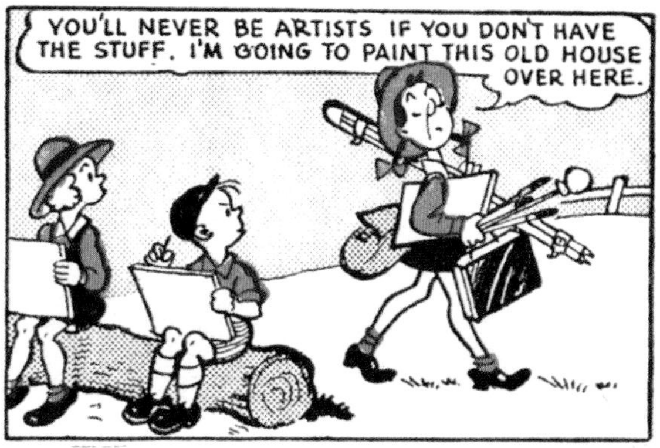
YOU'LL NEVER BE ARTISTS IF YOU DON'T HAVE THE STUFF. I'M GOING TO PAINT THIS OLD HOUSE OVER HERE.

The kids are going out to sketch,
But Liz is looking snooty.
" What drawing-boards !" she says. " I'll fetch
My own, for it's a beauty."

Out in the country then the class
All start to sketch away.
But Liz just looks and makes to pass.
" You're no good," hear her say.

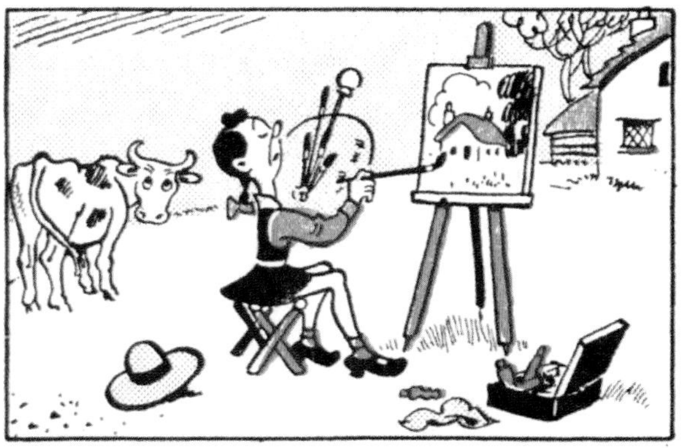

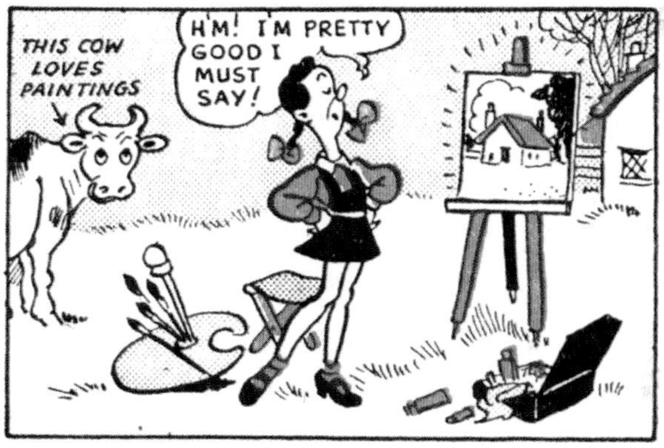
THIS COW LOVES PAINTINGS
H'M! I'M PRETTY GOOD I MUST SAY!

Then setting up her board and stand,
Liz paints a country scene.
She holds the palette in her hand
And paints the foreground green.

Her picture done, Liz gives a smile.
She says, " I'm pretty good."
A cow who's watching her the while,
Likes paint instead of food.

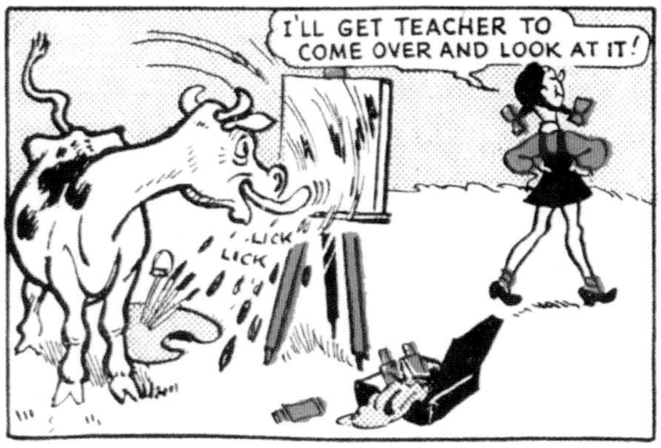
I'LL GET TEACHER TO COME OVER AND LOOK AT IT!
LICK
LICK

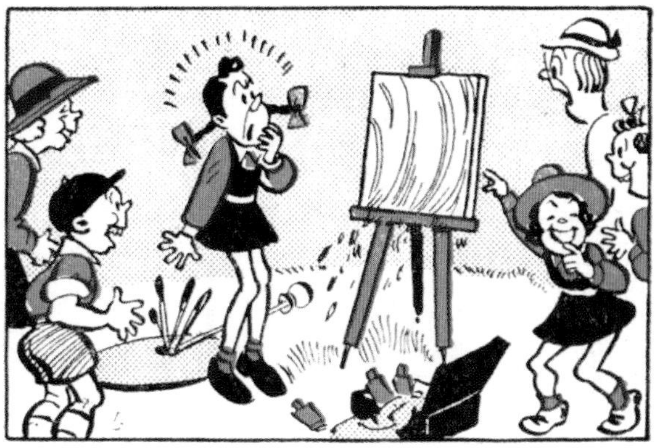

Liz says, " I'll go for teacher now
And let her see real art."
She walks away, and then the cow
On her work makes a start.

When Liz comes back—oh, what a shock !
The teacher's looking wild.
The pupils then with laughter rock.
Liz feels a stupid child.

Dickie tries to do his duty — But Old Ma Murphy is no beauty!

OLD MA MURPHY
THE STRONG-ARM SCHOOL-MA'RM
YOU WILL STAY IN, DICKIE DOPE, AND DRAW A REALLY PRETTY PICTURE.
I'LL BE BACK IN TEN MINUTES— SO GET BUSY!

THE biggest dunce at Old Ma's school
Is Dickie Dope, the champion fool.
He's being kept in at school today
And it looks like being a long, long stay.

For Dickie's got to make a sketch
Before he goes — Unlucky wretch!
His breath is all that he can draw,
Or lemonade up through a straw!

SILLY ISLES
OH DEAR— THIS IS GOING TO BE HARD.
SILLY ISLES
I'LL HAVE TO DRAW SOME-THING.

So Dickie thinks and Dickie ponders,
The minutes tick past as he wonders;
But on the paper — not a stroke!
Come on, lad, give your brains a poke!

Hooray! At last he's made a start
To this outstanding work of art.
What will it be, do you suppose?
A landscape view? — A blooming rose?

WELL - WHERE IS THAT PRETTY PICTURE?
I COULDN'T DRAW A PRETTY PICTURE SO I SKETCHED YOU!
A.M.

Well, Dick, we hope your picture's good
For teacher's in an angry mood;
Her brow is set, she wears a frown —
Your sketch will maybe soothe her down.

Alas, poor Dick! He's very rude,
Although he's done the best he could;
And surely you'll agree with him —
That face ain't pretty — it's pretty GRIM!

Dennis is dressed up — but he'd rather be messed up!

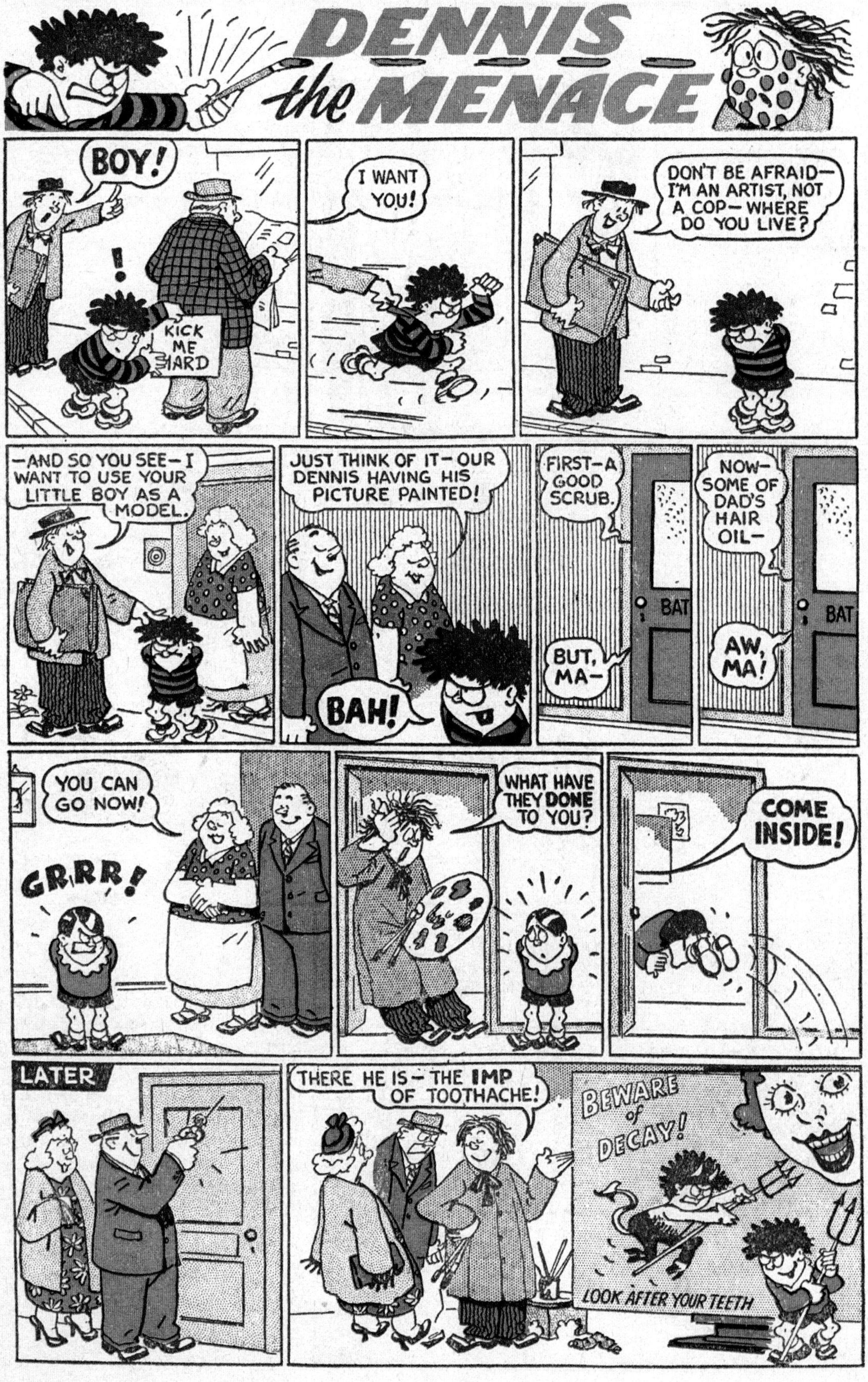
DENNIS the MENACE
BOY!
KICK ME
I WANT YOU!
DON'T BE AFRAID— I'M AN ARTIST, NOT A COP— WHERE DO YOU LIVE?
—AND SO YOU SEE— I WANT TO USE YOUR LITTLE BOY AS A MODEL.
JUST THINK OF IT— OUR DENNIS HAVING HIS PICTURE PAINTED!
BAH!
FIRST— A GOOD SCRUB.
BUT, MA—
BAT
NOW— SOME OF DAD'S HAIR OIL—
AW, MA!
BAT
YOU CAN GO NOW!
GRRR!
WHAT HAVE THEY DONE TO YOU?
COME INSIDE!
LATER
THERE HE IS— THE IMP OF TOOTHACHE!
BEWARE of DECAY!
LOOK AFTER YOUR TEETH

Dennis has no " Beano." WOW! — There's going to be big trouble now!

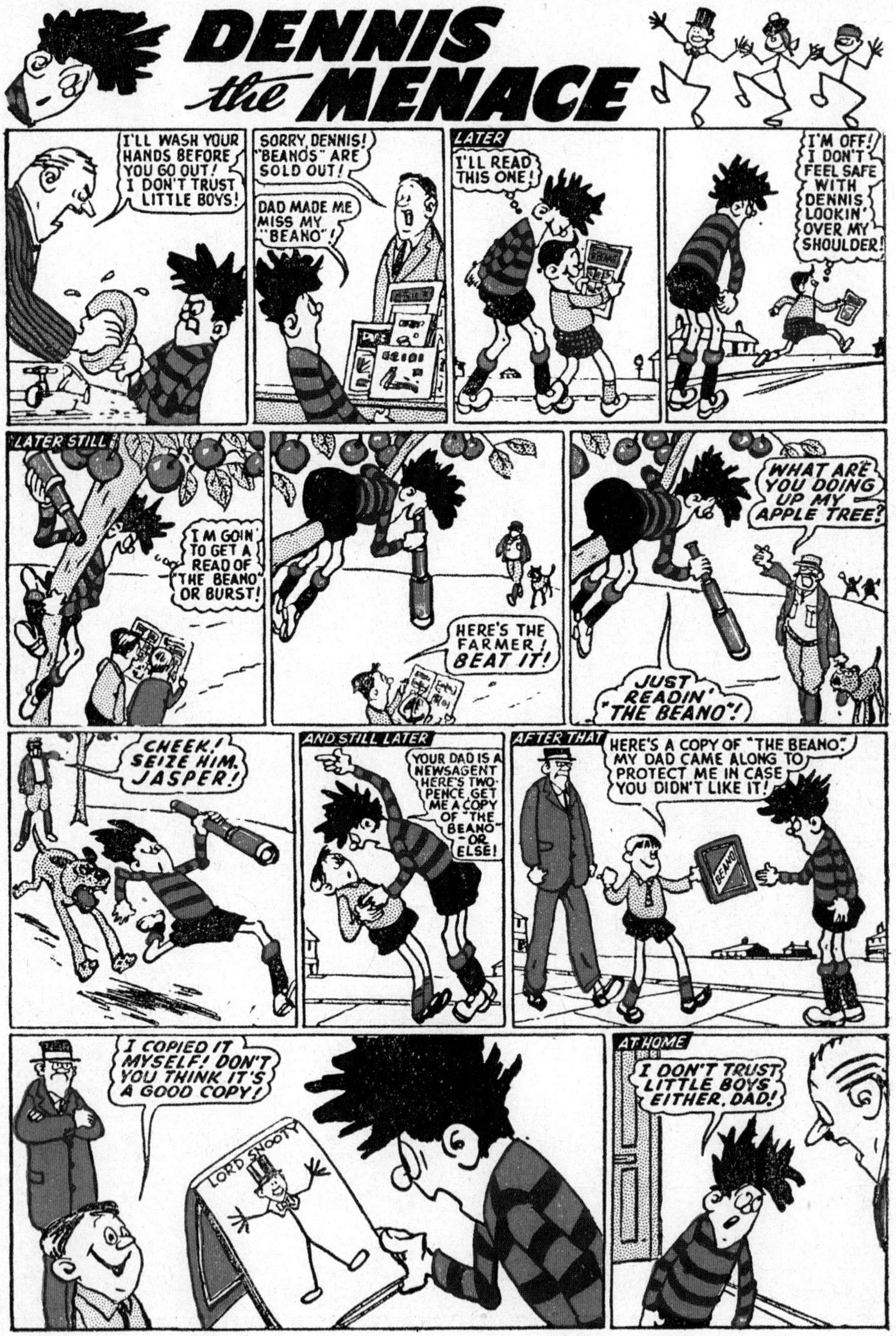
DENNIS the MENACE
I'LL WASH YOUR HANDS BEFORE YOU GO OUT! I DON'T TRUST LITTLE BOYS!
SORRY, DENNIS! "BEANOS" ARE SOLD OUT!
DAD MADE ME MISS MY "BEANO"!
LATER
I'LL READ THIS ONE!
I'M OFF! I DON'T FEEL SAFE WITH DENNIS LOOKIN' OVER MY SHOULDER!
LATER STILL
I'M GOIN' TO GET A READ OF "THE BEANO" OR BURST!
HERE'S THE FARMER! BEAT IT!
WHAT ARE YOU DOING UP MY APPLE TREE?
JUST READIN' "THE BEANO"!
CHEEK! SEIZE HIM, JASPER!
AND STILL LATER
YOUR DAD IS A NEWSAGENT. HERE'S TWOPENCE. GET ME A COPY OF "THE BEANO" —OR ELSE!
AFTER THAT
HERE'S A COPY OF "THE BEANO". MY DAD CAME ALONG TO PROTECT ME IN CASE YOU DIDN'T LIKE IT!
BEANO
I COPIED IT MYSELF! DON'T YOU THINK IT'S A GOOD COPY?
LORD SNOOTY
AT HOME
I DON'T TRUST LITTLE BOYS EITHER, DAD!

Out of the museum poor Dad goes — For tampering with Cromwell's nose.

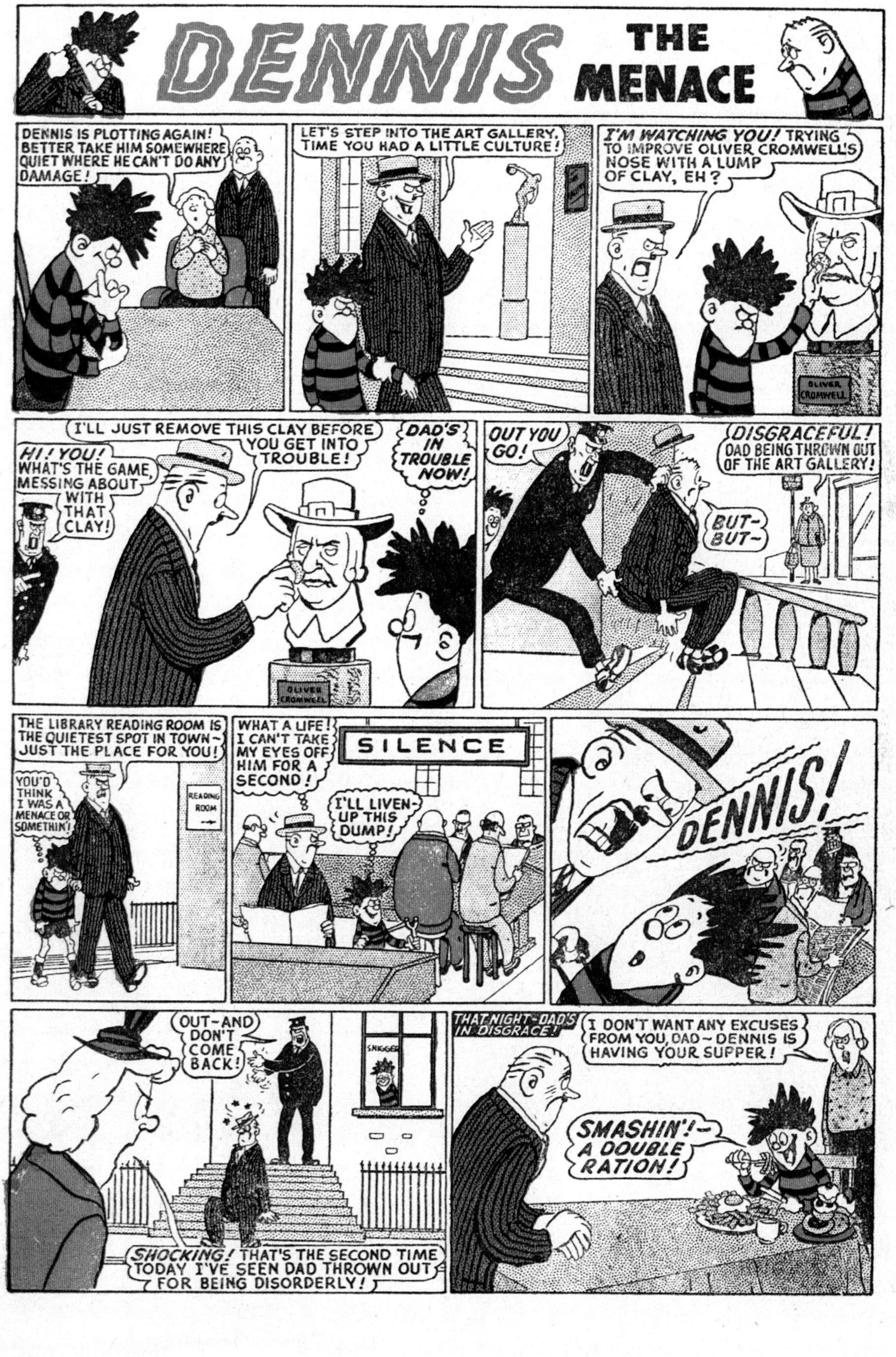
DENNIS THE MENACE
DENNIS IS PLOTTING AGAIN! BETTER TAKE HIM SOMEWHERE QUIET WHERE HE CAN'T DO ANY DAMAGE!
LET'S STEP INTO THE ART GALLERY. TIME YOU HAD A LITTLE CULTURE!
I'M WATCHING YOU! TRYING TO IMPROVE OLIVER CROMWELL'S NOSE WITH A LUMP OF CLAY, EH?
OLIVER CROMWELL
I'LL JUST REMOVE THIS CLAY BEFORE YOU GET INTO TROUBLE!
HI! YOU! WHAT'S THE GAME, MESSING ABOUT WITH THAT CLAY!
DAD'S IN TROUBLE NOW!
OLIVER CROMWELL
OUT YOU GO!
DISGRACEFUL! DAD BEING THROWN OUT OF THE ART GALLERY!
BUT-BUT-
THE LIBRARY READING ROOM IS THE QUIETEST SPOT IN TOWN~ JUST THE PLACE FOR YOU!
YOU'D THINK I WAS A MENACE OR SOMETHIN'!
READING ROOM
WHAT A LIFE! I CAN'T TAKE MY EYES OFF HIM FOR A SECOND!
SILENCE
I'LL LIVEN-UP THIS DUMP!
DENNIS!
OUT-AND DON'T COME BACK!
SNIGGER
SHOCKING! THAT'S THE SECOND TIME TODAY I'VE SEEN DAD THROWN OUT FOR BEING DISORDERLY!
THAT NIGHT-DAD'S IN DISGRACE!
I DON'T WANT ANY EXCUSES FROM YOU, DAD~ DENNIS IS HAVING YOUR SUPPER!
SMASHIN'!- A DOUBLE RATION!

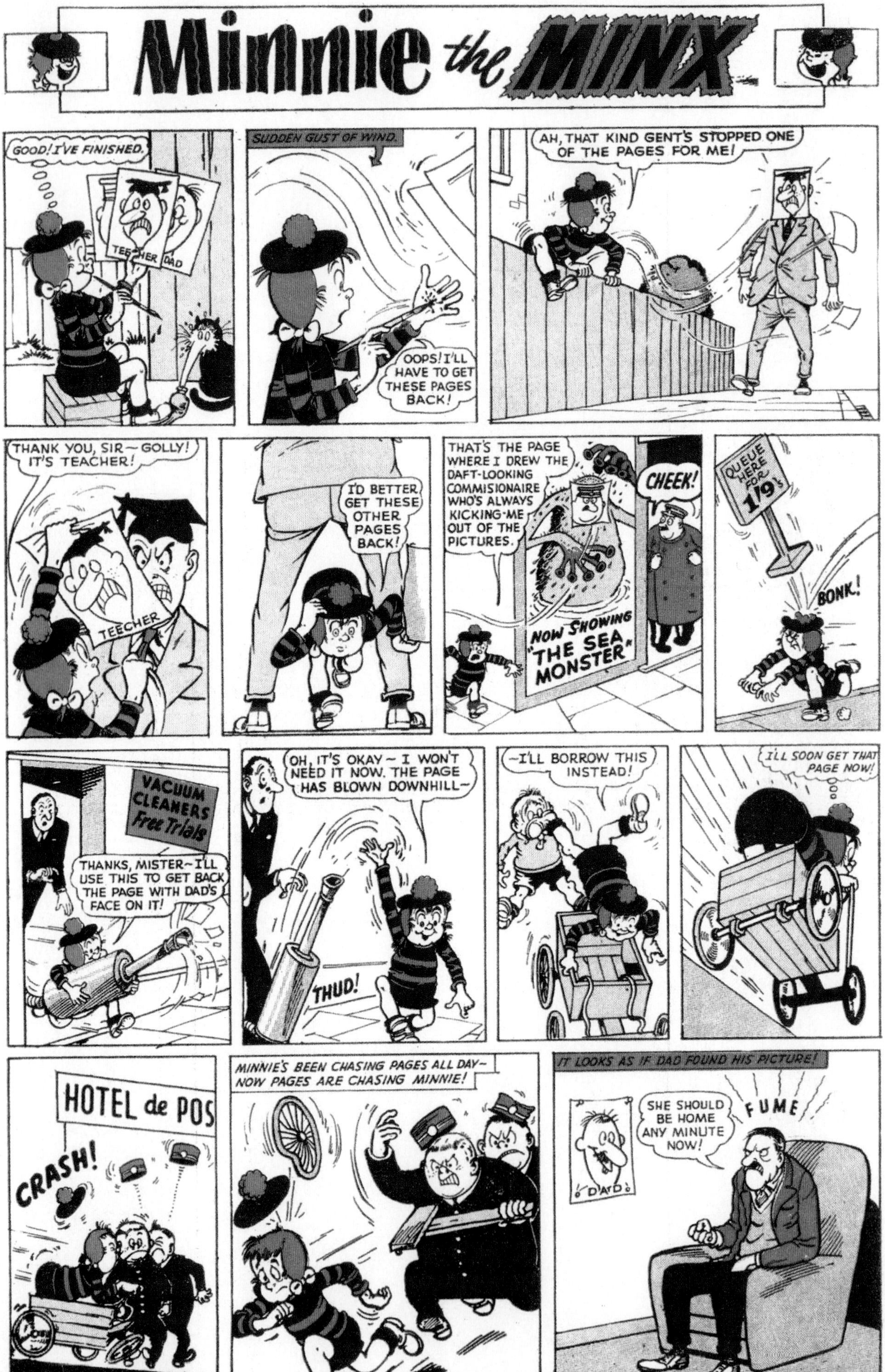
Minnie the MINX
GOOD! I'VE FINISHED.
TEECHER
DAD
SUDDEN GUST OF WIND.
OOPS! I'LL HAVE TO GET THESE PAGES BACK!
AH, THAT KIND GENT'S STOPPED ONE OF THE PAGES FOR ME!
THANK YOU, SIR ~ GOLLY! IT'S TEACHER!
TEECHER
I'D BETTER GET THESE OTHER PAGES BACK!
THAT'S THE PAGE WHERE I DREW THE DAFT-LOOKING COMMISIONAIRE WHO'S ALWAYS KICKING ME OUT OF THE PICTURES.
CHEEK!
NOW SHOWING "THE SEA MONSTER"
QUEUE HERE FOR 1/9's
BONK!
VACUUM CLEANERS Free Trials
THANKS, MISTER ~ I'LL USE THIS TO GET BACK THE PAGE WITH DAD'S FACE ON IT!
OH, IT'S OKAY ~ I WON'T NEED IT NOW. THE PAGE HAS BLOWN DOWNHILL ~
THUD!
~ I'LL BORROW THIS INSTEAD!
I'LL SOON GET THAT PAGE NOW!
HOTEL de POS
CRASH!
MINNIE'S BEEN CHASING PAGES ALL DAY ~ NOW PAGES ARE CHASING MINNIE!
IT LOOKS AS IF DAD FOUND HIS PICTURE!
DAD
SHE SHOULD BE HOME ANY MINUTE NOW!
FUME

Look out for laughs—SHE's taking photographs.

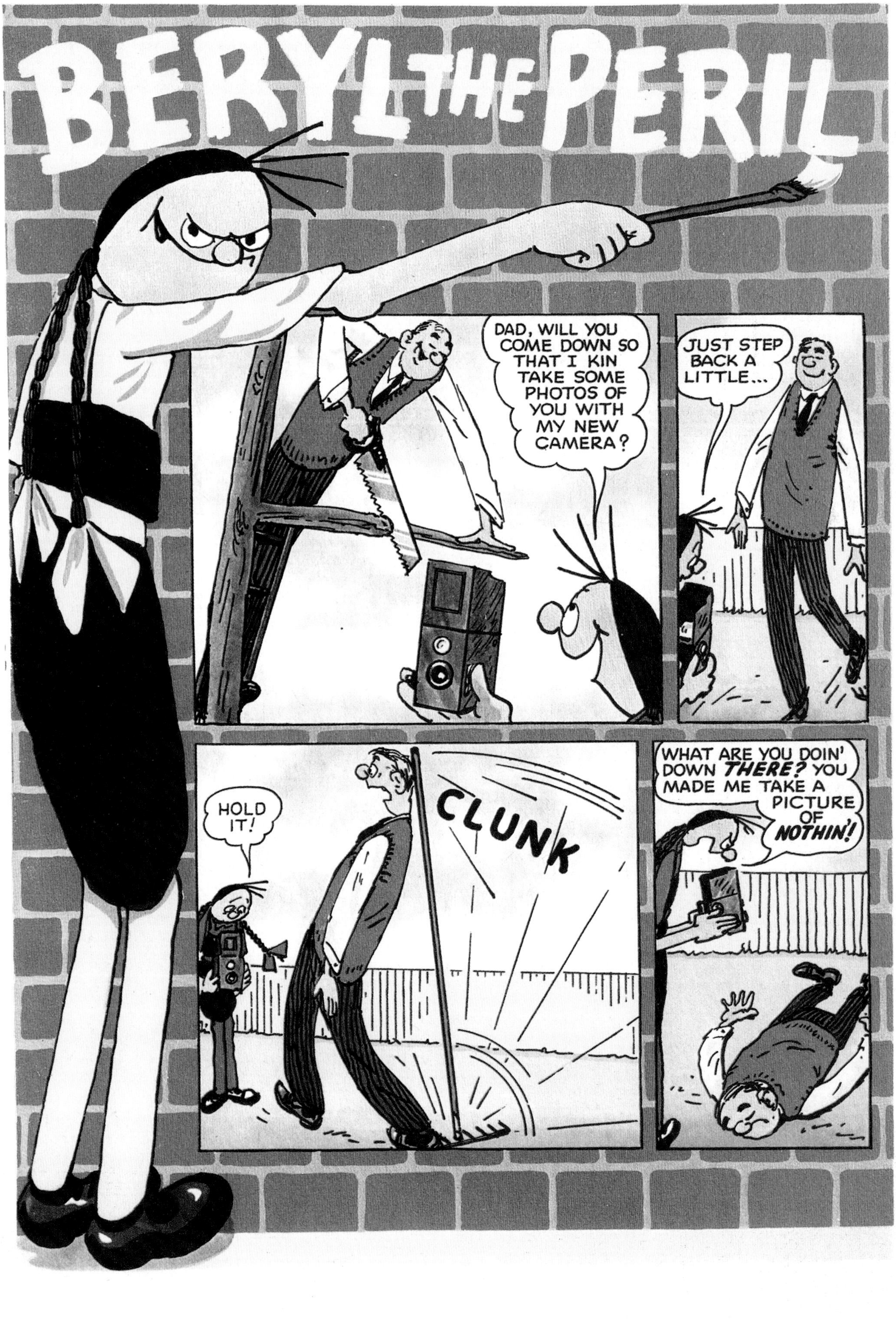
BERYL THE PERIL
DAD, WILL YOU COME DOWN SO THAT I KIN TAKE SOME PHOTOS OF YOU WITH MY NEW CAMERA?
JUST STEP BACK A LITTLE...
HOLD IT!
CLUNK
WHAT ARE YOU DOIN' DOWN THERE? YOU MADE ME TAKE A PICTURE OF NOTHIN'!

Dad's doing fine—till he casts his line.

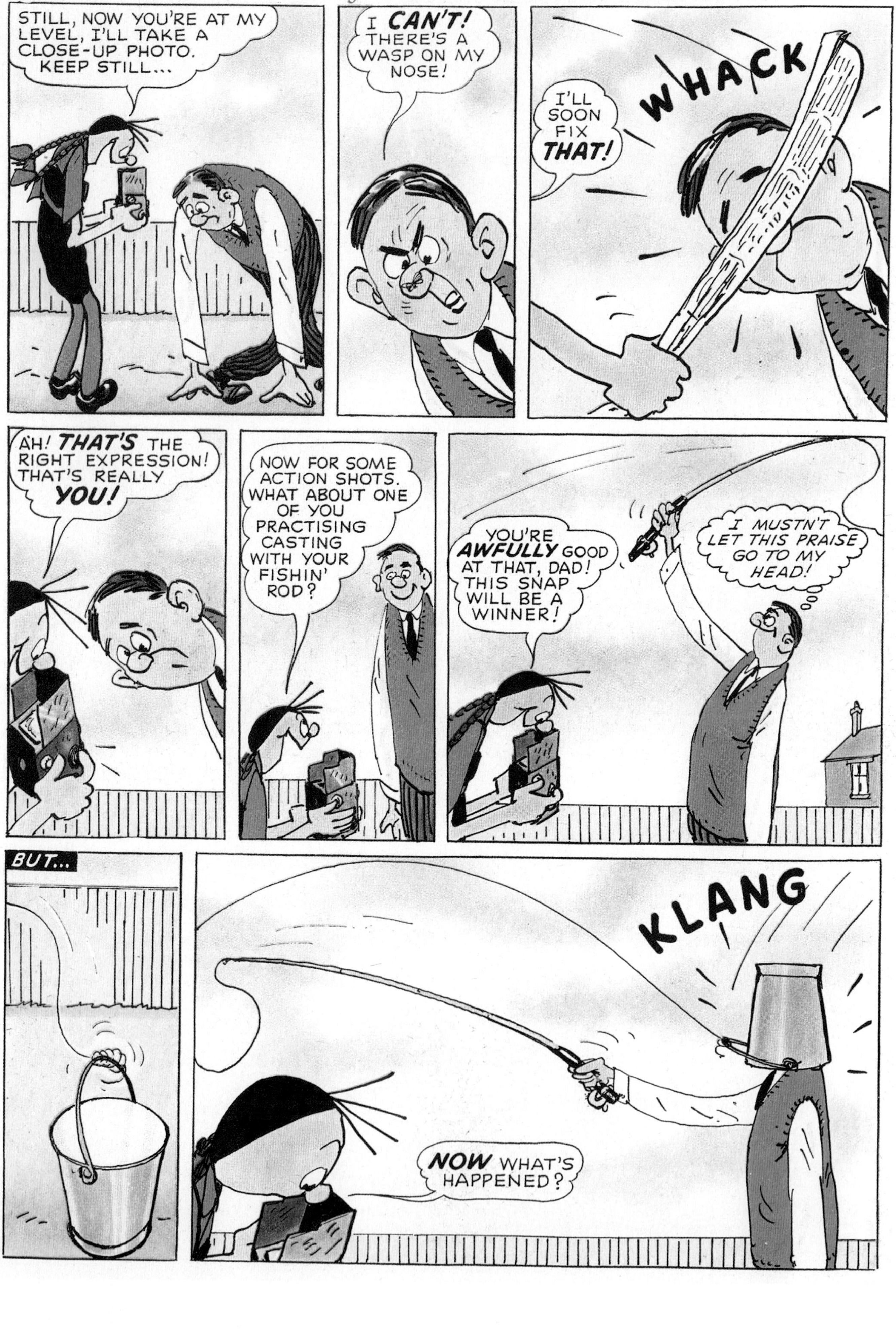
STILL, NOW YOU'RE AT MY LEVEL, I'LL TAKE A CLOSE-UP PHOTO. KEEP STILL...
I CAN'T! THERE'S A WASP ON MY NOSE!
I'LL SOON FIX THAT!
WHACK
AH! THAT'S THE RIGHT EXPRESSION! THAT'S REALLY YOU!
NOW FOR SOME ACTION SHOTS. WHAT ABOUT ONE OF YOU PRACTISING CASTING WITH YOUR FISHIN' ROD?
YOU'RE AWFULLY GOOD AT THAT, DAD! THIS SNAP WILL BE A WINNER!
I MUSTN'T LET THIS PRAISE GO TO MY HEAD!
BUT...
KLANG
NOW WHAT'S HAPPENED?

Trust Beryl to make—a big mistake.

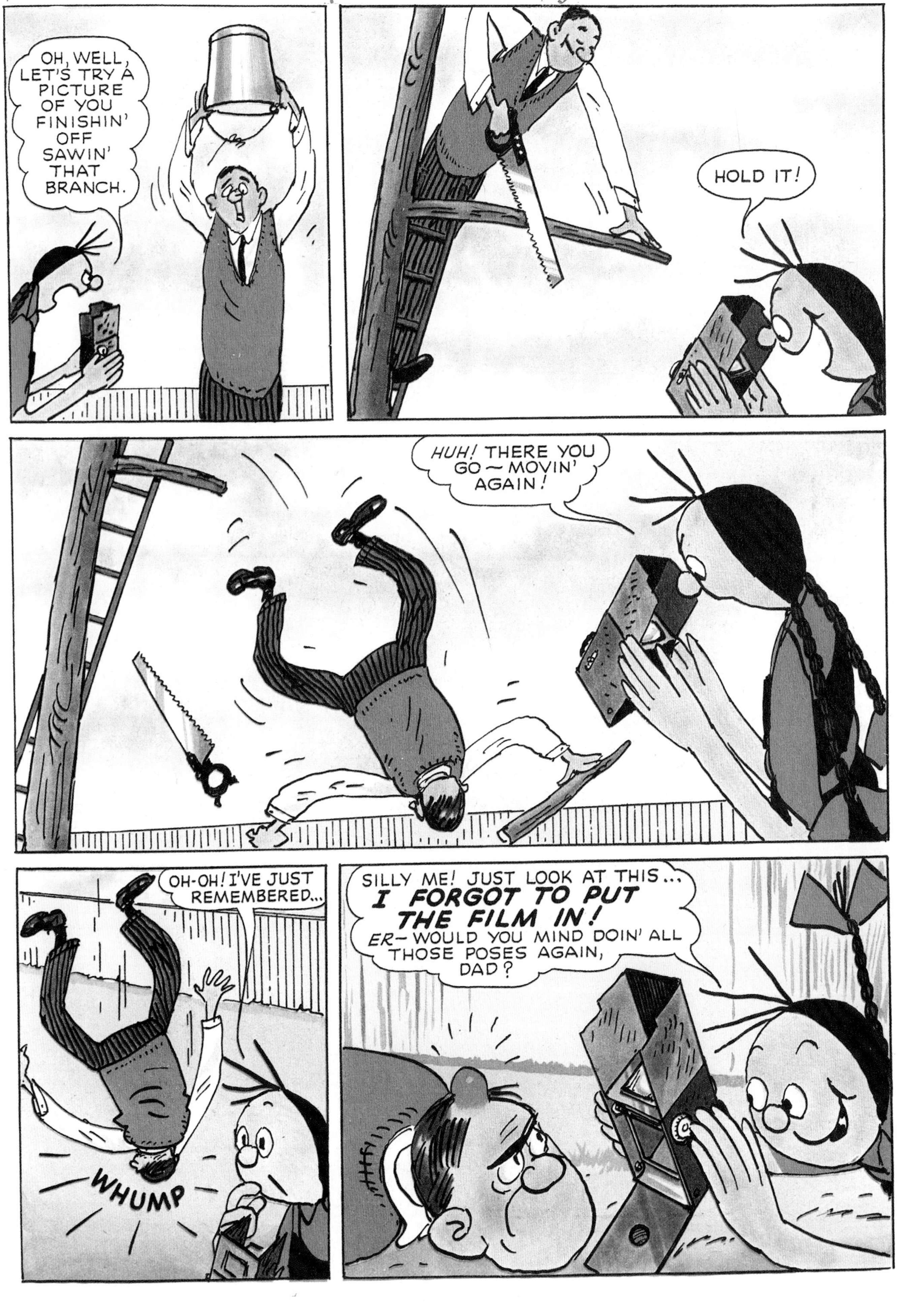
OH, WELL, LET'S TRY A PICTURE OF YOU FINISHIN' OFF SAWIN' THAT BRANCH.
HOLD IT!
HUH! THERE YOU GO ~ MOVIN' AGAIN!
OH-OH! I'VE JUST REMEMBERED...
WHUMP
SILLY ME! JUST LOOK AT THIS... I FORGOT TO PUT THE FILM IN! ER— WOULD YOU MIND DOIN' ALL THOSE POSES AGAIN, DAD?

Bash Street poetry will make you laugh all day!

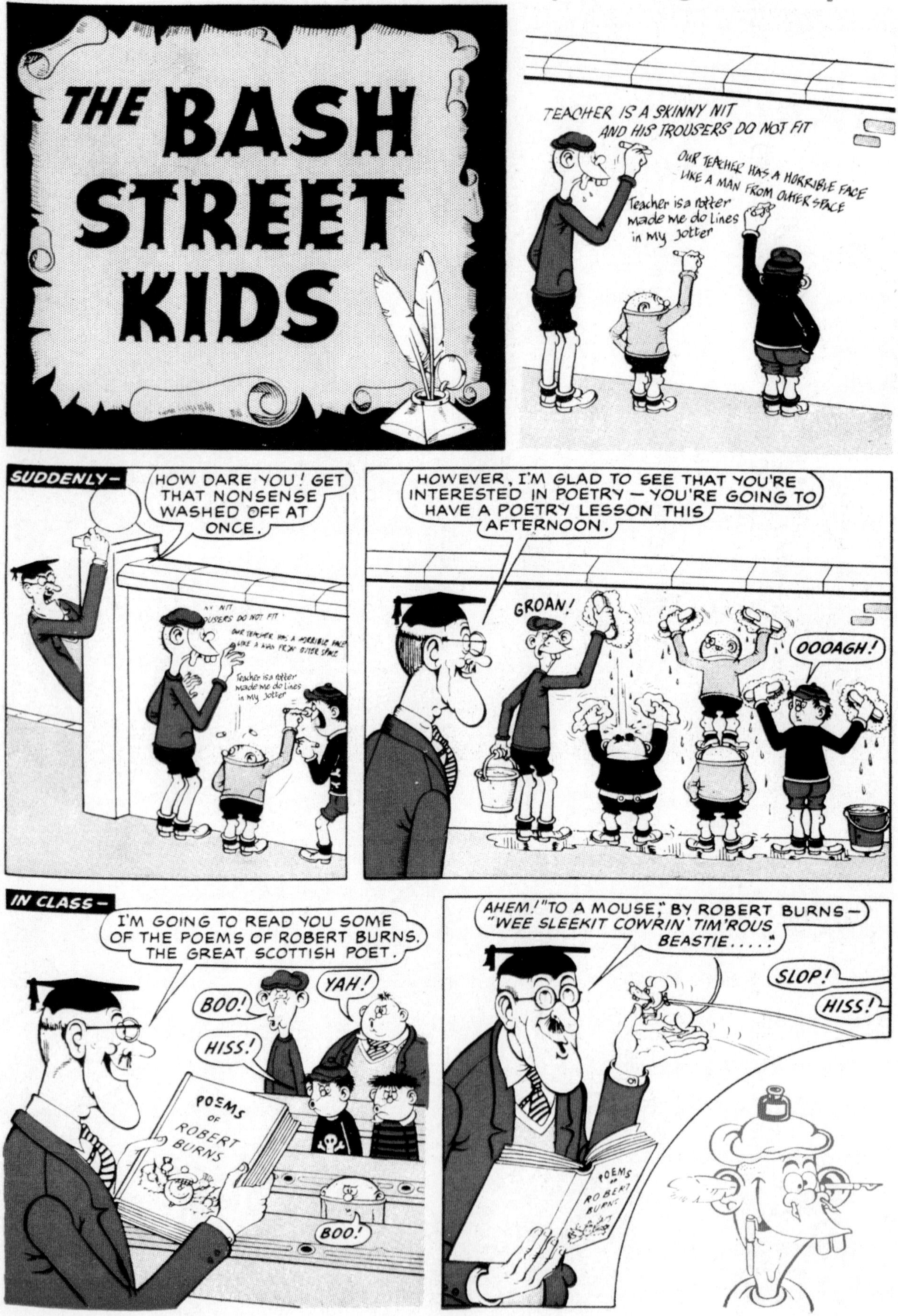
THE BASH STREET KIDS
TEACHER IS A SKINNY NIT
AND HIS TROUSERS DO NOT FIT
OUR TEACHER HAS A HORRIBLE FACE
LIKE A MAN FROM OUTER SPACE
Teacher is a rotter
made me do lines
in my Jotter
SUDDENLY—
HOW DARE YOU! GET THAT NONSENSE WASHED OFF AT ONCE.
HOWEVER, I'M GLAD TO SEE THAT YOU'RE INTERESTED IN POETRY — YOU'RE GOING TO HAVE A POETRY LESSON THIS AFTERNOON.
GROAN!
OOOAGH!
IN CLASS—
I'M GOING TO READ YOU SOME OF THE POEMS OF ROBERT BURNS, THE GREAT SCOTTISH POET.
BOO!
YAH!
HISS!
POEMS OF ROBERT BURNS
BOO!
AHEM! "TO A MOUSE," BY ROBERT BURNS— "WEE SLEEKIT COWRIN' TIM'ROUS BEASTIE....."
SLOP!
HISS!
POEMS OF ROBERT BURNS

A big feed is a prize indeed!

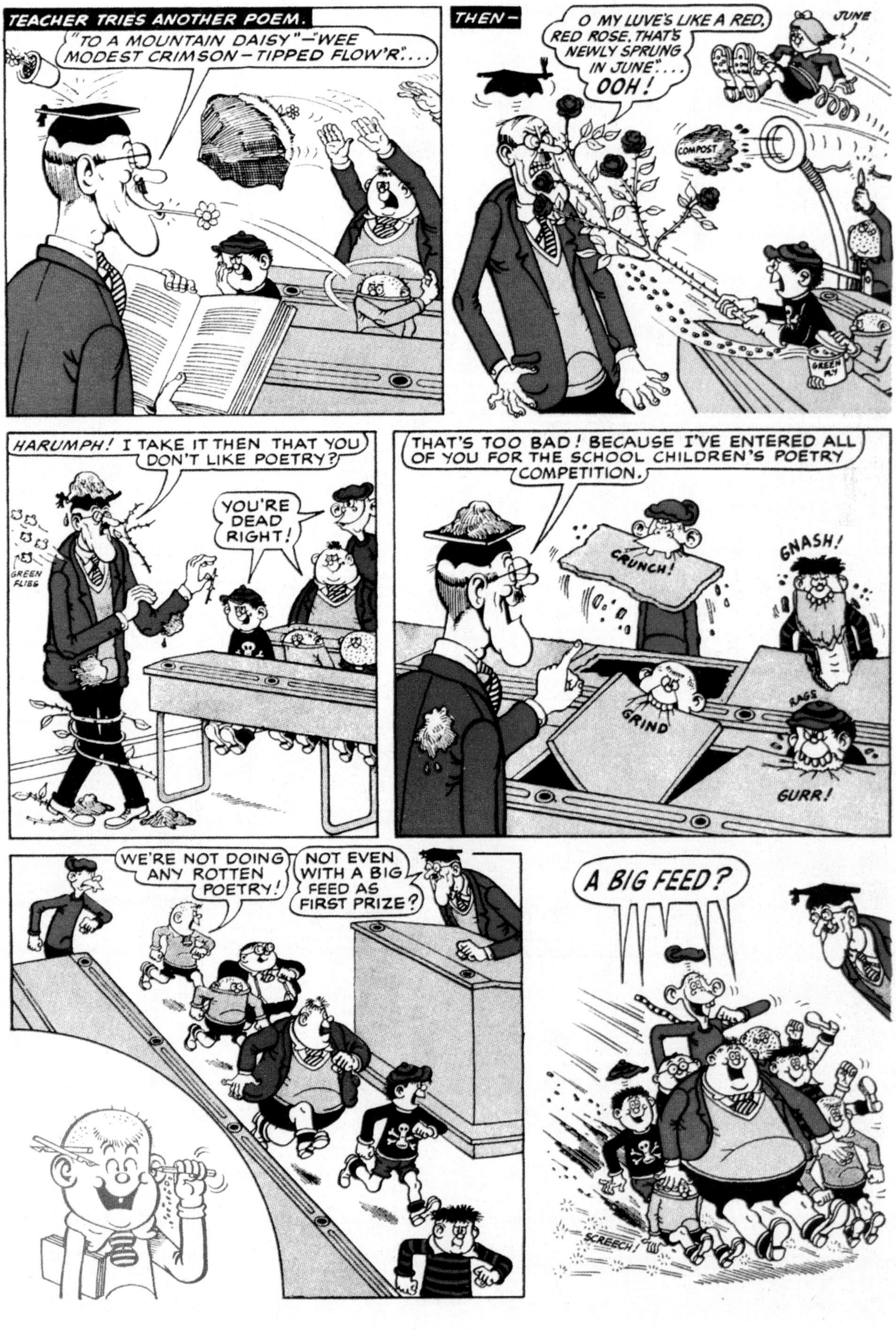

TEACHER TRIES ANOTHER POEM.
"TO A MOUNTAIN DAISY"—"WEE MODEST CRIMSON—TIPPED FLOW'R"....
THEN—
O MY LUVE'S LIKE A RED, RED ROSE, THAT'S NEWLY SPRUNG IN JUNE"....
OOH!
JUNE
COMPOST
GREEN FLY
HARUMPH! I TAKE IT THEN THAT YOU DON'T LIKE POETRY?
YOU'RE DEAD RIGHT!
GREEN FLIES
THAT'S TOO BAD! BECAUSE I'VE ENTERED ALL OF YOU FOR THE SCHOOL CHILDREN'S POETRY COMPETITION.
CRUNCH!
GNASH!
GRIND
RAGS
GURR!
WE'RE NOT DOING ANY ROTTEN POETRY!
NOT EVEN WITH A BIG FEED AS FIRST PRIZE?
A BIG FEED?
SCREECH!

Teacher has some fun when the writing's done!

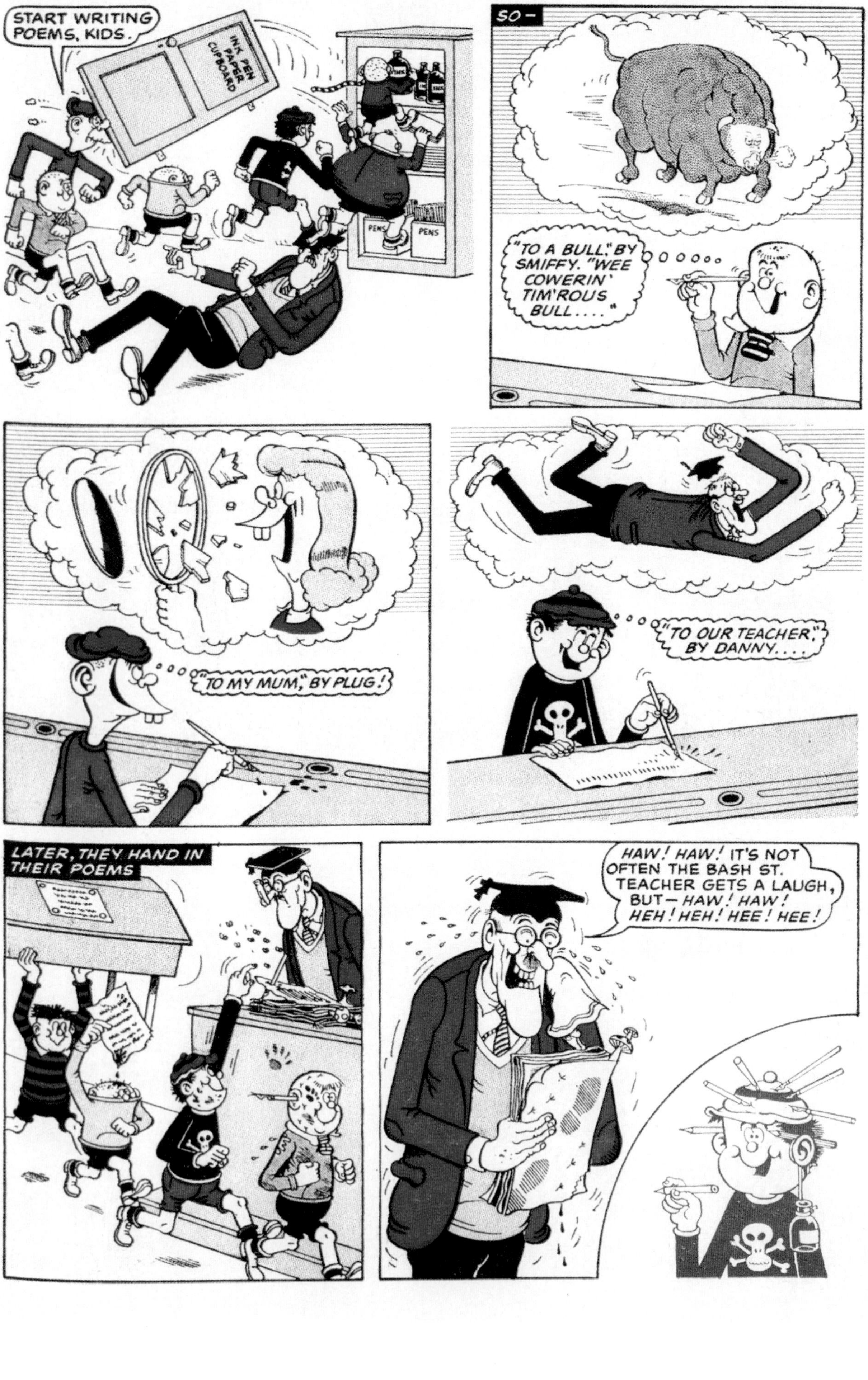
START WRITING POEMS, KIDS.
INK PEN PAPER CUPBOARD
PENS
PENS
SO—
"TO A BULL," BY SMIFFY. "WEE COWERIN' TIM'ROUS BULL...."
"TO MY MUM," BY PLUG!
"TO OUR TEACHER," BY DANNY....
LATER, THEY HAND IN THEIR POEMS
HAW! HAW! IT'S NOT OFTEN THE BASH ST. TEACHER GETS A LAUGH, BUT— HAW! HAW! HEH! HEH! HEE! HEE!

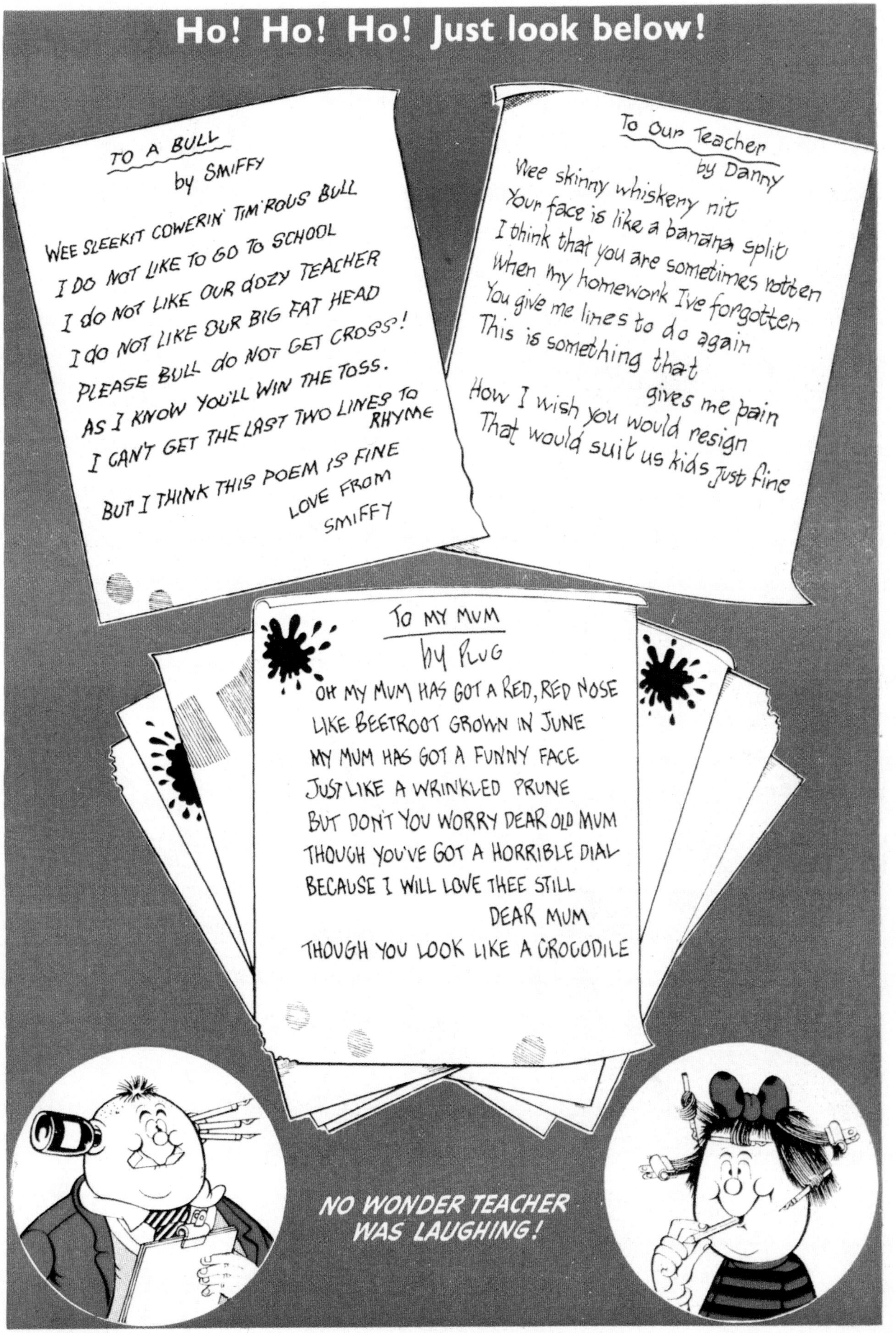
Ho! Ho! Ho! Just look below!
TO A BULL
by SMIFFY
WEE SLEEKIT COWERIN' TIM'ROUS BULL
I DO NOT LIKE TO GO TO SCHOOL
I do NOT LIKE OUR dozy TEACHER
I do NOT LIKE OUR BIG FAT HEAD
PLEASE BULL do NOT GET CROSS!
AS I KNOW YOU'LL WIN THE TOSS.
I CAN'T GET THE LAST TWO LINES TO RHYME
BUT I THINK THIS POEM IS FINE
LOVE FROM
SMIFFY
To Our Teacher
by Danny
Wee skinny whiskery nit
Your face is like a banana split
I think that you are sometimes rotten
When my homework I've forgotten
You give me lines to do again
This is something that
gives me pain
How I wish you would resign
That would suit us kids just fine
TO MY MUM
by PLUG
OH MY MUM HAS GOT A RED, RED NOSE
LIKE BEETROOT GROWN IN JUNE
MY MUM HAS GOT A FUNNY FACE
JUST LIKE A WRINKLED PRUNE
BUT DON'T YOU WORRY DEAR OLD MUM
THOUGH YOU'VE GOT A HORRIBLE DIAL
BECAUSE I WILL LOVE THEE STILL
DEAR MUM
THOUGH YOU LOOK LIKE A CROCODILE
NO WONDER TEACHER WAS LAUGHING!

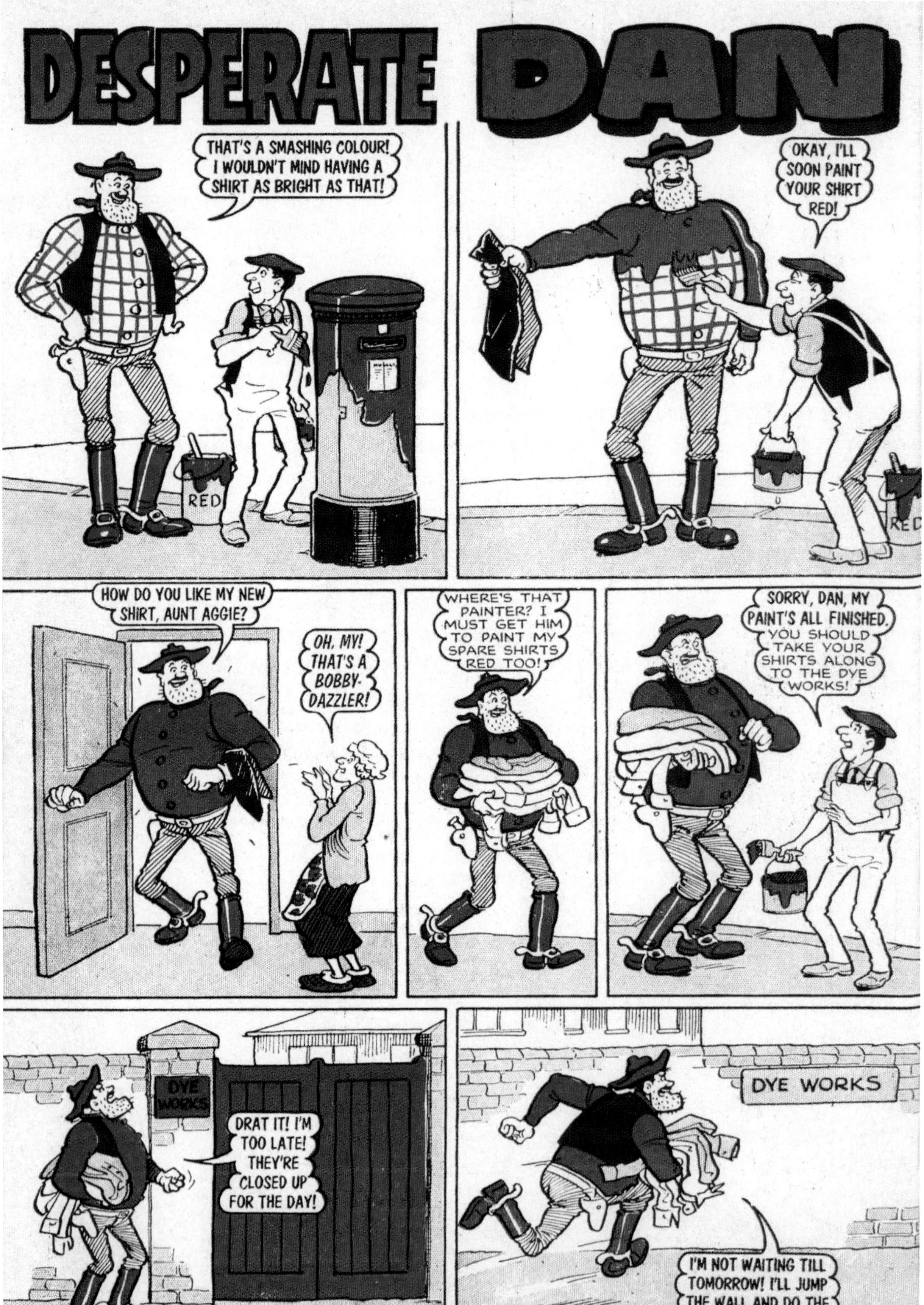
DESPERATE DAN
THAT'S A SMASHING COLOUR! I WOULDN'T MIND HAVING A SHIRT AS BRIGHT AS THAT!
RED
OKAY, I'LL SOON PAINT YOUR SHIRT RED!
RED
HOW DO YOU LIKE MY NEW SHIRT, AUNT AGGIE?
OH, MY! THAT'S A BOBBY-DAZZLER!
WHERE'S THAT PAINTER? I MUST GET HIM TO PAINT MY SPARE SHIRTS RED TOO!
SORRY, DAN, MY PAINT'S ALL FINISHED. YOU SHOULD TAKE YOUR SHIRTS ALONG TO THE DYE WORKS!
DYE WORKS
DRAT IT! I'M TOO LATE! THEY'RE CLOSED UP FOR THE DAY!
DYE WORKS
I'M NOT WAITING TILL TOMORROW! I'LL JUMP THE WALL AND DO THE DYEING MYSELF!

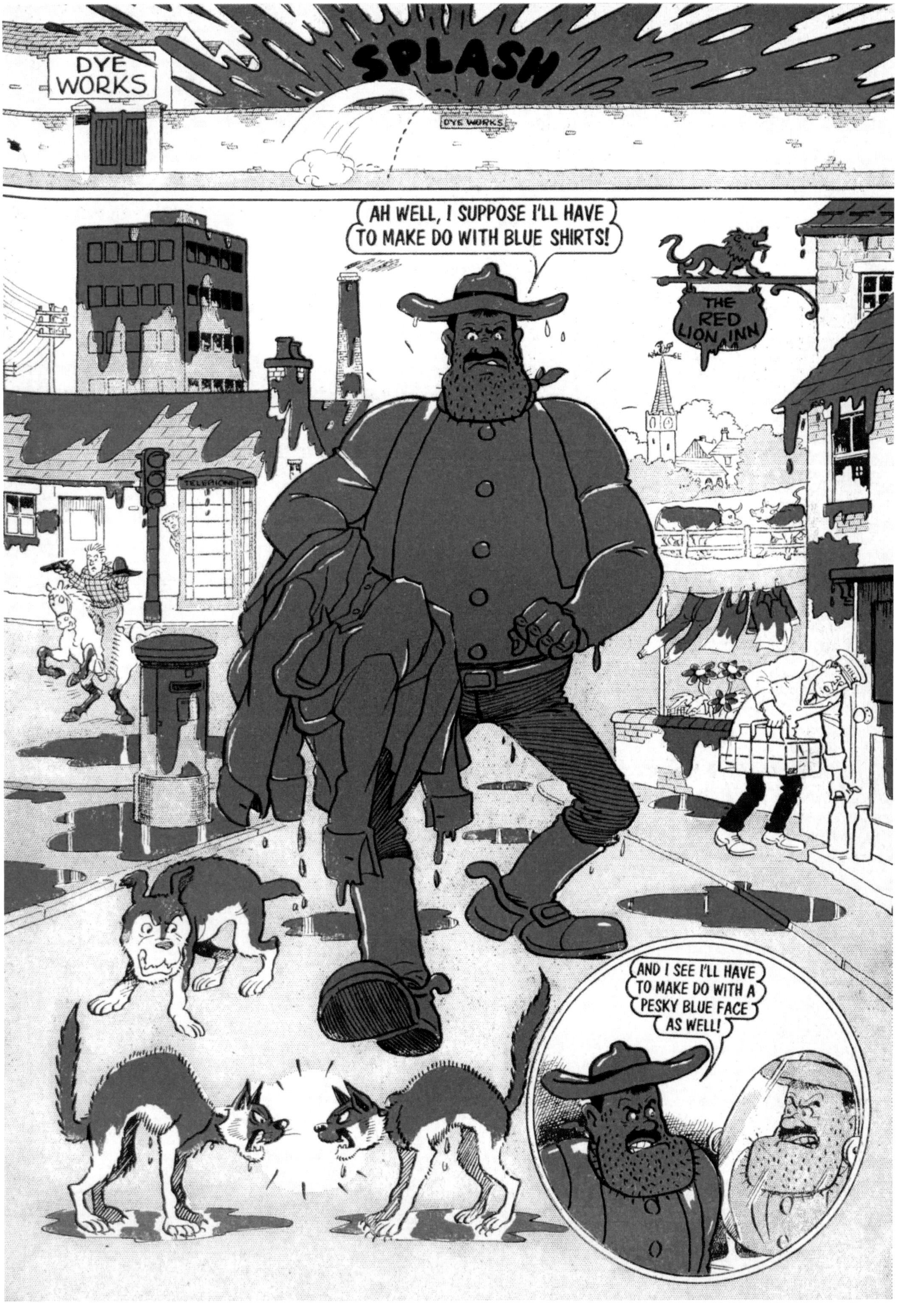

DYE WORKS
SPLASH
DYE WORKS
AH WELL, I SUPPOSE I'LL HAVE TO MAKE DO WITH BLUE SHIRTS!
THE RED LION INN
TELEPHONE
AND I SEE I'LL HAVE TO MAKE DO WITH A PESKY BLUE FACE AS WELL!

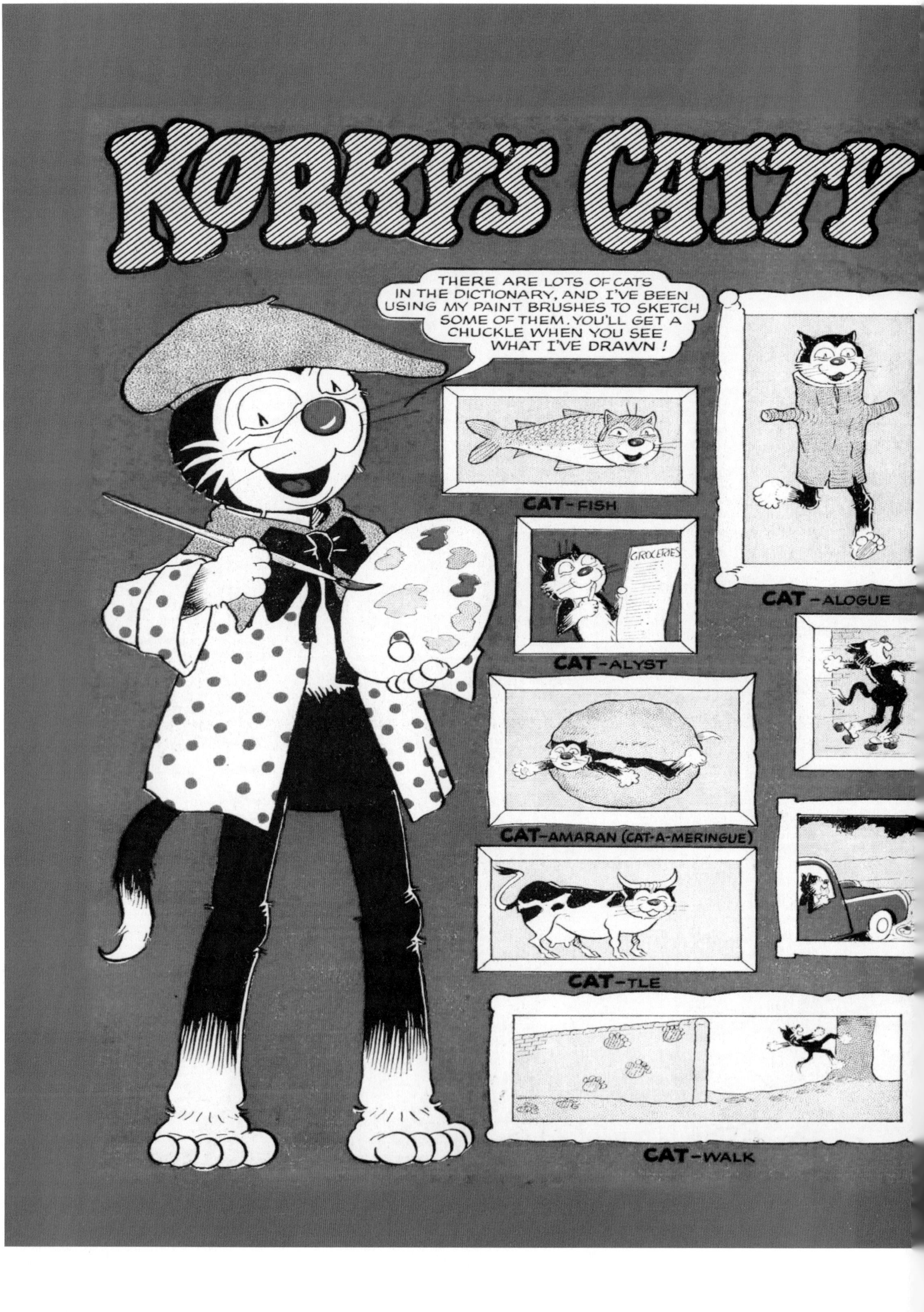
KORKY'S CATTY
THERE ARE LOTS OF CATS IN THE DICTIONARY, AND I'VE BEEN USING MY PAINT BRUSHES TO SKETCH SOME OF THEM. YOU'LL GET A CHUCKLE WHEN YOU SEE WHAT I'VE DRAWN!
CAT-FISH
GROCERIES
CAT-ALYST
CAT-ALOGUE
CAT-AMARAN (CAT-A-MERINGUE)
CAT-TLE
CAT-WALK

DICTIONARY

CAT-ARRH
CAT-ACOMB
MIAOW
CAT-CALL
CAT-ERING CORPS
ONK
HOWL!
CAT-ERWAUL
CAT-ASTROPHE
CAT-ERPILLAR
CAT'S-EYES
CAT-APULT
NO FISHING
CAT-O'NINE TAILS
CAT-KING
SWAG
CAT-FOOTED

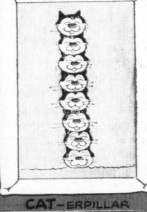

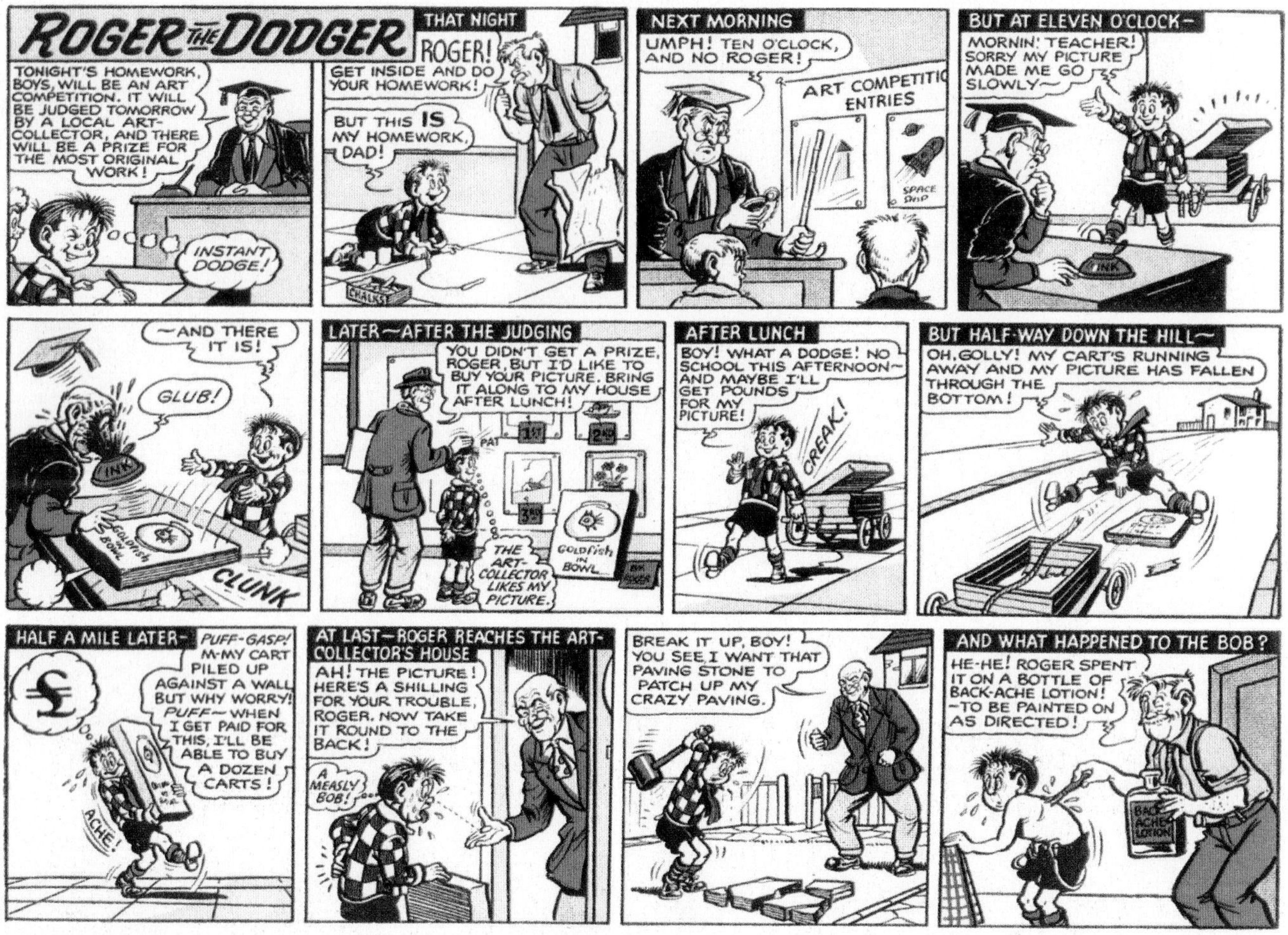
ROGER THE DODGER
TONIGHT'S HOMEWORK, BOYS, WILL BE AN ART COMPETITION. IT WILL BE JUDGED TOMORROW BY A LOCAL ART-COLLECTOR, AND THERE WILL BE A PRIZE FOR THE MOST ORIGINAL WORK!
INSTANT DODGE!
THAT NIGHT
ROGER! GET INSIDE AND DO YOUR HOMEWORK!
BUT THIS IS MY HOMEWORK, DAD!
CHALKS
NEXT MORNING
UMPH! TEN O'CLOCK, AND NO ROGER!
ART COMPETITIO
ENTRIES
SPACE SHIP
BUT AT ELEVEN O'CLOCK—
MORNIN' TEACHER! SORRY MY PICTURE MADE ME GO SLOWLY~
INK
~AND THERE IT IS!
GLUB!
INK
GOLDFISH IN BOWL
CLUNK
LATER—AFTER THE JUDGING
YOU DIDN'T GET A PRIZE, ROGER, BUT I'D LIKE TO BUY YOUR PICTURE. BRING IT ALONG TO MY HOUSE AFTER LUNCH!
PAT
1ST
2ND
3RD
THE ART-COLLECTOR LIKES MY PICTURE.
GOLDFISH IN BOWL
BY ROGER
AFTER LUNCH
BOY! WHAT A DODGE! NO SCHOOL THIS AFTERNOON~ AND MAYBE I'LL GET POUNDS FOR MY PICTURE!
CREAK!
BUT HALF-WAY DOWN THE HILL~
OH, GOLLY! MY CART'S RUNNING AWAY AND MY PICTURE HAS FALLEN THROUGH THE BOTTOM!
HALF A MILE LATER—
PUFF-GASP! M-MY CART PILED UP AGAINST A WALL BUT WHY WORRY! PUFF~ WHEN I GET PAID FOR THIS, I'LL BE ABLE TO BUY A DOZEN CARTS!
£
ACHE!
AT LAST—ROGER REACHES THE ART-COLLECTOR'S HOUSE
AH! THE PICTURE! HERE'S A SHILLING FOR YOUR TROUBLE, ROGER. NOW TAKE IT ROUND TO THE BACK!
A MEASLY BOB!
BREAK IT UP, BOY! YOU SEE, I WANT THAT PAVING STONE TO PATCH UP MY CRAZY PAVING.
AND WHAT HAPPENED TO THE BOB?
HE-HE! ROGER SPENT IT ON A BOTTLE OF BACK-ACHE LOTION! —TO BE PAINTED ON AS DIRECTED!
BACK-ACHE LOTION

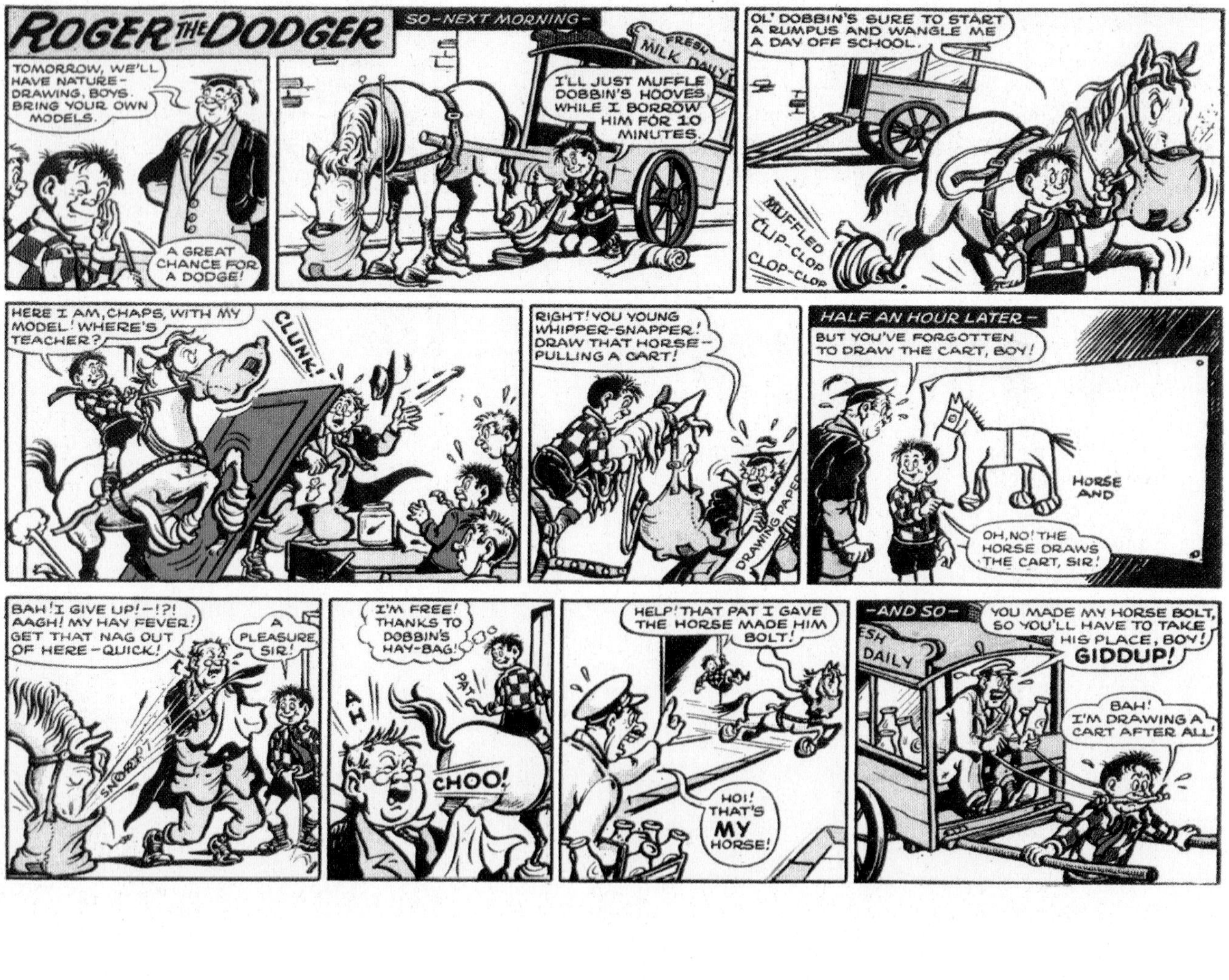
ROGER THE DODGER
TOMORROW, WE'LL HAVE NATURE-DRAWING, BOYS. BRING YOUR OWN MODELS.
A GREAT CHANCE FOR A DODGE!
SO—NEXT MORNING—
FRESH MILK DAILY
I'LL JUST MUFFLE DOBBIN'S HOOVES WHILE I BORROW HIM FOR 10 MINUTES.
OL' DOBBIN'S SURE TO START A RUMPUS AND WANGLE ME A DAY OFF SCHOOL.
MUFFLED CLIP-CLOP CLOP-CLOP
HERE I AM, CHAPS, WITH MY MODEL! WHERE'S TEACHER?
CLUNK!
RIGHT! YOU YOUNG WHIPPER-SNAPPER! DRAW THAT HORSE—PULLING A CART!
DRAWING PAPER
HALF AN HOUR LATER—
BUT YOU'VE FORGOTTEN TO DRAW THE CART, BOY!
HORSE AND
OH, NO! THE HORSE DRAWS THE CART, SIR!
BAH! I GIVE UP!—!?! AAGH! MY HAY FEVER! GET THAT NAG OUT OF HERE—QUICK!
A PLEASURE, SIR!
I'M FREE! THANKS TO DOBBIN'S HAY-BAG!
PAT
AH
CHOO!
HELP! THAT PAT I GAVE THE HORSE MADE HIM BOLT!
HOI! THAT'S MY HORSE!
—AND SO—
DAILY
YOU MADE MY HORSE BOLT, SO YOU'LL HAVE TO TAKE HIS PLACE, BOY! GIDDUP!
BAH! I'M DRAWING A CART AFTER ALL!

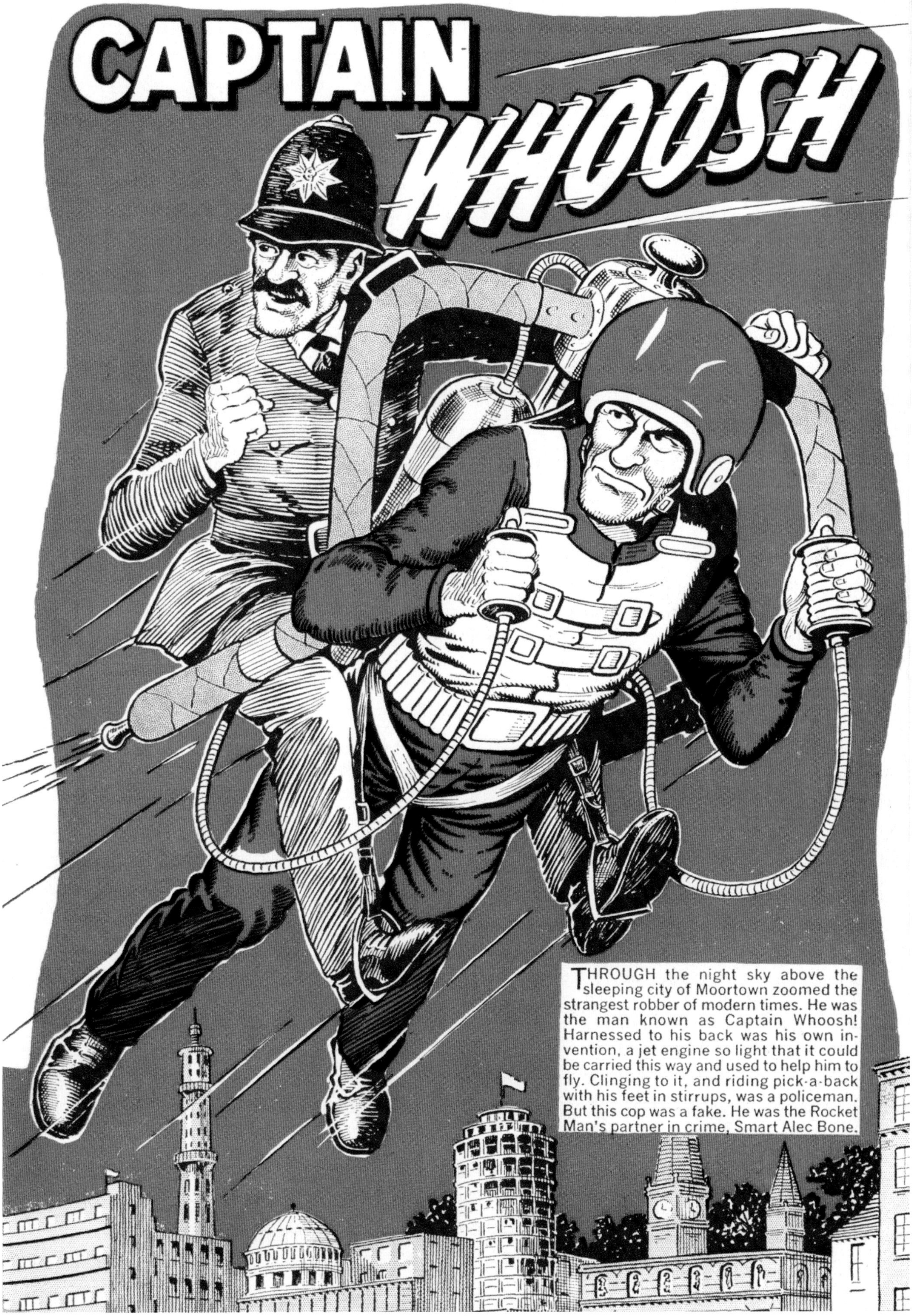
CAPTAIN WHOOOSH
THROUGH the night sky above the sleeping city of Moortown zoomed the strangest robber of modern times. He was the man known as Captain Whoosh! Harnessed to his back was his own invention, a jet engine so light that it could be carried this way and used to help him to fly. Clinging to it, and riding pick-a-back with his feet in stirrups, was a policeman. But this cop was a fake. He was the Rocket Man's partner in crime, Smart Alec Bone.

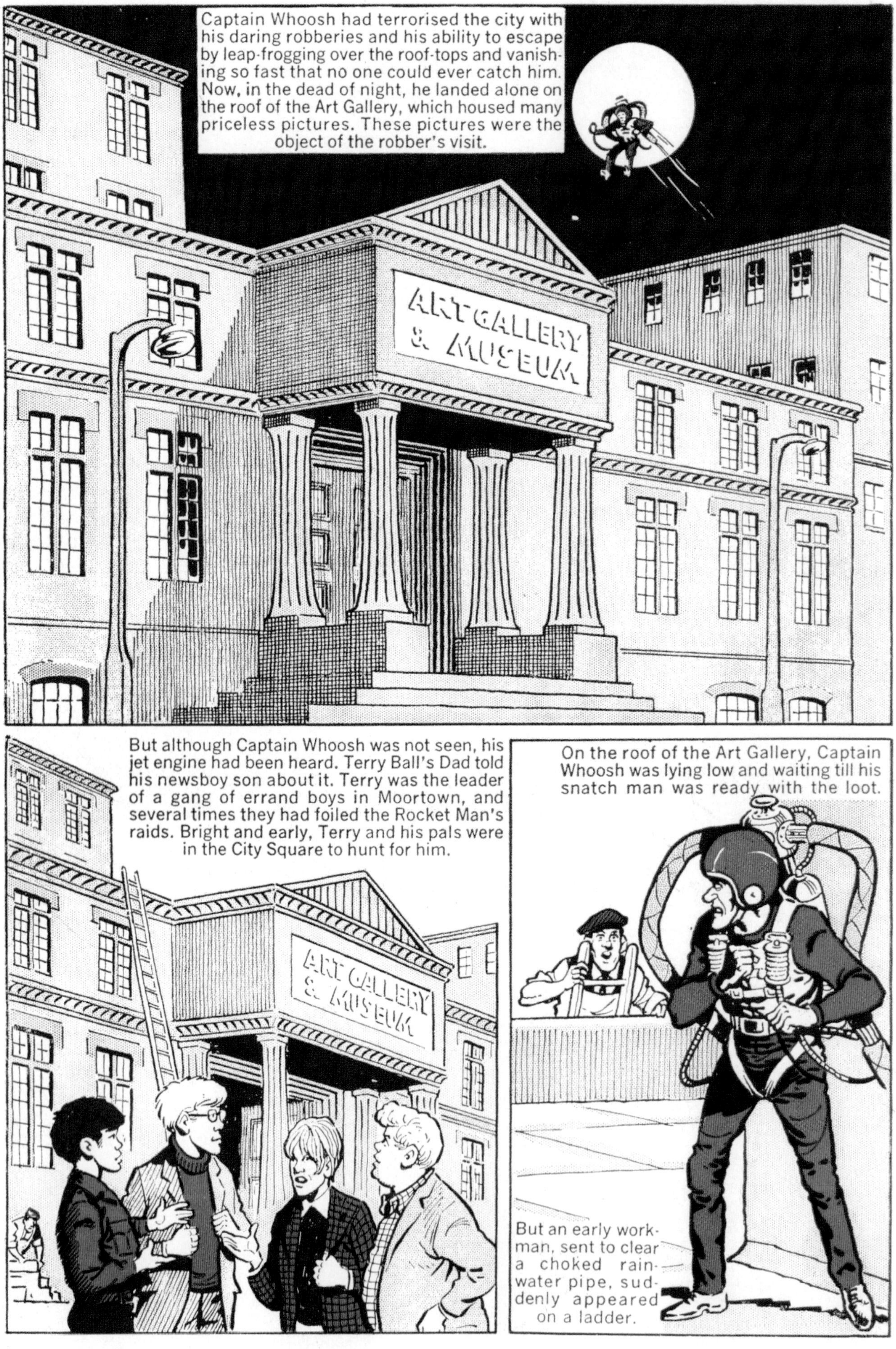
Captain Whoosh had terrorised the city with his daring robberies and his ability to escape by leap-frogging over the roof-tops and vanishing so fast that no one could ever catch him. Now, in the dead of night, he landed alone on the roof of the Art Gallery, which housed many priceless pictures. These pictures were the object of the robber's visit.
ART GALLERY & MUSEUM
But although Captain Whoosh was not seen, his jet engine had been heard. Terry Ball's Dad told his newsboy son about it. Terry was the leader of a gang of errand boys in Moortown, and several times they had foiled the Rocket Man's raids. Bright and early, Terry and his pals were in the City Square to hunt for him.
ART GALLERY & MUSEUM
On the roof of the Art Gallery, Captain Whoosh was lying low and waiting till his snatch man was ready with the loot.
But an early workman, sent to clear a choked rain-water pipe, suddenly appeared on a ladder.

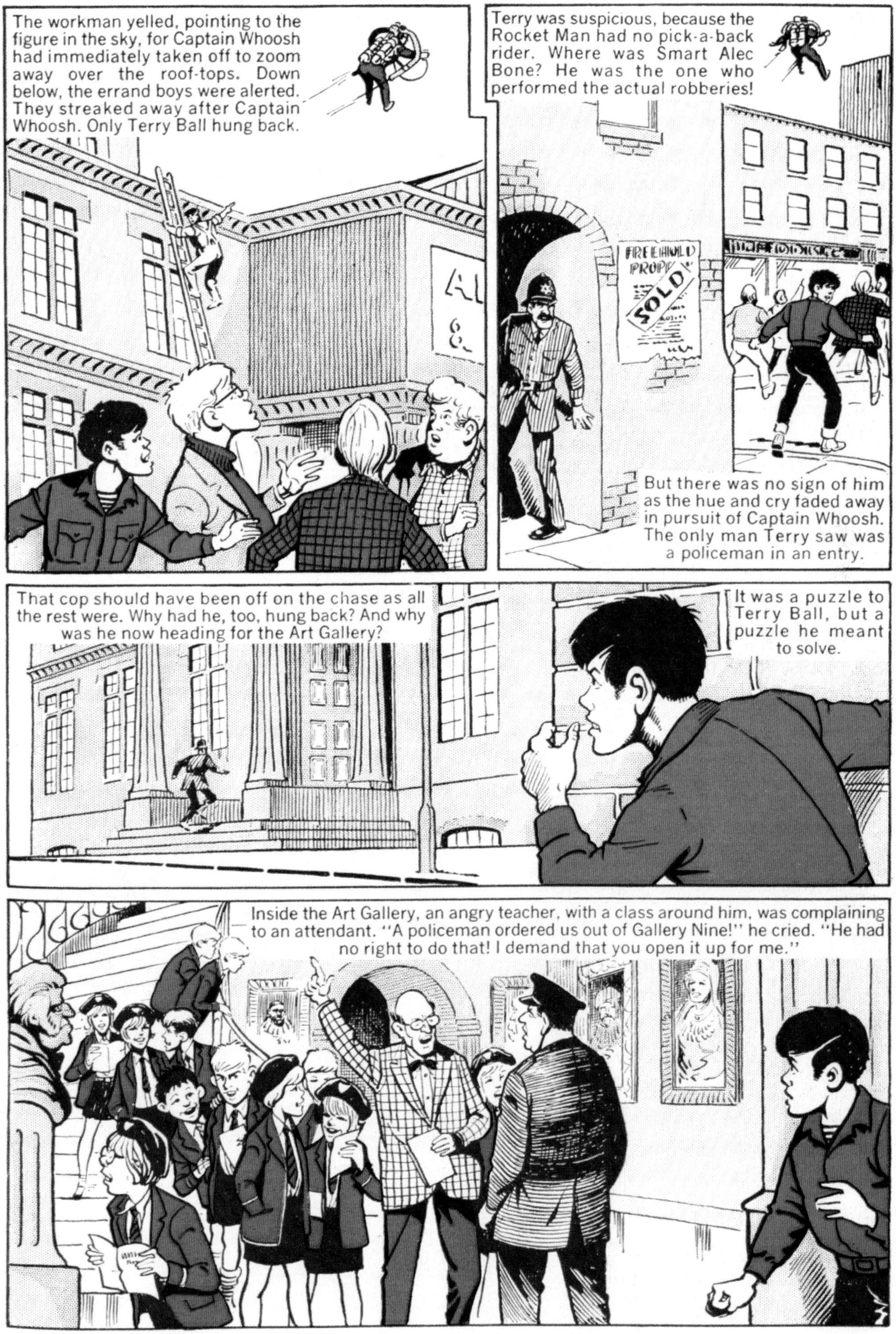

The workman yelled, pointing to the figure in the sky, for Captain Whoosh had immediately taken off to zoom away over the roof-tops. Down below, the errand boys were alerted. They streaked away after Captain Whoosh. Only Terry Ball hung back.
Terry was suspicious, because the Rocket Man had no pick-a-back rider. Where was Smart Alec Bone? He was the one who performed the actual robberies!
SOLD
But there was no sign of him as the hue and cry faded away in pursuit of Captain Whoosh. The only man Terry saw was a policeman in an entry.
That cop should have been off on the chase as all the rest were. Why had he, too, hung back? And why was he now heading for the Art Gallery?
It was a puzzle to Terry Ball, but a puzzle he meant to solve.
Inside the Art Gallery, an angry teacher, with a class around him, was complaining to an attendant. "A policeman ordered us out of Gallery Nine!" he cried. "He had no right to do that! I demand that you open it up for me."

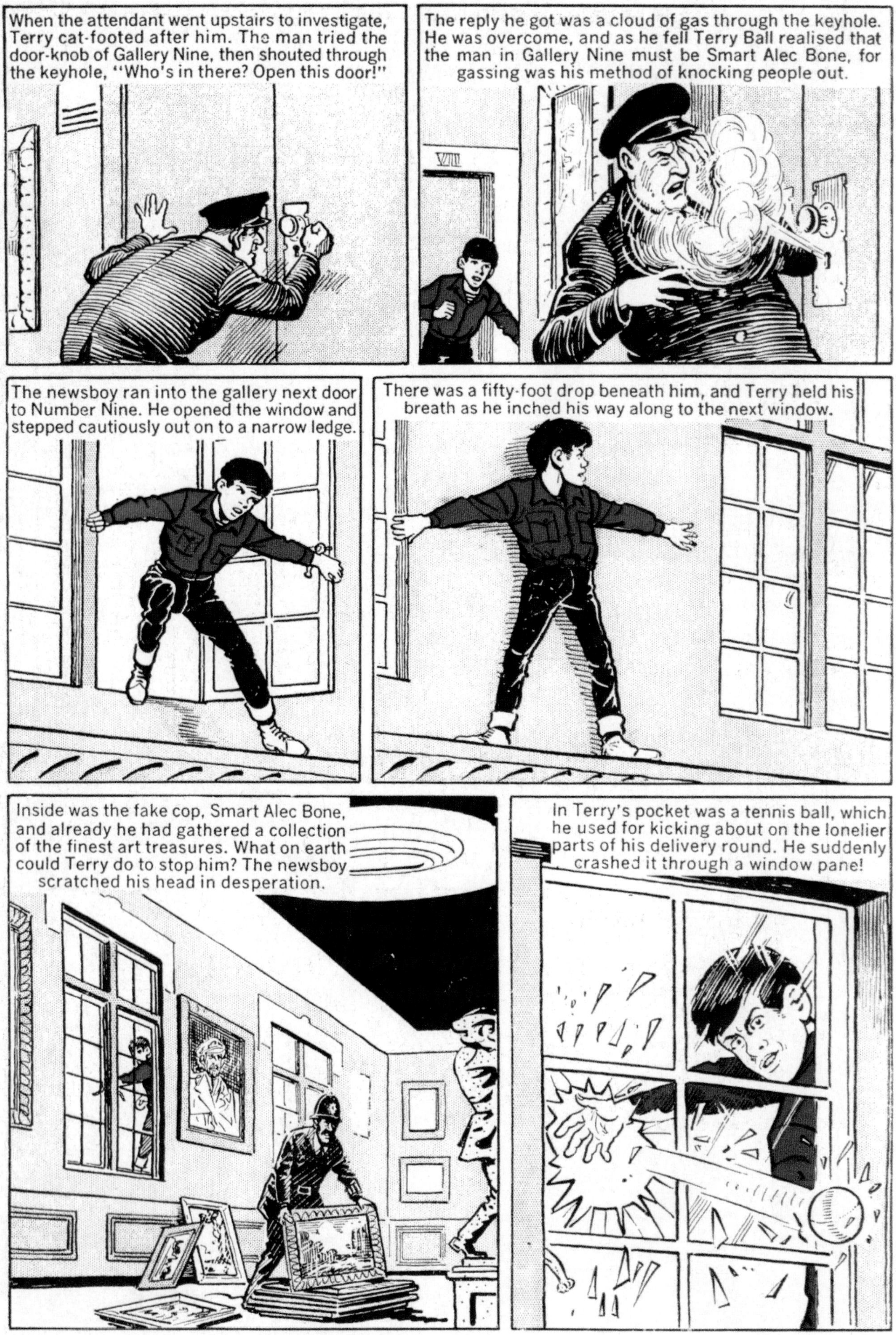
When the attendant went upstairs to investigate, Terry cat-footed after him. The man tried the door-knob of Gallery Nine, then shouted through the keyhole, "Who's in there? Open this door!"
The reply he got was a cloud of gas through the keyhole. He was overcome, and as he fell Terry Ball realised that the man in Gallery Nine must be Smart Alec Bone, for gassing was his method of knocking people out.
VII
The newsboy ran into the gallery next door to Number Nine. He opened the window and stepped cautiously out on to a narrow ledge.
There was a fifty-foot drop beneath him, and Terry held his breath as he inched his way along to the next window.
Inside was the fake cop, Smart Alec Bone, and already he had gathered a collection of the finest art treasures. What on earth could Terry do to stop him? The newsboy scratched his head in desperation.
In Terry's pocket was a tennis ball, which he used for kicking about on the lonelier parts of his delivery round. He suddenly crashed it through a window pane!

Smart Alec whirled to glare at the window, but Terry had edged out of view. Thinking some boy had accidentally kicked the ball at the window from below, Smart Alec ignored it.

When all the pictures were parcelled up, the robber went across to a window on the gallery's far side. And Terry silently opened the catch on his window.

The noise of traffic drowned the scrape of Terry's feet as he climbed inside. Smart Alec stood on the sill of the open window with a hooked rope in his hand, and the other end of the rope was secured to the parcel of pictures.

Now the hum of the marvellous jet engine was heard close by. Here came Captain Whoosh, returning to collect Smart Alec and his loot.

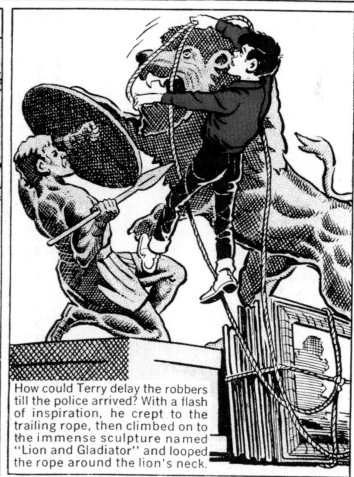

How could Terry delay the robbers till the police arrived? With a flash of inspiration, he crept to the trailing rope, then climbed on to the immense sculpture named "Lion and Gladiator" and looped the rope around the lion's neck.

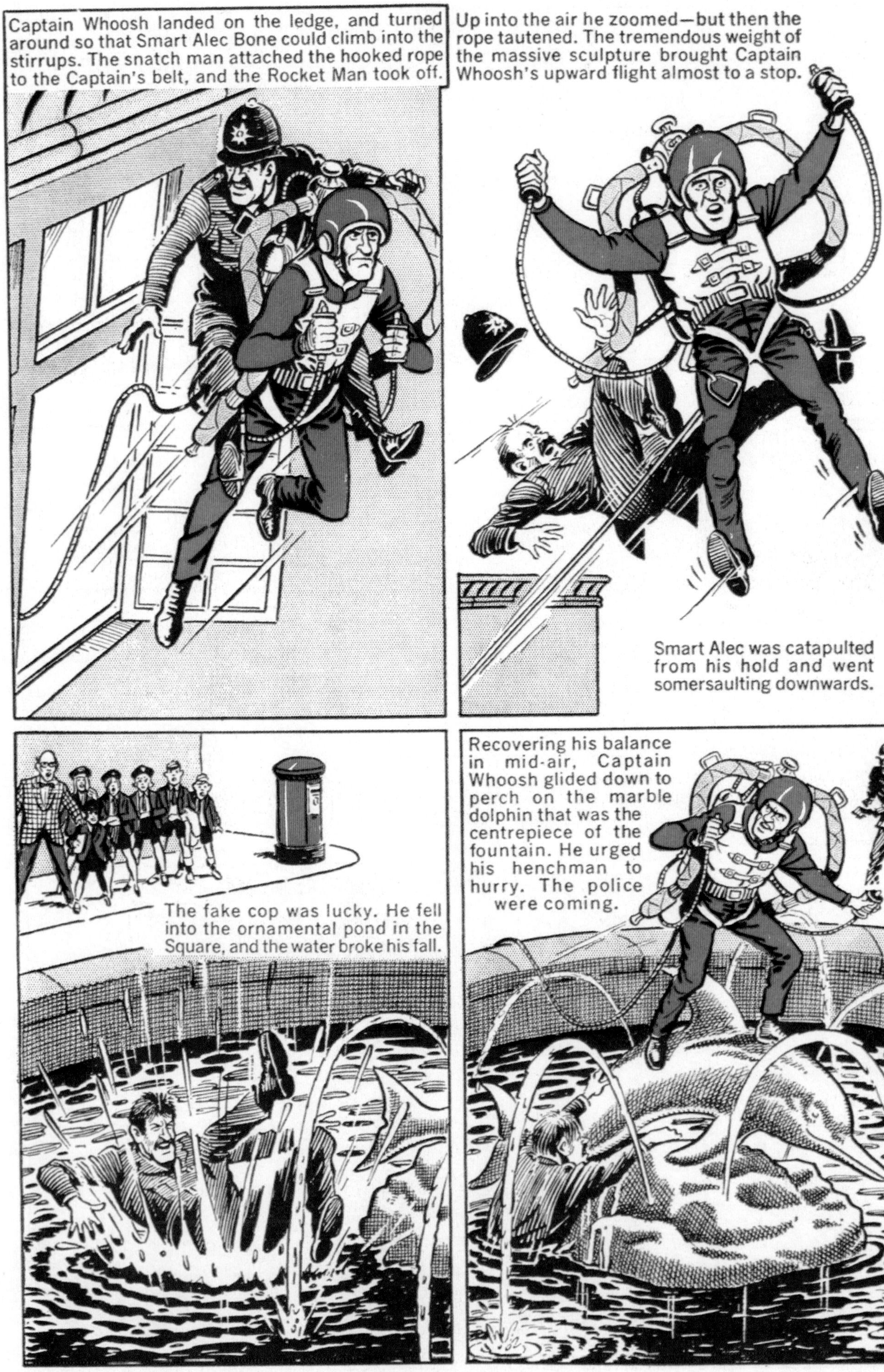
Captain Whoosh landed on the ledge, and turned around so that Smart Alec Bone could climb into the stirrups. The snatch man attached the hooked rope to the Captain's belt, and the Rocket Man took off.
Up into the air he zoomed—but then the rope tautened. The tremendous weight of the massive sculpture brought Captain Whoosh's upward flight almost to a stop.
Smart Alec was catapulted from his hold and went somersaulting downwards.
The fake cop was lucky. He fell into the ornamental pond in the Square, and the water broke his fall.
Recovering his balance in mid-air, Captain Whoosh glided down to perch on the marble dolphin that was the centrepiece of the fountain. He urged his henchman to hurry. The police were coming.

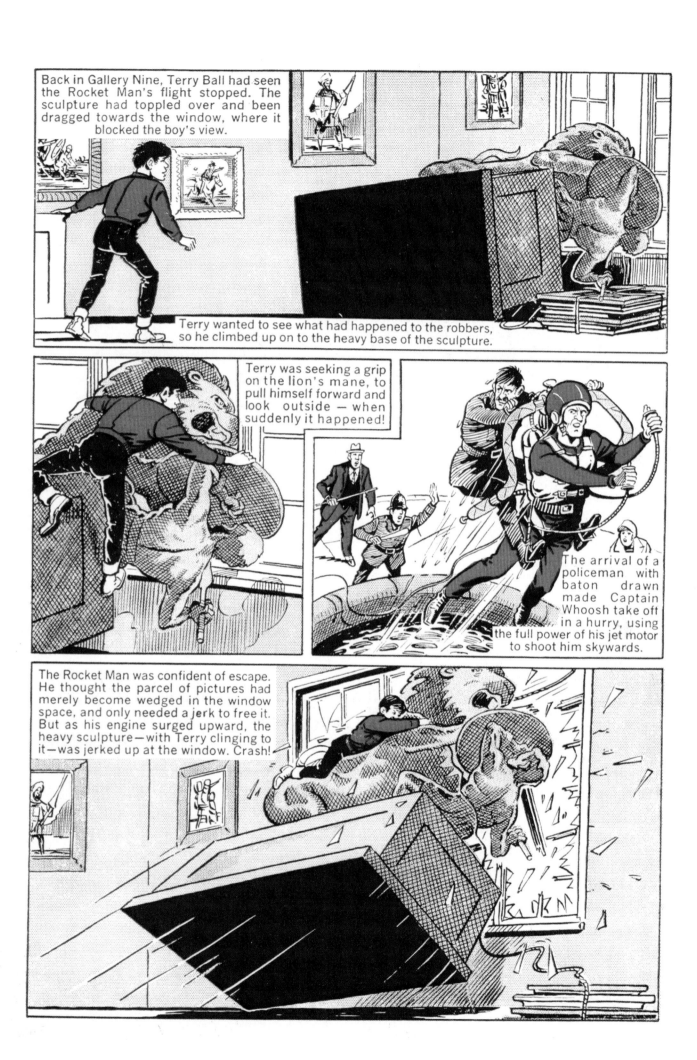

Back in Gallery Nine, Terry Ball had seen the Rocket Man's flight stopped. The sculpture had toppled over and been dragged towards the window, where it blocked the boy's view.

Terry wanted to see what had happened to the robbers, so he climbed up on to the heavy base of the sculpture.

Terry was seeking a grip on the lion's mane, to pull himself forward and look outside — when suddenly it happened!

The arrival of a policeman with baton drawn made Captain Whoosh take off in a hurry, using the full power of his jet motor to shoot him skywards.

The Rocket Man was confident of escape. He thought the parcel of pictures had merely become wedged in the window space, and only needed a jerk to free it. But as his engine surged upward, the heavy sculpture—with Terry clinging to it—was jerked up at the window. Crash!

Bricks, mortar, window frames, all were torn out as the mighty stone figures of lion and gladiator burst through the wall of the Art Gallery! Smart Alec Bone turned in horror and pointed frantically backwards. Captain Whoosh, struggling to maintain his balance and to coax more power from his jet motor, saw the lumbering mass of stone come hurtling after him. Behind the sculpture trailed the parcel of looted pictures on the end of the rope. But what made Captain Whoosh more than ever furious was the sight of the boy who clung between the battling figures of man and beast, the boy he hated more than anyone in the world—Terry Ball!

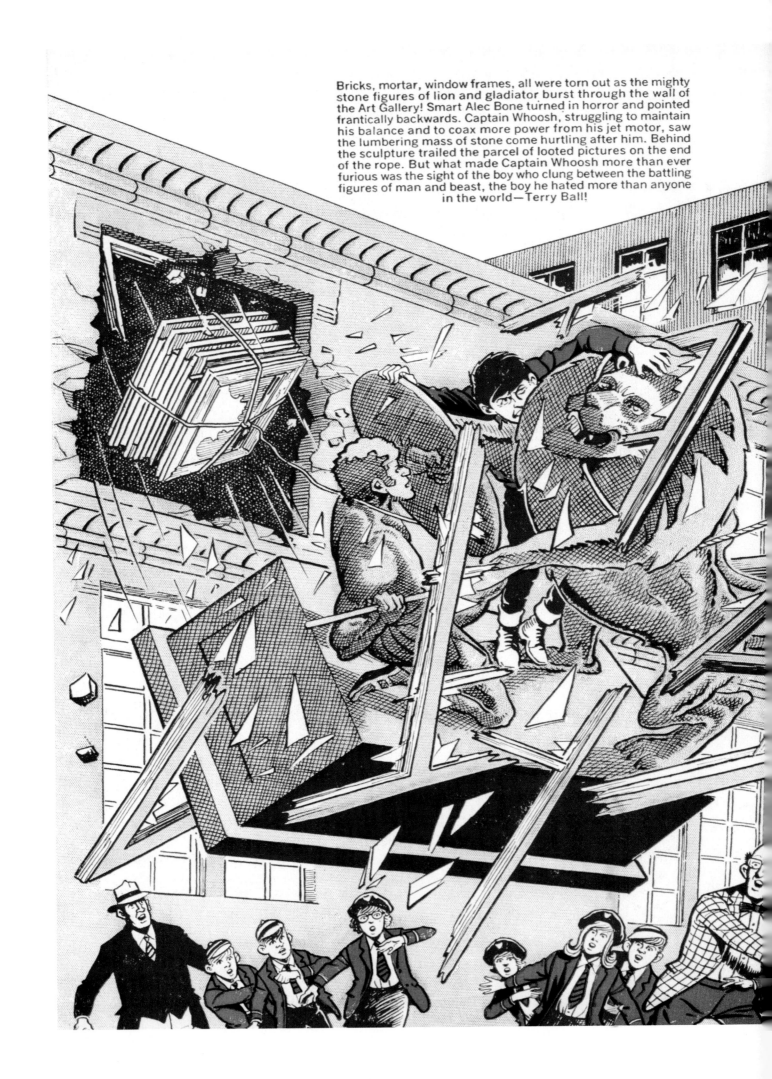

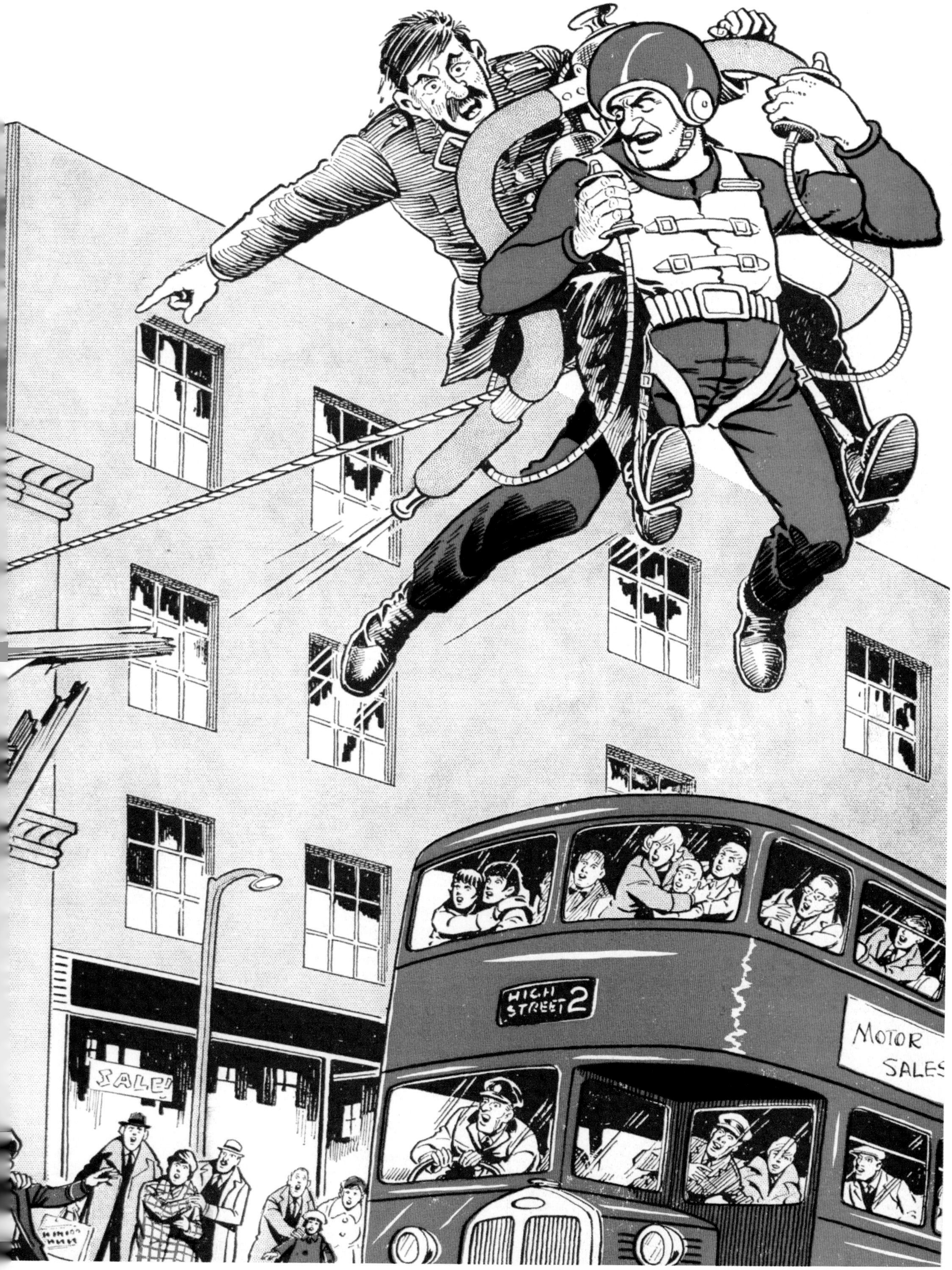
HIGH STREET 2
MOTOR SALES
SALE

Terry's brain was in a whirl after this sudden jerk into open space, but in a split second he glimpsed the ornamental pond below. Letting go his hold, he flung himself clear and plunged downwards.

Like Smart Alec Bone, Terry was lucky enough to land in open water and it was deep enough to break his fall. He let his knees bend and his body go limp as he dropped in.

Beyond the pond, Captain Whoosh fought desperately to keep his jet engine at full power. But the tremendous drag on the rope was too much. The sculptured figures hurtled over the ornamental pond in a pendulum swing that ended with the heavy stone base crashing like thunder into a double-deck bus that was circling the pond. Screams of terror rang out as the bus overturned.

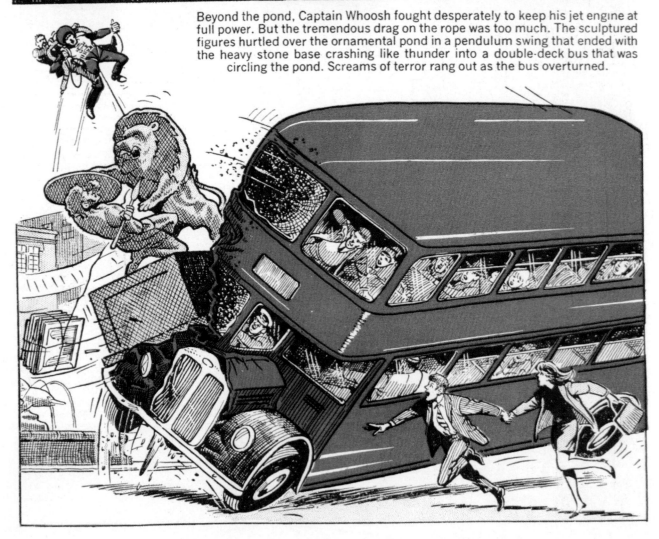

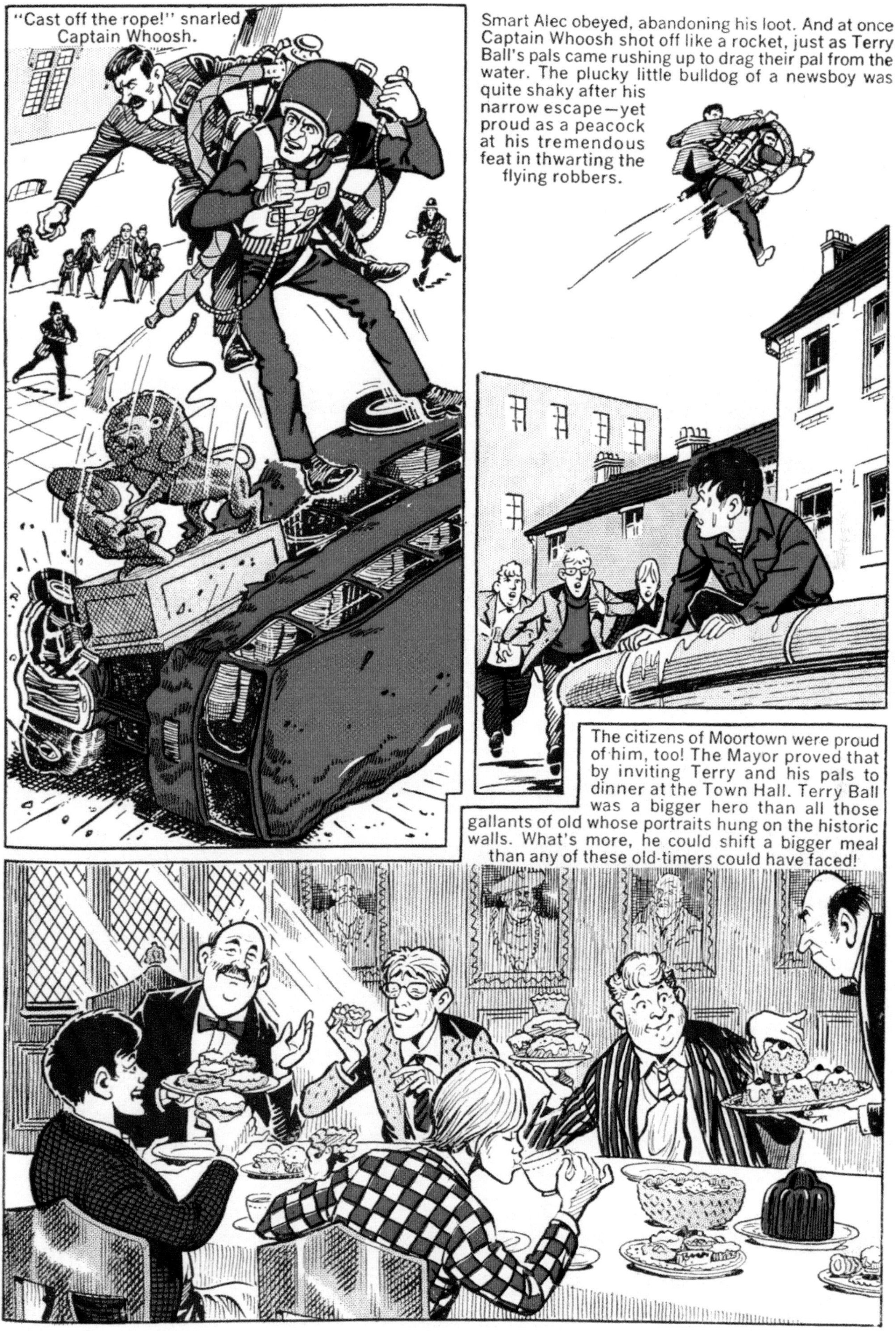
"Cast off the rope!" snarled Captain Whoosh.
Smart Alec obeyed, abandoning his loot. And at once Captain Whoosh shot off like a rocket, just as Terry Ball's pals came rushing up to drag their pal from the water. The plucky little bulldog of a newsboy was quite shaky after his narrow escape—yet proud as a peacock at his tremendous feat in thwarting the flying robbers.
The citizens of Moortown were proud of him, too! The Mayor proved that by inviting Terry and his pals to dinner at the Town Hall. Terry Ball was a bigger hero than all those gallants of old whose portraits hung on the historic walls. What's more, he could shift a bigger meal than any of these old-timers could have faced!

This class'll make you laugh — not half!

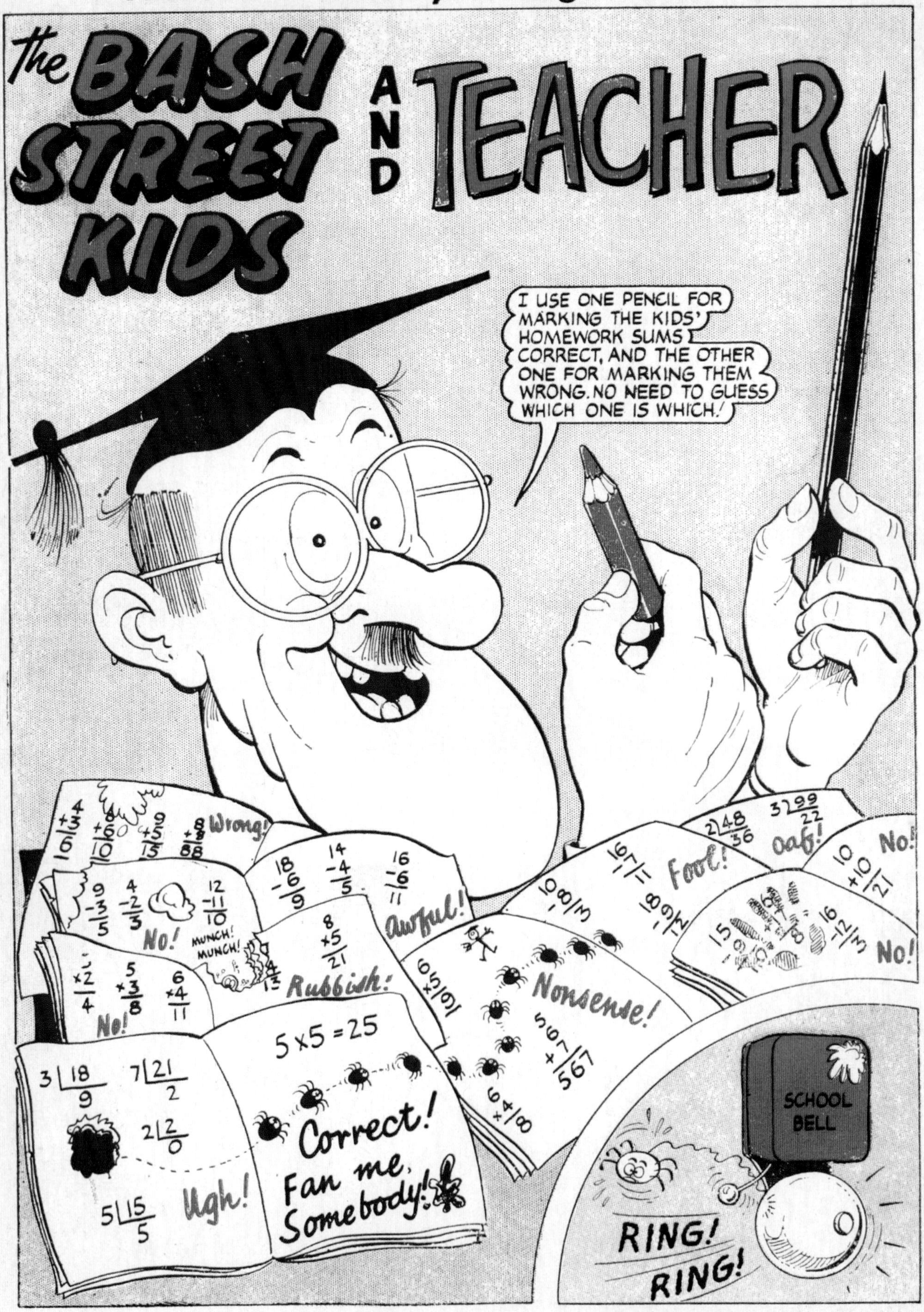

the BASH STREET KIDS AND TEACHER
I USE ONE PENCIL FOR MARKING THE KIDS' HOMEWORK SUMS CORRECT, AND THE OTHER ONE FOR MARKING THEM WRONG. NO NEED TO GUESS WHICH ONE IS WHICH!
Wrong!
No!
MUNCH! MUNCH!
Awful!
Rubbish!
Fool!
oaf!
No!
No!
Nonsense!
No!
5 x 5 = 25
Correct!
Fan me, Somebody!
Ugh!
SCHOOL BELL
RING! RING!

A lesson in art will do for a start.

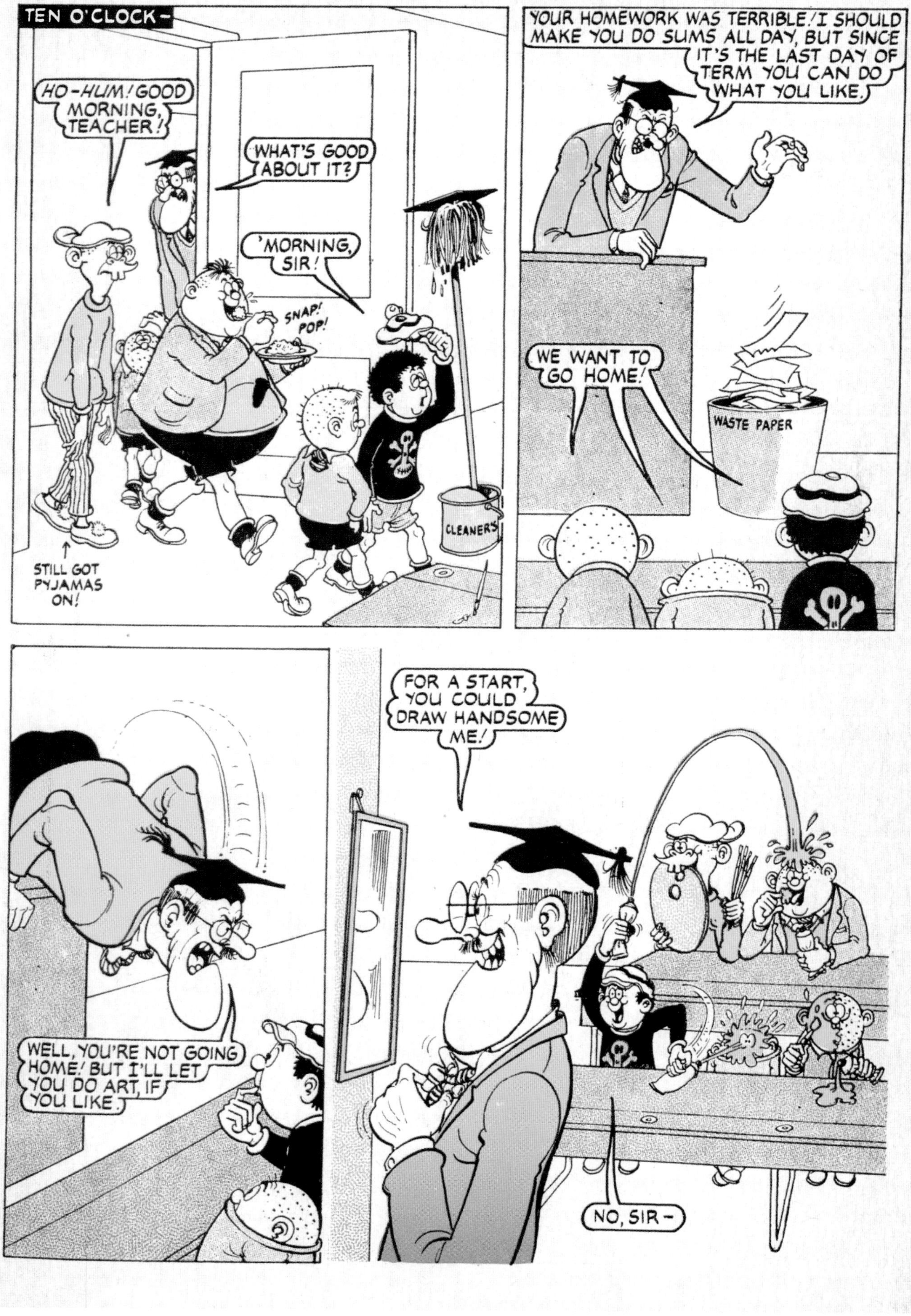

TEN O'CLOCK–
HO-HUM! GOOD MORNING, TEACHER!
WHAT'S GOOD ABOUT IT?
'MORNING, SIR!
SNAP! POP!
CLEANER'S
STILL GOT PYJAMAS ON!
YOUR HOMEWORK WAS TERRIBLE! I SHOULD MAKE YOU DO SUMS ALL DAY, BUT SINCE IT'S THE LAST DAY OF TERM YOU CAN DO WHAT YOU LIKE.
WE WANT TO GO HOME!
WASTE PAPER
WELL, YOU'RE NOT GOING HOME! BUT I'LL LET YOU DO ART, IF YOU LIKE.
FOR A START, YOU COULD DRAW HANDSOME ME!
NO, SIR –

Oh, what a caper, drawing Plug on paper!

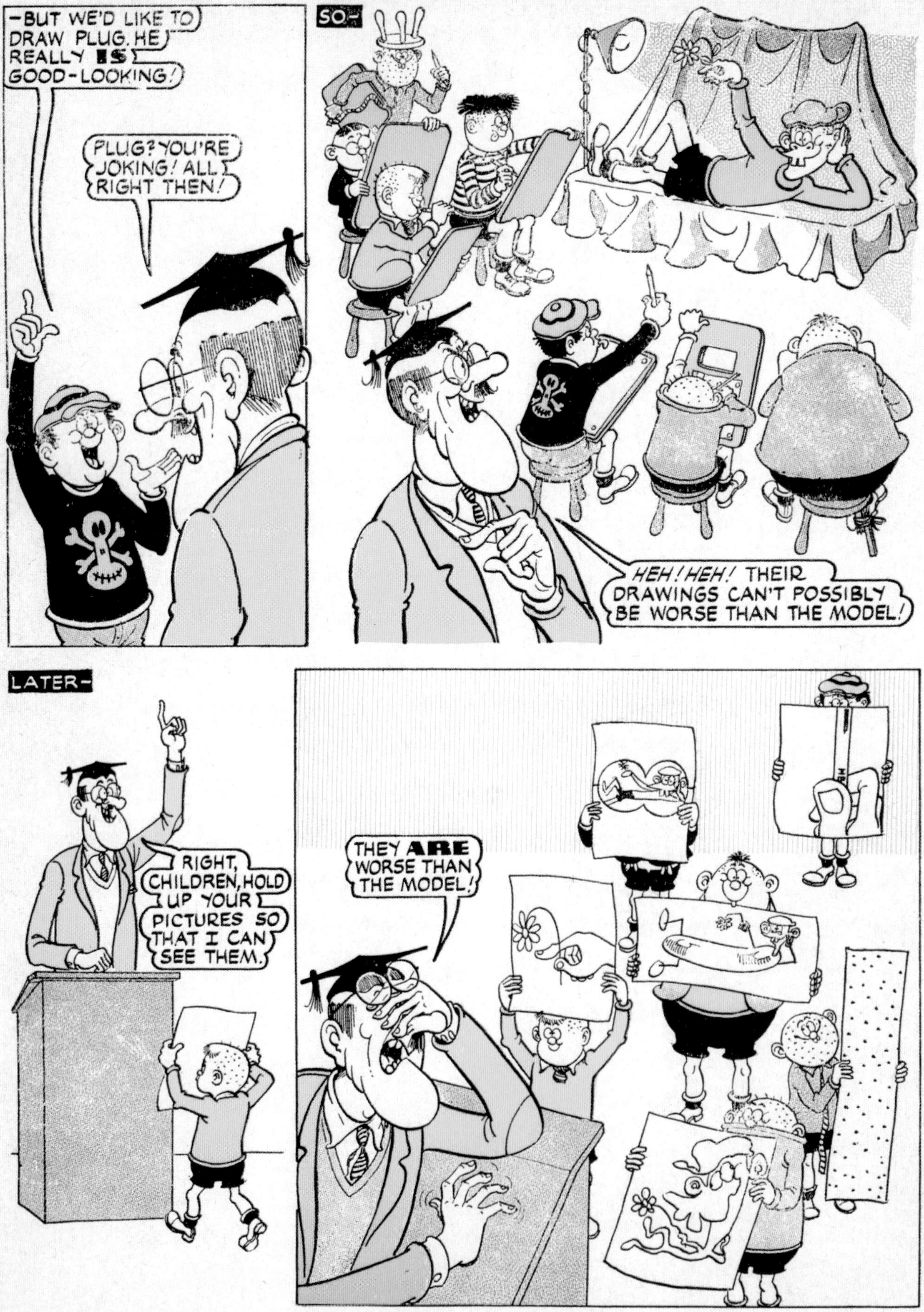

-BUT WE'D LIKE TO DRAW PLUG. HE REALLY IS GOOD-LOOKING!
PLUG? YOU'RE JOKING! ALL RIGHT THEN!
SO-
HEH! HEH! THEIR DRAWINGS CAN'T POSSIBLY BE WORSE THAN THE MODEL!
LATER-
RIGHT, CHILDREN, HOLD UP YOUR PICTURES SO THAT I CAN SEE THEM.
THEY ARE WORSE THAN THE MODEL!

More funny drawing has Teacher haw-hawing.

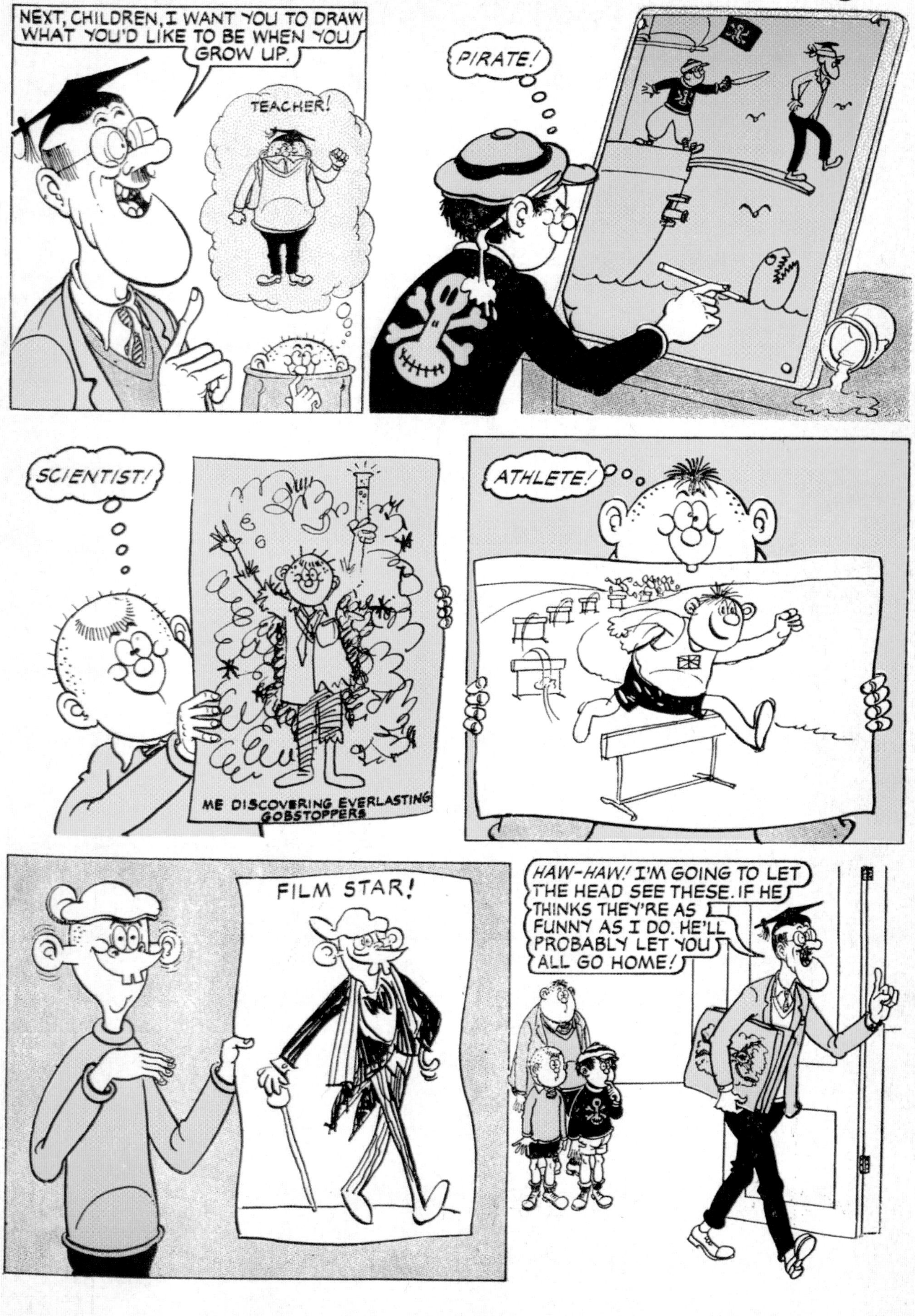
NEXT, CHILDREN, I WANT YOU TO DRAW WHAT YOU'D LIKE TO BE WHEN YOU GROW UP.
TEACHER!
PIRATE!
SCIENTIST!
ME DISCOVERING EVERLASTING GOBSTOPPERS
ATHLETE!
FILM STAR!
HAW-HAW! I'M GOING TO LET THE HEAD SEE THESE. IF HE THINKS THEY'RE AS FUNNY AS I DO, HE'LL PROBABLY LET YOU ALL GO HOME!

Smiffy hasn't a care, swinging through the air!

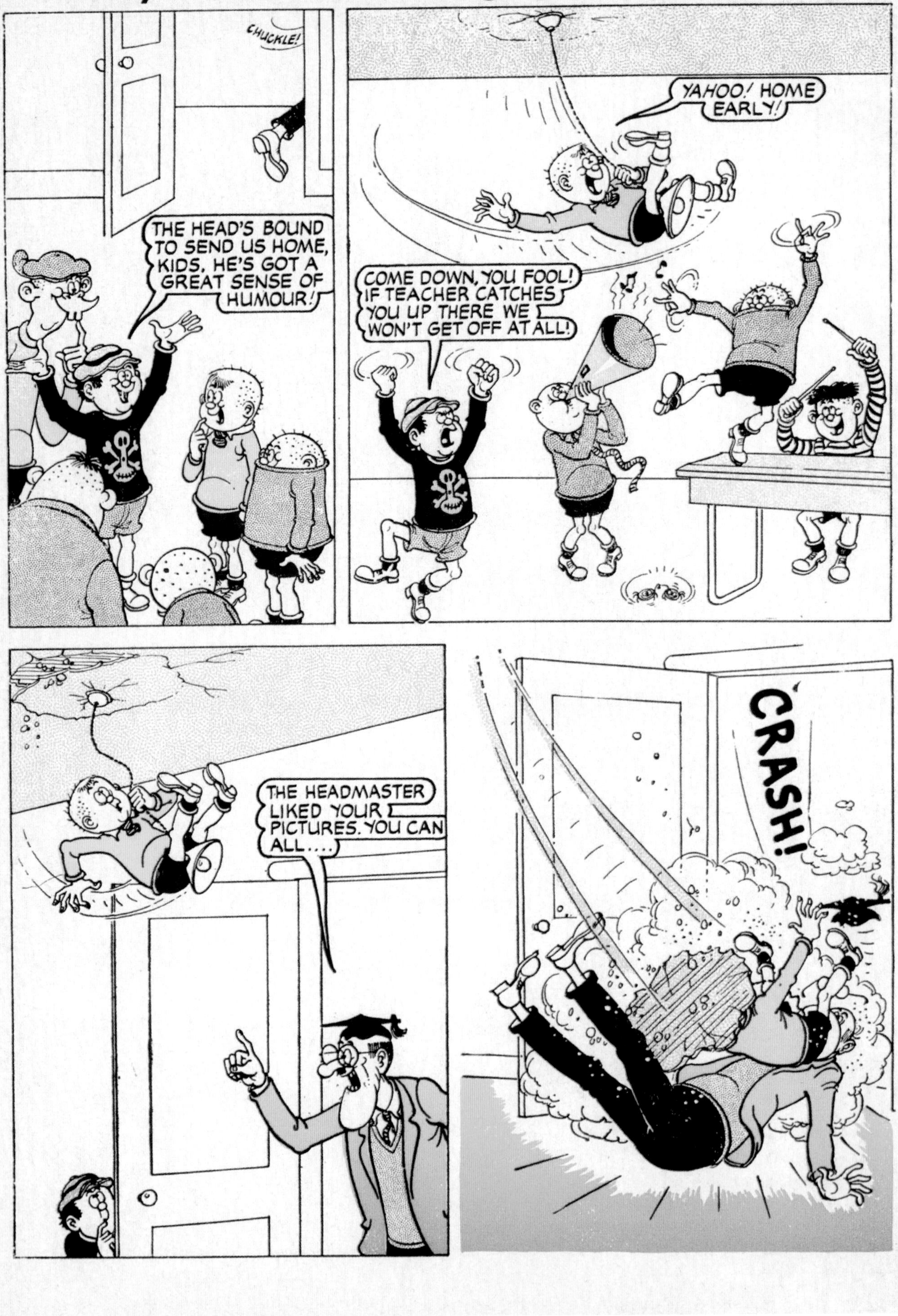
CHUCKLE!
THE HEAD'S BOUND TO SEND US HOME, KIDS, HE'S GOT A GREAT SENSE OF HUMOUR!
YAHOO! HOME EARLY!
COME DOWN, YOU FOOL! IF TEACHER CATCHES YOU UP THERE WE WON'T GET OFF AT ALL!
THE HEADMASTER LIKED YOUR PICTURES. YOU CAN ALL....
CRASH!

Sums galore — and maybe more!

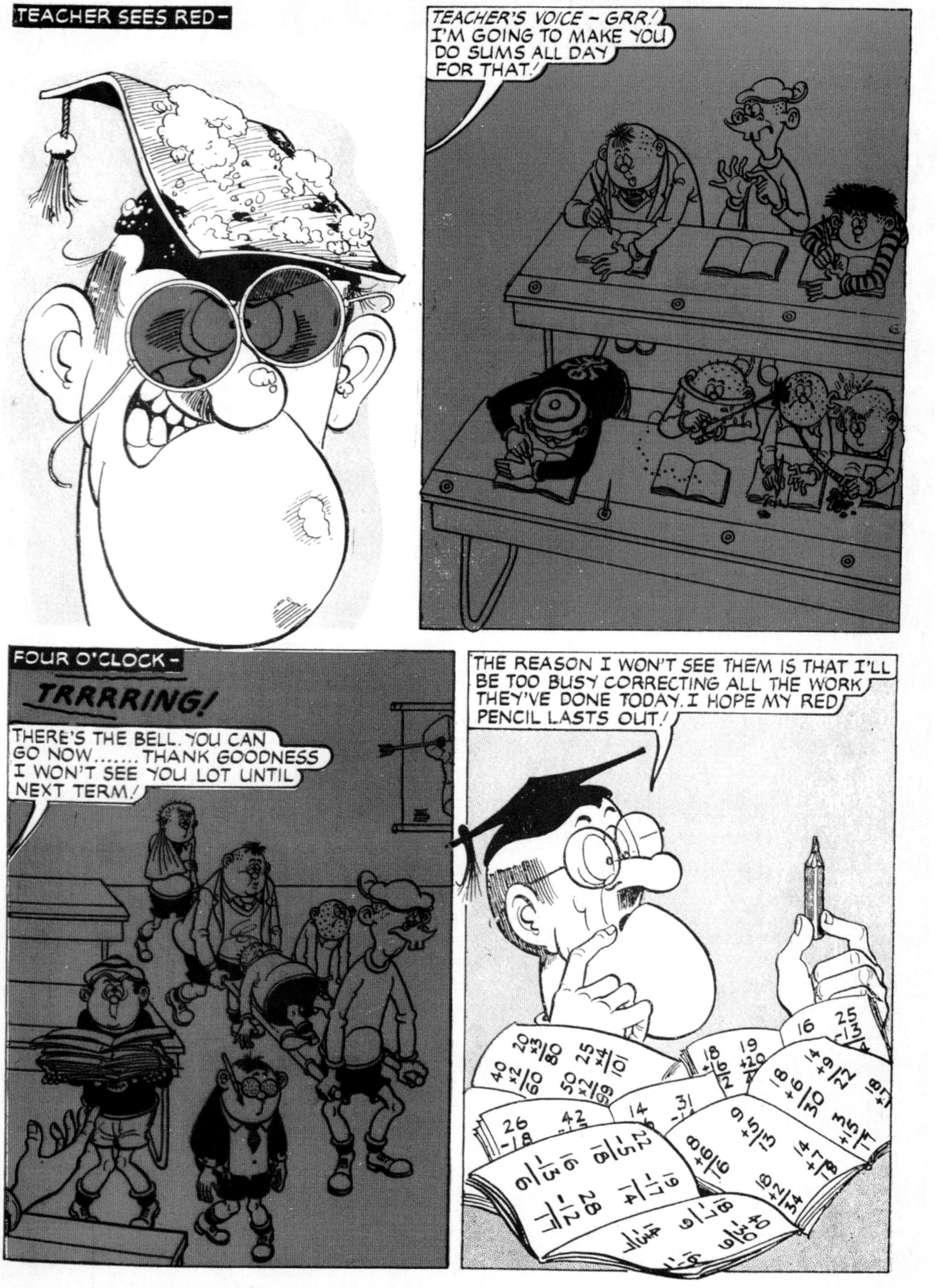
TEACHER SEES RED-
TEACHER'S VOICE - GRR! I'M GOING TO MAKE YOU DO SUMS ALL DAY FOR THAT!
FOUR O'CLOCK-
TRRRRING!
THERE'S THE BELL. YOU CAN GO NOW....... THANK GOODNESS I WON'T SEE YOU LOT UNTIL NEXT TERM!
THE REASON I WON'T SEE THEM IS THAT I'LL BE TOO BUSY CORRECTING ALL THE WORK THEY'VE DONE TODAY. I HOPE MY RED PENCIL LASTS OUT!

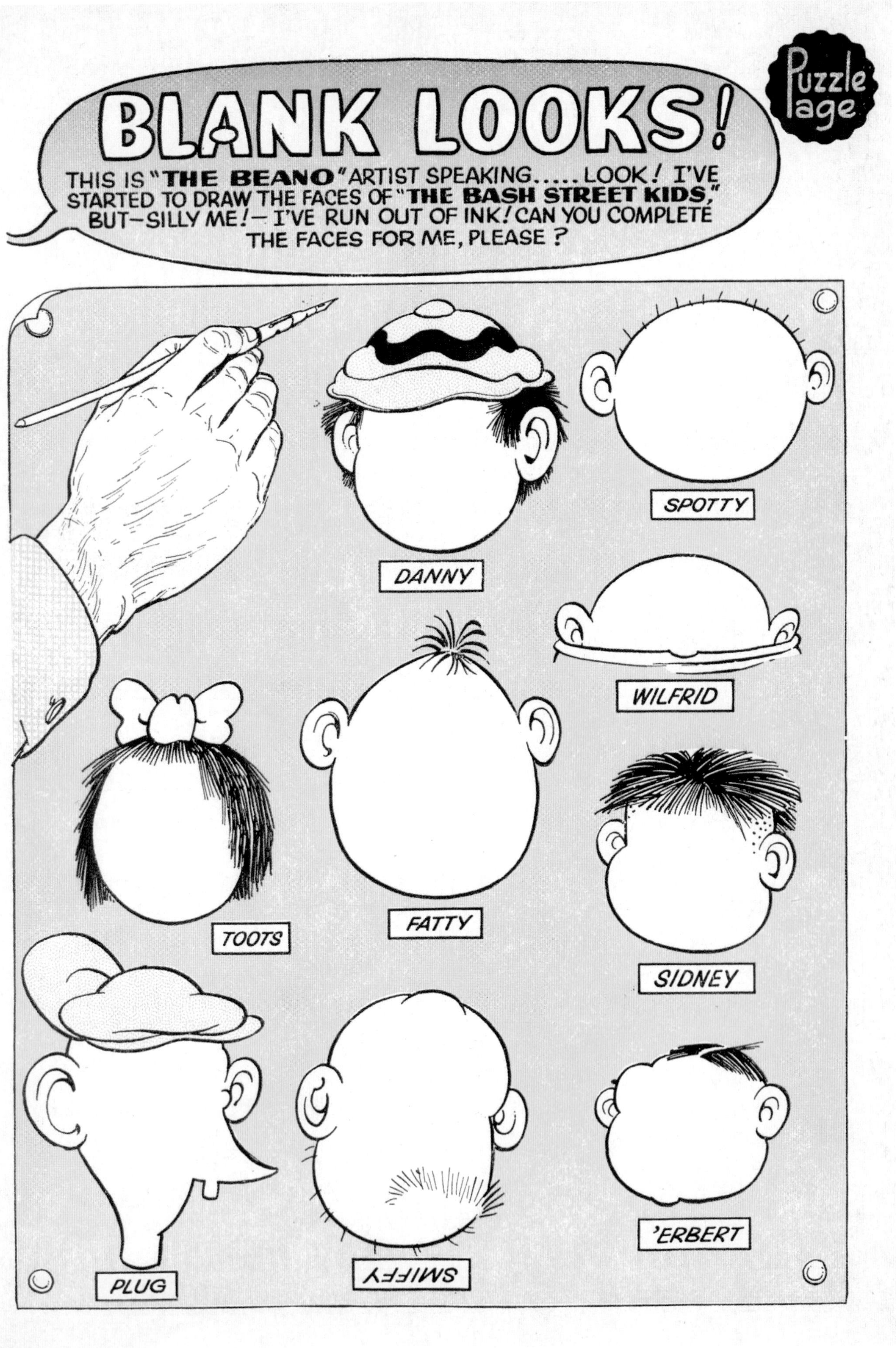
Puzzle Page
BLANK LOOKS!
THIS IS "THE BEANO" ARTIST SPEAKING..... LOOK! I'VE STARTED TO DRAW THE FACES OF "THE BASH STREET KIDS," BUT—SILLY ME!—I'VE RUN OUT OF INK! CAN YOU COMPLETE THE FACES FOR ME, PLEASE?
DANNY
SPOTTY
WILFRID
TOOTS
FATTY
SIDNEY
PLUG
SMIFFY
'ERBERT

YOU CAN DRAW ME!

FIRST, A CIRCLE FOR MY HANDSOME FACE —	— THEN TWO LINES FOR MY BEEE-OOTIFUL EYEBROWS —	— ADD A FEW CIRCLES AND YOU'VE DRAWN MY PEEPERS —
— ANOTHER CIRCLE FOR MY FAMOUS CONK —	— NEXT, SOME CURVED LINES MAKE MY MOUTH AND EARS —	— FINALLY ADD MY LOVELY LOCKS!

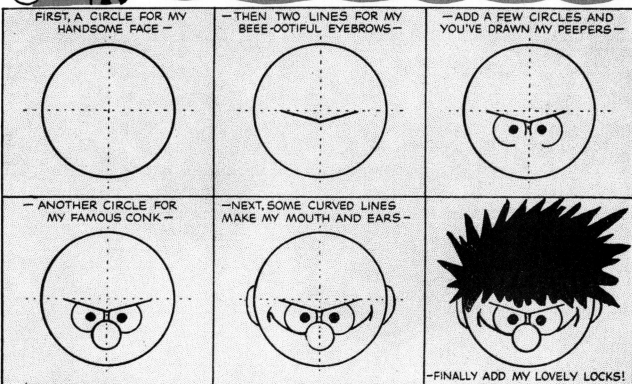

← YOU CAN ALSO PAINT ME →

USE PAINTS OR CRAYONS TO COLOUR THIS PICTURE — AND THE BEST OF LUCK, PALS!

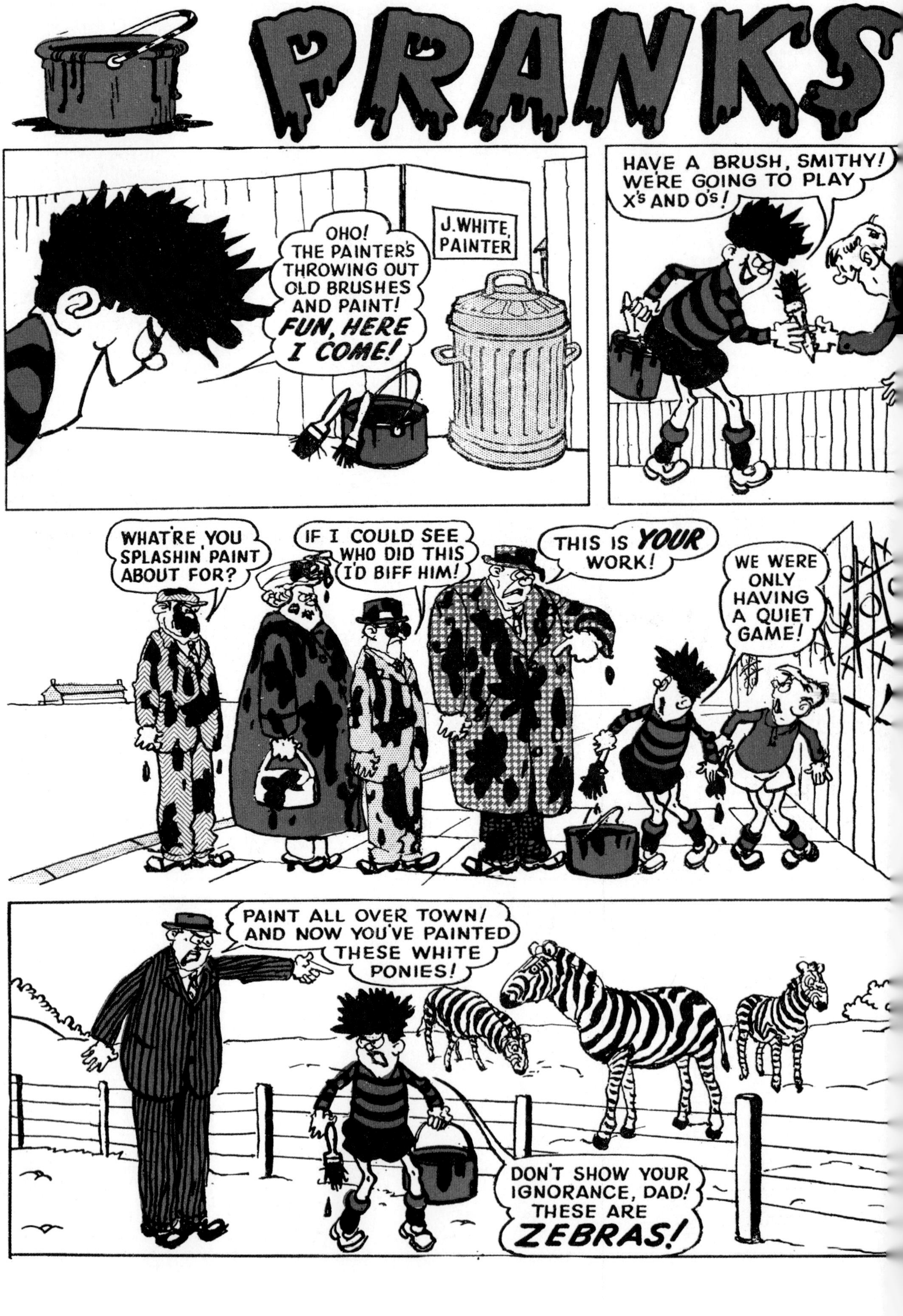
PRANKS
OHO! THE PAINTER'S THROWING OUT OLD BRUSHES AND PAINT! FUN, HERE I COME!
J. WHITE, PAINTER
HAVE A BRUSH, SMITHY! WE'RE GOING TO PLAY X's AND O's!
WHAT'RE YOU SPLASHIN' PAINT ABOUT FOR?
IF I COULD SEE WHO DID THIS I'D BIFF HIM!
THIS IS YOUR WORK!
WE WERE ONLY HAVING A QUIET GAME!
PAINT ALL OVER TOWN! AND NOW YOU'VE PAINTED THESE WHITE PONIES!
DON'T SHOW YOUR IGNORANCE, DAD! THESE ARE ZEBRAS!

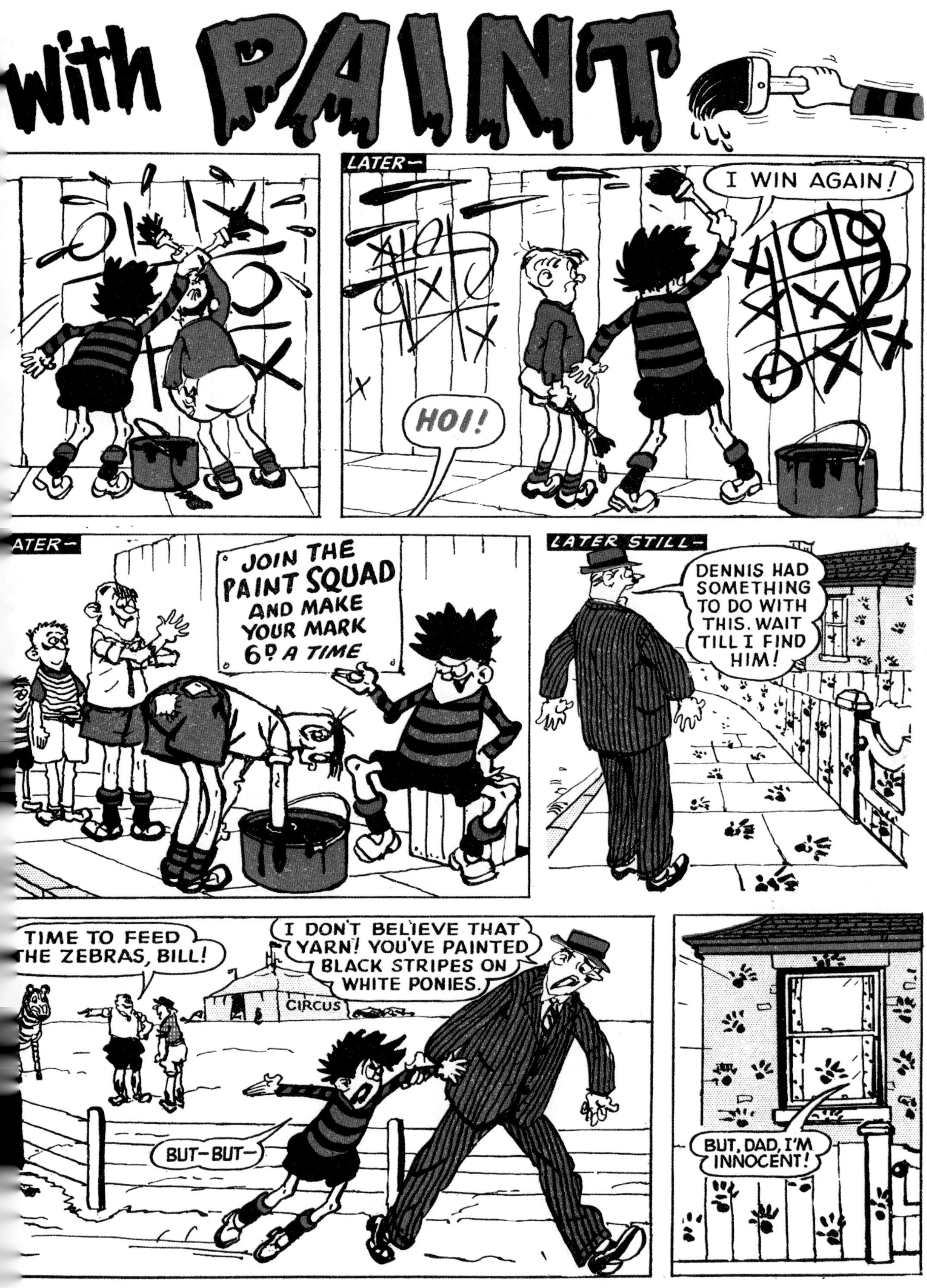
with PAINT
LATER—
I WIN AGAIN!
HOI!
ATER—
JOIN THE PAINT SQUAD AND MAKE YOUR MARK 6D A TIME
LATER STILL—
DENNIS HAD SOMETHING TO DO WITH THIS. WAIT TILL I FIND HIM!
TIME TO FEED THE ZEBRAS, BILL!
I DON'T BELIEVE THAT YARN! YOU'VE PAINTED BLACK STRIPES ON WHITE PONIES.
CIRCUS
BUT—BUT—
BUT, DAD, I'M INNOCENT!

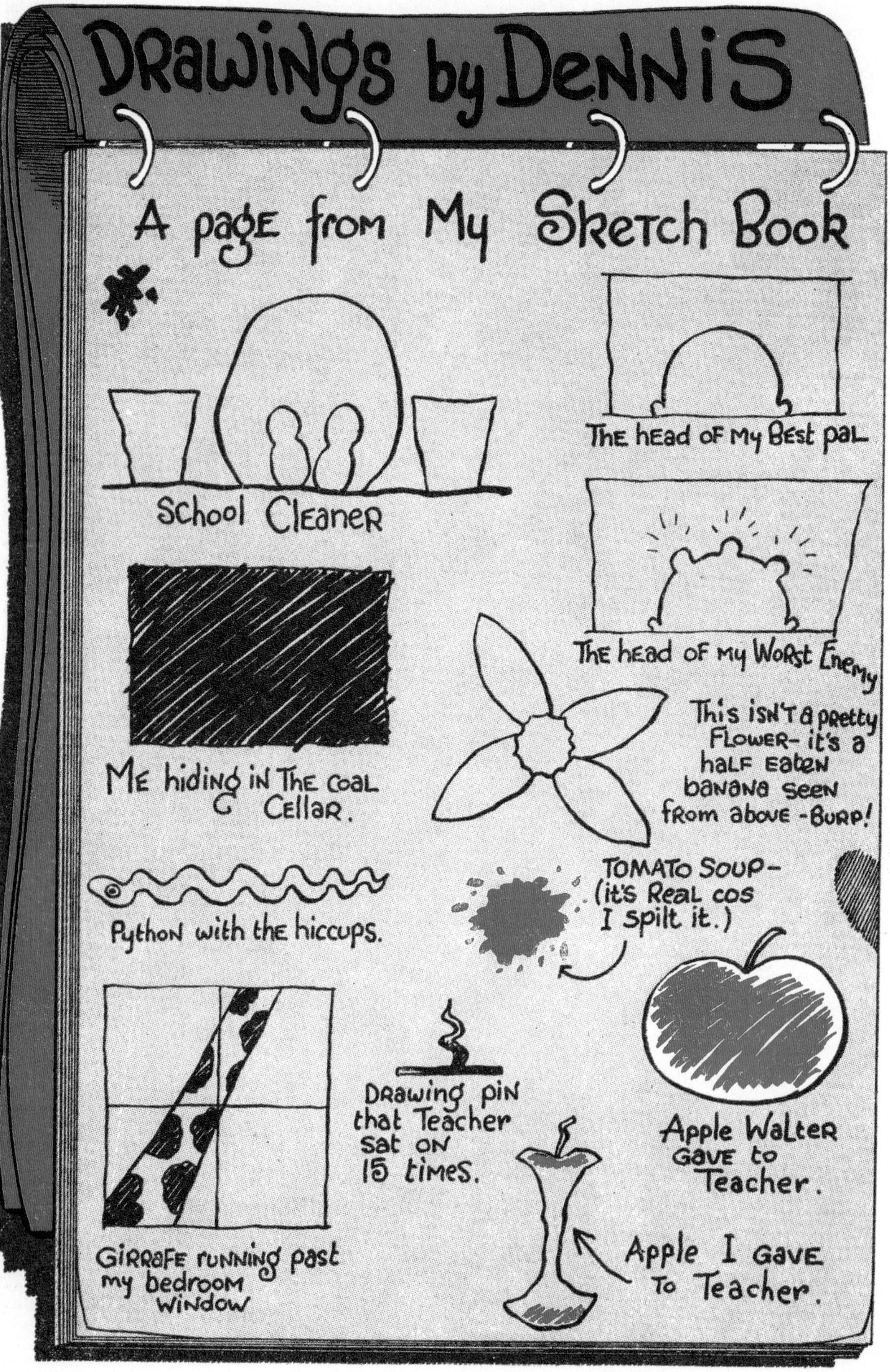

DRAWINGS by DENNIS

A page from My Sketch Book

School Cleaner

The head of My Best Pal

The head of My Worst Enemy

Me hiding in The coal Cellar.

This isn't a pretty FLOWER - it's a half eaten banana seen from above - Burp!

Python with the hiccups.

TOMATO SOUP - (it's Real cos I spilt it.)

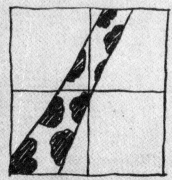

Girrafe running past my bedroom Window

Drawing pin that Teacher sat on 15 times.

Apple Walter Gave to Teacher.

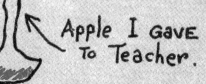

Apple I Gave To Teacher.

None but D. D. would dare — To smack the chin of a marble bear!

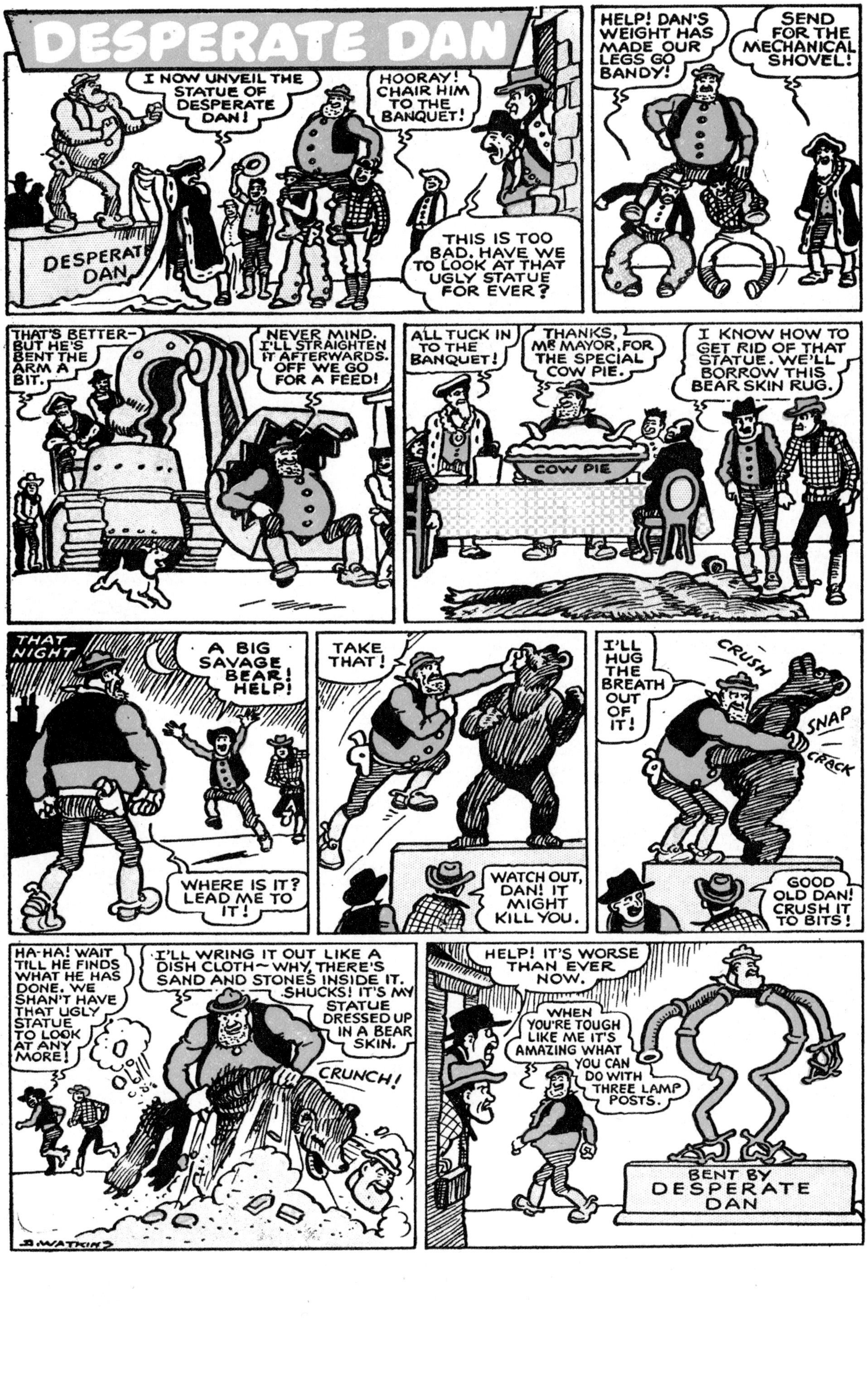
DESPERATE DAN
I NOW UNVEIL THE STATUE OF DESPERATE DAN!
DESPERATE DAN
HOORAY! CHAIR HIM TO THE BANQUET!
THIS IS TOO BAD. HAVE WE TO LOOK AT THAT UGLY STATUE FOR EVER?
HELP! DAN'S WEIGHT HAS MADE OUR LEGS GO BANDY!
SEND FOR THE MECHANICAL SHOVEL!
THAT'S BETTER— BUT HE'S BENT THE ARM A BIT.
NEVER MIND. I'LL STRAIGHTEN IT AFTERWARDS. OFF WE GO FOR A FEED!
ALL TUCK IN TO THE BANQUET!
THANKS, MR MAYOR, FOR THE SPECIAL COW PIE.
COW PIE
I KNOW HOW TO GET RID OF THAT STATUE. WE'LL BORROW THIS BEAR SKIN RUG.
THAT NIGHT
A BIG SAVAGE BEAR! HELP!
WHERE IS IT? LEAD ME TO IT!
TAKE THAT!
WATCH OUT, DAN! IT MIGHT KILL YOU.
I'LL HUG THE BREATH OUT OF IT!
CRUSH
SNAP
CRACK
GOOD OLD DAN! CRUSH IT TO BITS!
HA-HA! WAIT TILL HE FINDS WHAT HE HAS DONE. WE SHAN'T HAVE THAT UGLY STATUE TO LOOK AT ANY MORE!
I'LL WRING IT OUT LIKE A DISH CLOTH~ WHY, THERE'S SAND AND STONES INSIDE IT. SHUCKS! IT'S MY STATUE DRESSED UP IN A BEAR SKIN.
CRUNCH!
D. WATKINS
HELP! IT'S WORSE THAN EVER NOW.
WHEN YOU'RE TOUGH LIKE ME IT'S AMAZING WHAT YOU CAN DO WITH THREE LAMP POSTS.
BENT BY DESPERATE DAN

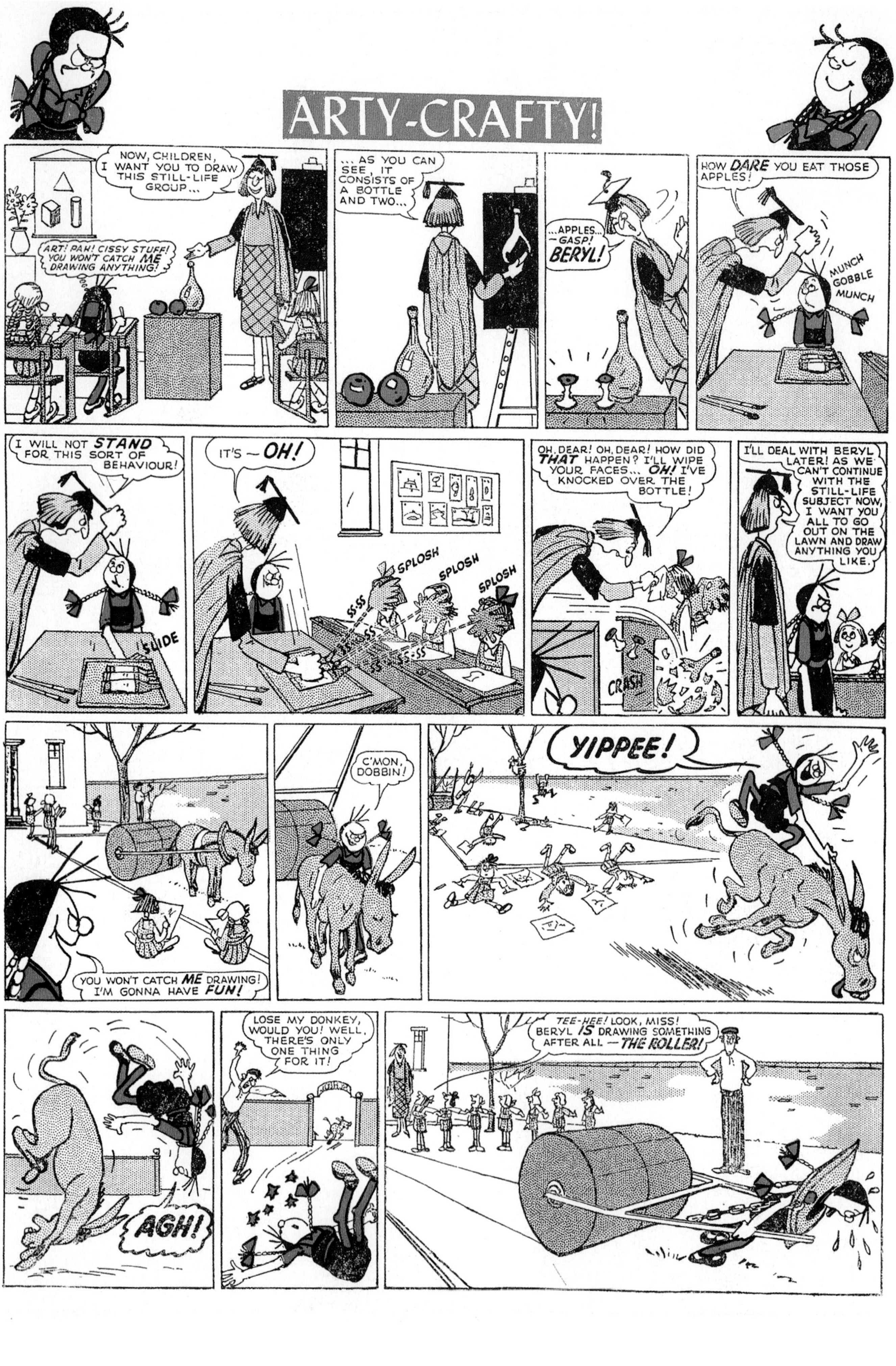
ARTY-CRAFTY!
NOW, CHILDREN, I WANT YOU TO DRAW THIS STILL-LIFE GROUP...
ART! PAH! CISSY STUFF! YOU WON'T CATCH ME DRAWING ANYTHING!
...AS YOU CAN SEE, IT CONSISTS OF A BOTTLE AND TWO...
...APPLES... —GASP! BERYL!
HOW DARE YOU EAT THOSE APPLES!
MUNCH
GOBBLE
MUNCH
I WILL NOT STAND FOR THIS SORT OF BEHAVIOUR!
SLIDE
IT'S — OH!
SPLOSH
SPLOSH
SPLOSH
OH, DEAR! OH, DEAR! HOW DID THAT HAPPEN? I'LL WIPE YOUR FACES... OH! I'VE KNOCKED OVER THE BOTTLE!
CRASH
I'LL DEAL WITH BERYL LATER! AS WE CAN'T CONTINUE WITH THE STILL-LIFE SUBJECT NOW, I WANT YOU ALL TO GO OUT ON THE LAWN AND DRAW ANYTHING YOU LIKE.
YOU WON'T CATCH ME DRAWING! I'M GONNA HAVE FUN!
C'MON, DOBBIN!
YIPPEE!
AGH!
LOSE MY DONKEY, WOULD YOU! WELL, THERE'S ONLY ONE THING FOR IT!
TEE-HEE! LOOK, MISS! BERYL IS DRAWING SOMETHING AFTER ALL — THE ROLLER!

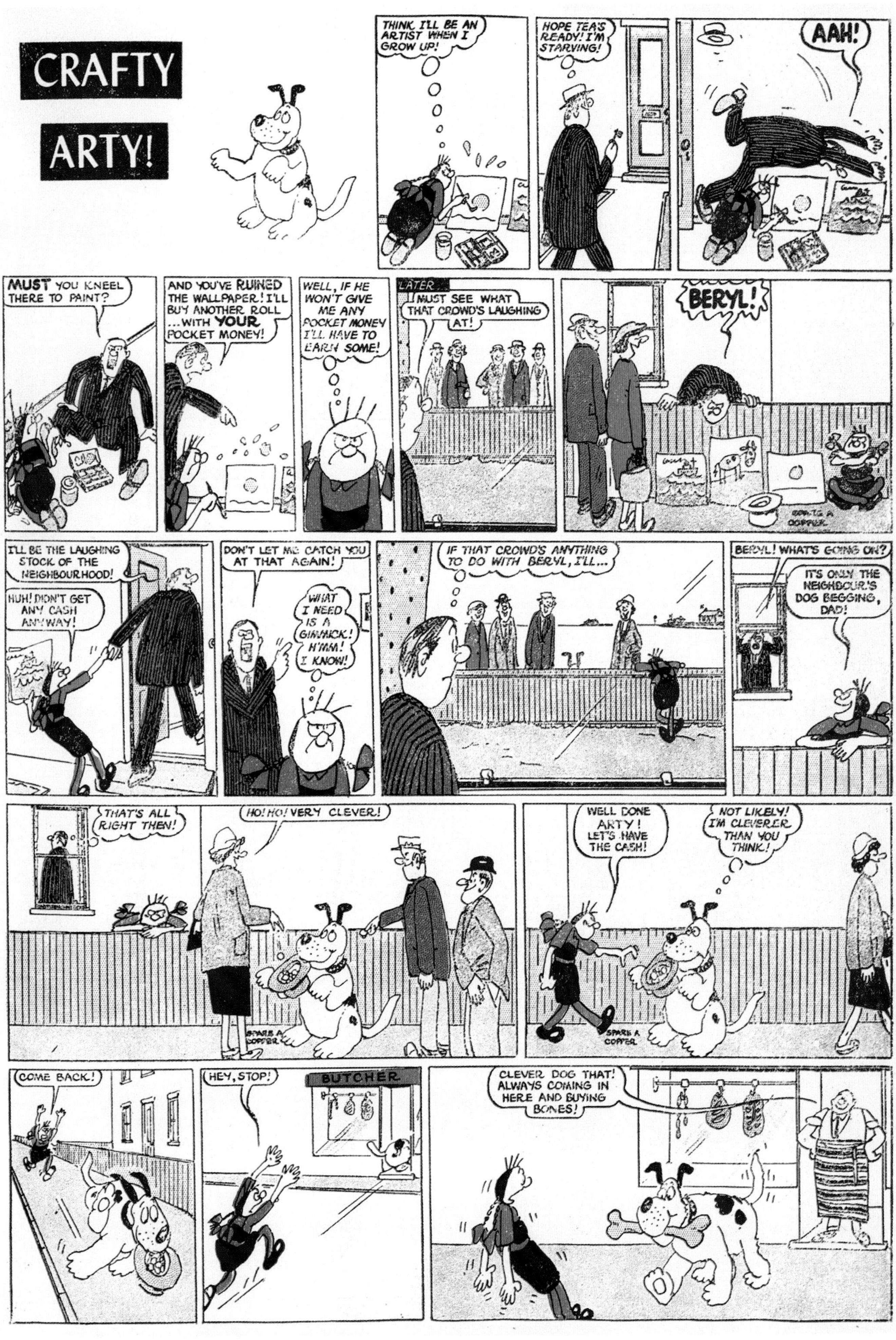
CRAFTY ARTY!
THINK I'LL BE AN ARTIST WHEN I GROW UP!
HOPE TEA'S READY! I'M STARVING!
AAH!
MUST YOU KNEEL THERE TO PAINT?
AND YOU'VE RUINED THE WALLPAPER! I'LL BUY ANOTHER ROLL ...WITH YOUR POCKET MONEY!
WELL, IF HE WON'T GIVE ME ANY POCKET MONEY I'LL HAVE TO EARN SOME!
LATER...
MUST SEE WHAT THAT CROWD'S LAUGHING AT!
BERYL!
SPARE A COPPER
I'LL BE THE LAUGHING STOCK OF THE NEIGHBOURHOOD!
HUH! DIDN'T GET ANY CASH ANYWAY!
DON'T LET ME CATCH YOU AT THAT AGAIN!
WHAT I NEED IS A GIMMICK! H'MM! I KNOW!
IF THAT CROWD'S ANYTHING TO DO WITH BERYL, I'LL...
BERYL! WHAT'S GOING ON?
IT'S ONLY THE NEIGHBOUR'S DOG BEGGING, DAD!
THAT'S ALL RIGHT THEN!
HO! HO! VERY CLEVER!
SPARE A COPPER
WELL DONE ARTY! LET'S HAVE THE CASH!
NOT LIKELY! I'M CLEVERER THAN YOU THINK!
SPARE A COPPER
COME BACK!
HEY, STOP!
BUTCHER
CLEVER DOG THAT! ALWAYS COMING IN HERE AND BUYING BONES!

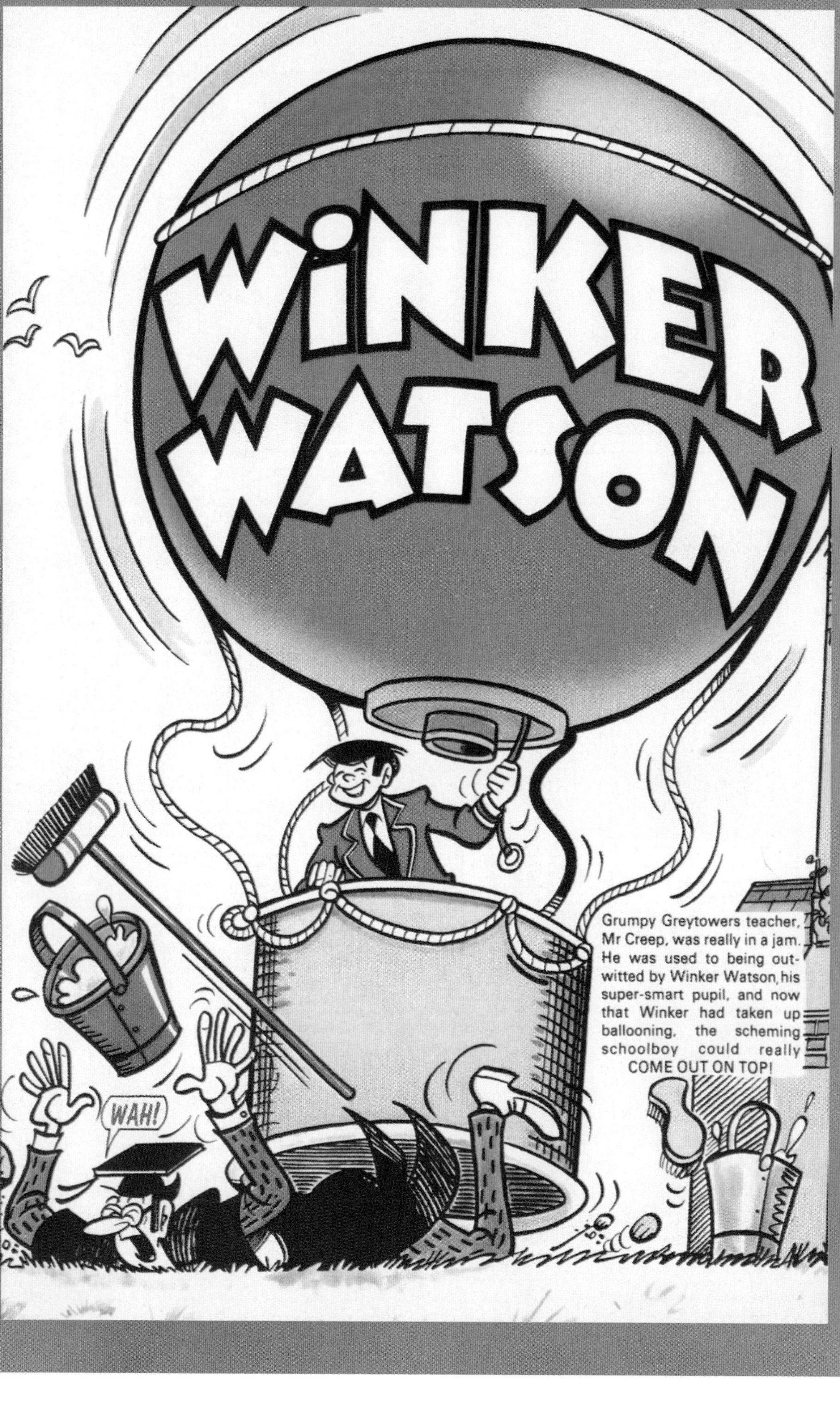
WINKER WATSON
Grumpy Greytowers teacher, Mr Creep, was really in a jam. He was used to being out-witted by Winker Watson, his super-smart pupil, and now that Winker had taken up ballooning, the scheming schoolboy could really COME OUT ON TOP!
WAH!

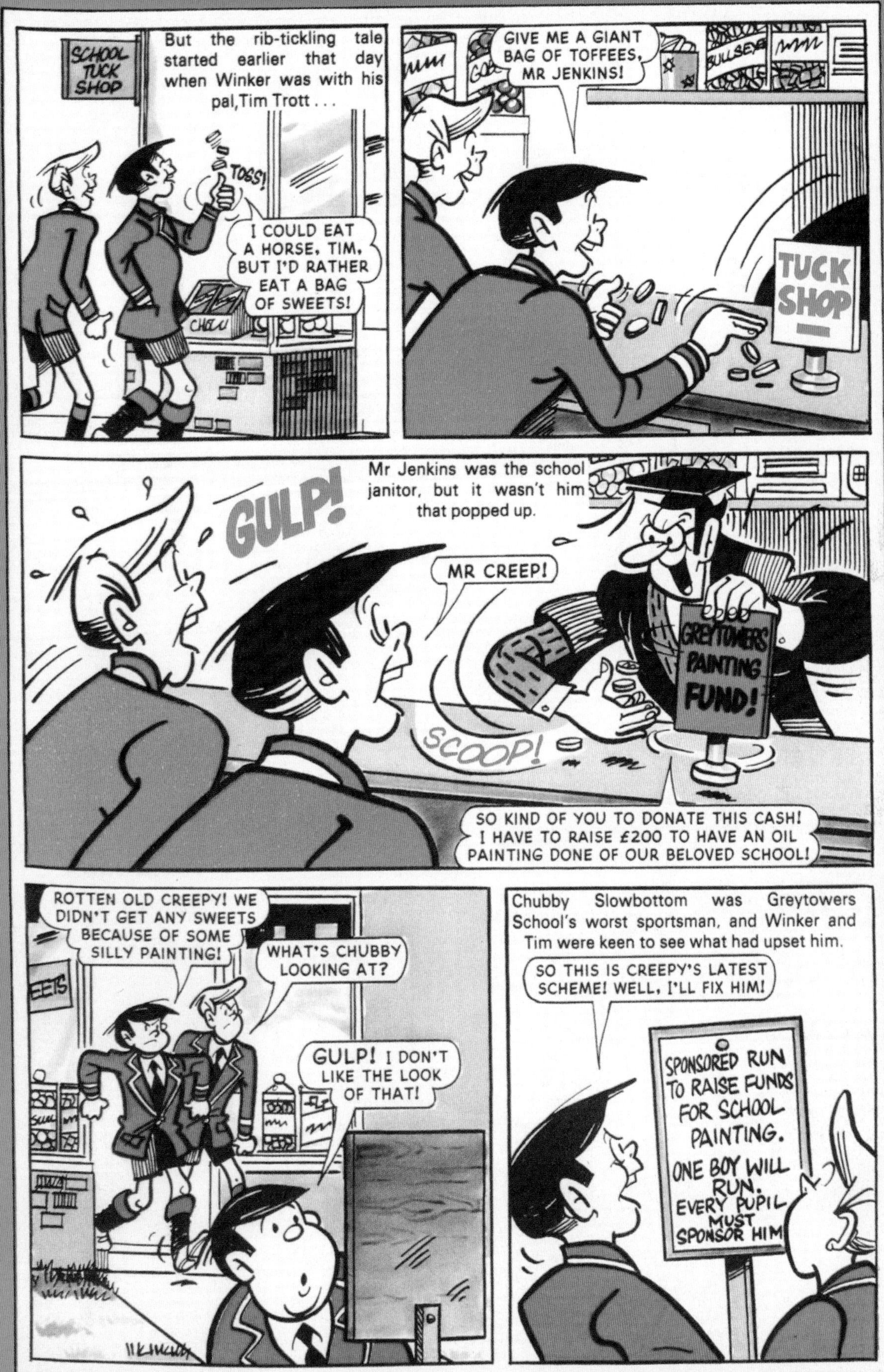
SCHOOL TUCK SHOP
But the rib-tickling tale started earlier that day when Winker was with his pal, Tim Trott . . .
TOSS!
I COULD EAT A HORSE, TIM, BUT I'D RATHER EAT A BAG OF SWEETS!
GIVE ME A GIANT BAG OF TOFFEES, MR JENKINS!
BULLSEYE
TUCK SHOP
Mr Jenkins was the school janitor, but it wasn't him that popped up.
GULP!
MR CREEP!
GREYTOWERS PAINTING FUND!
SCOOP!
SO KIND OF YOU TO DONATE THIS CASH! I HAVE TO RAISE £200 TO HAVE AN OIL PAINTING DONE OF OUR BELOVED SCHOOL!
ROTTEN OLD CREEPY! WE DIDN'T GET ANY SWEETS BECAUSE OF SOME SILLY PAINTING!
WHAT'S CHUBBY LOOKING AT?
GULP! I DON'T LIKE THE LOOK OF THAT!
Chubby Slowbottom was Greytowers School's worst sportsman, and Winker and Tim were keen to see what had upset him.
SO THIS IS CREEPY'S LATEST SCHEME! WELL, I'LL FIX HIM!
SPONSORED RUN TO RAISE FUNDS FOR SCHOOL PAINTING. ONE BOY WILL RUN. EVERY PUPIL MUST SPONSOR HIM

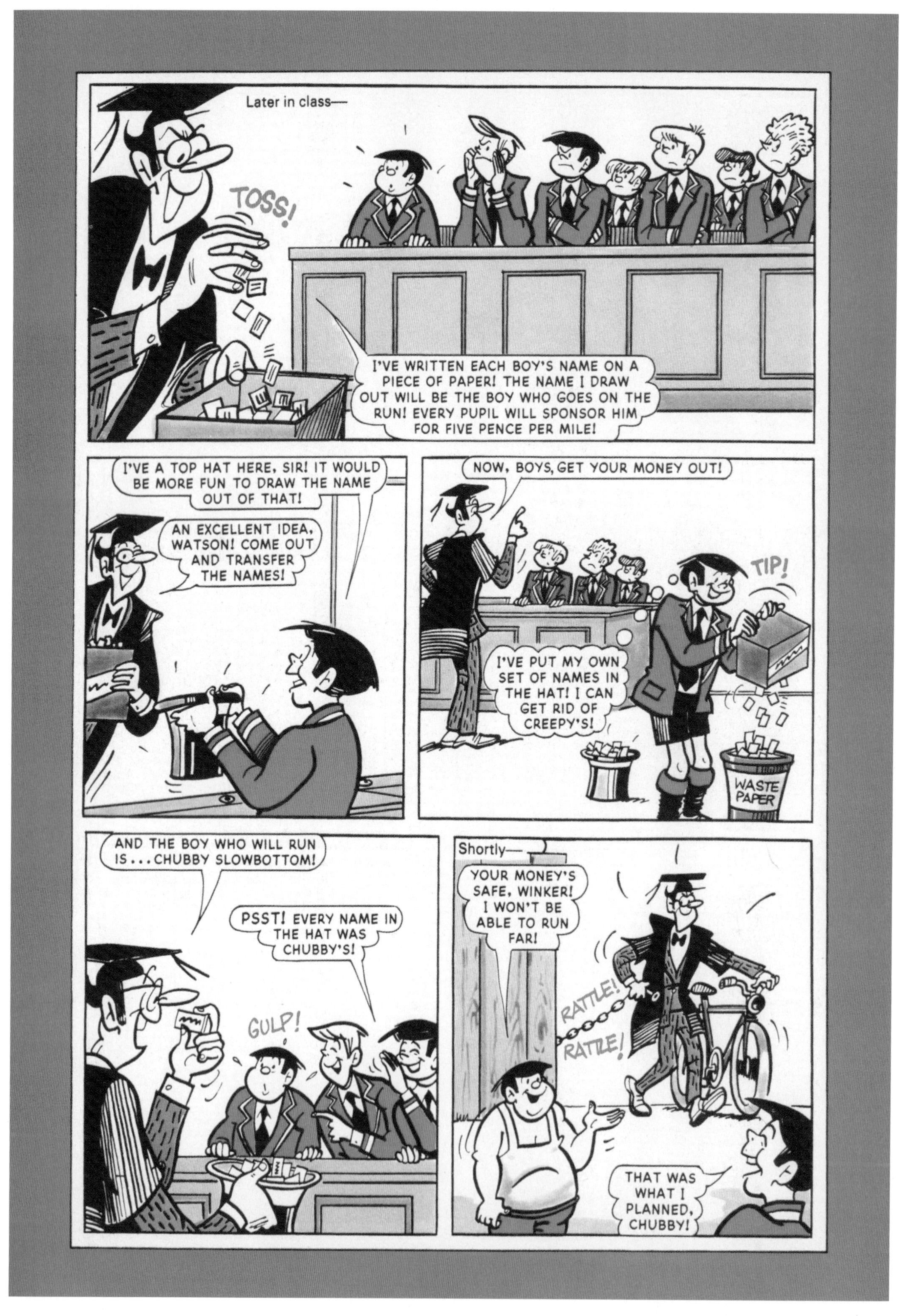
Later in class—
TOSS!
I'VE WRITTEN EACH BOY'S NAME ON A PIECE OF PAPER! THE NAME I DRAW OUT WILL BE THE BOY WHO GOES ON THE RUN! EVERY PUPIL WILL SPONSOR HIM FOR FIVE PENCE PER MILE!
I'VE A TOP HAT HERE, SIR! IT WOULD BE MORE FUN TO DRAW THE NAME OUT OF THAT!
AN EXCELLENT IDEA, WATSON! COME OUT AND TRANSFER THE NAMES!
NOW, BOYS, GET YOUR MONEY OUT!
TIP!
I'VE PUT MY OWN SET OF NAMES IN THE HAT! I CAN GET RID OF CREEPY'S!
WASTE PAPER
AND THE BOY WHO WILL RUN IS . . . CHUBBY SLOWBOTTOM!
PSST! EVERY NAME IN THE HAT WAS CHUBBY'S!
GULP!
Shortly—
YOUR MONEY'S SAFE, WINKER! I WON'T BE ABLE TO RUN FAR!
RATTLE! RATTLE!
THAT WAS WHAT I PLANNED, CHUBBY!

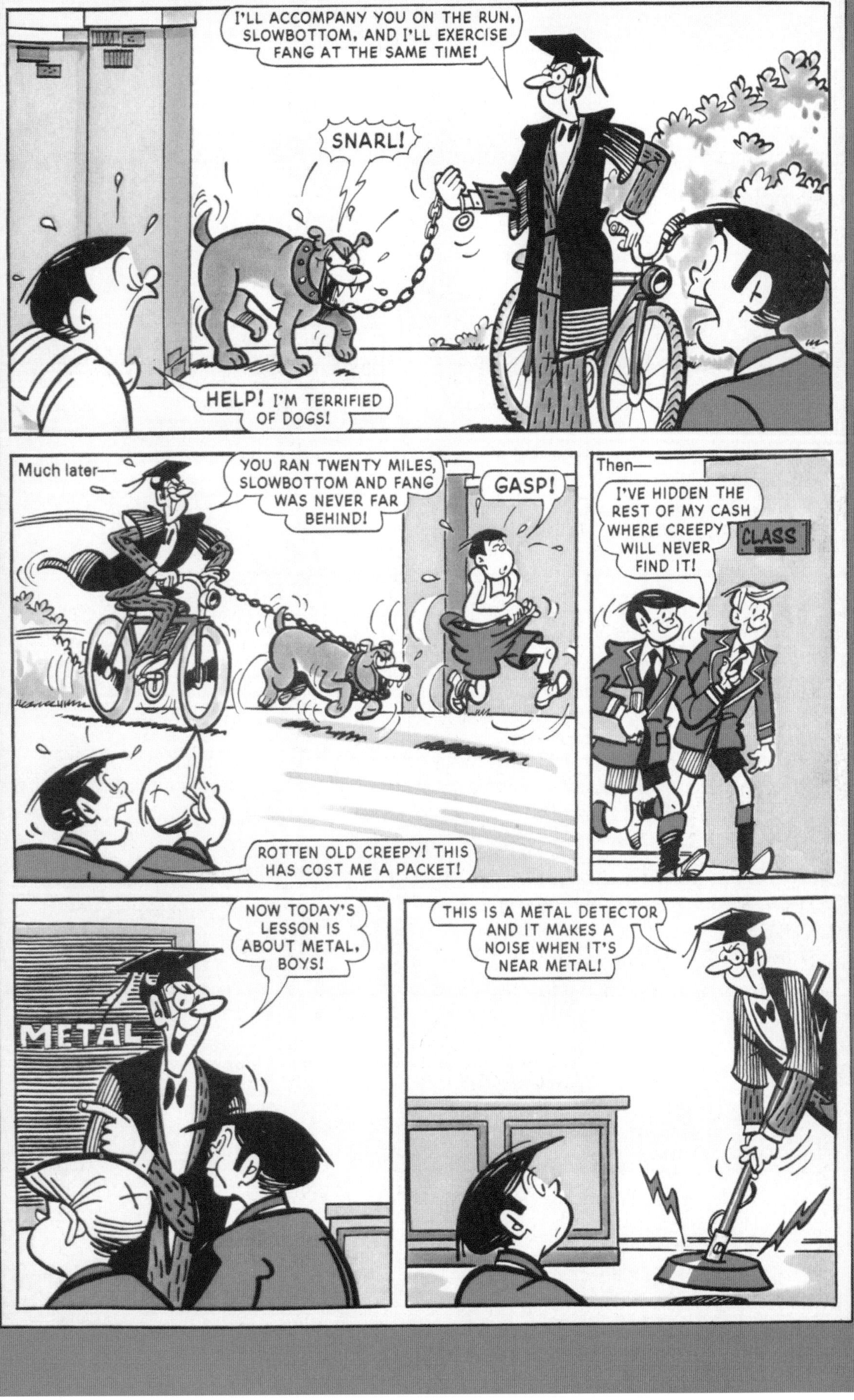
I'LL ACCOMPANY YOU ON THE RUN, SLOWBOTTOM, AND I'LL EXERCISE FANG AT THE SAME TIME!
SNARL!
HELP! I'M TERRIFIED OF DOGS!
Much later—
YOU RAN TWENTY MILES, SLOWBOTTOM AND FANG WAS NEVER FAR BEHIND!
GASP!
ROTTEN OLD CREEPY! THIS HAS COST ME A PACKET!
Then—
I'VE HIDDEN THE REST OF MY CASH WHERE CREEPY WILL NEVER FIND IT!
CLASS
NOW TODAY'S LESSON IS ABOUT METAL, BOYS!
METAL
THIS IS A METAL DETECTOR AND IT MAKES A NOISE WHEN IT'S NEAR METAL!

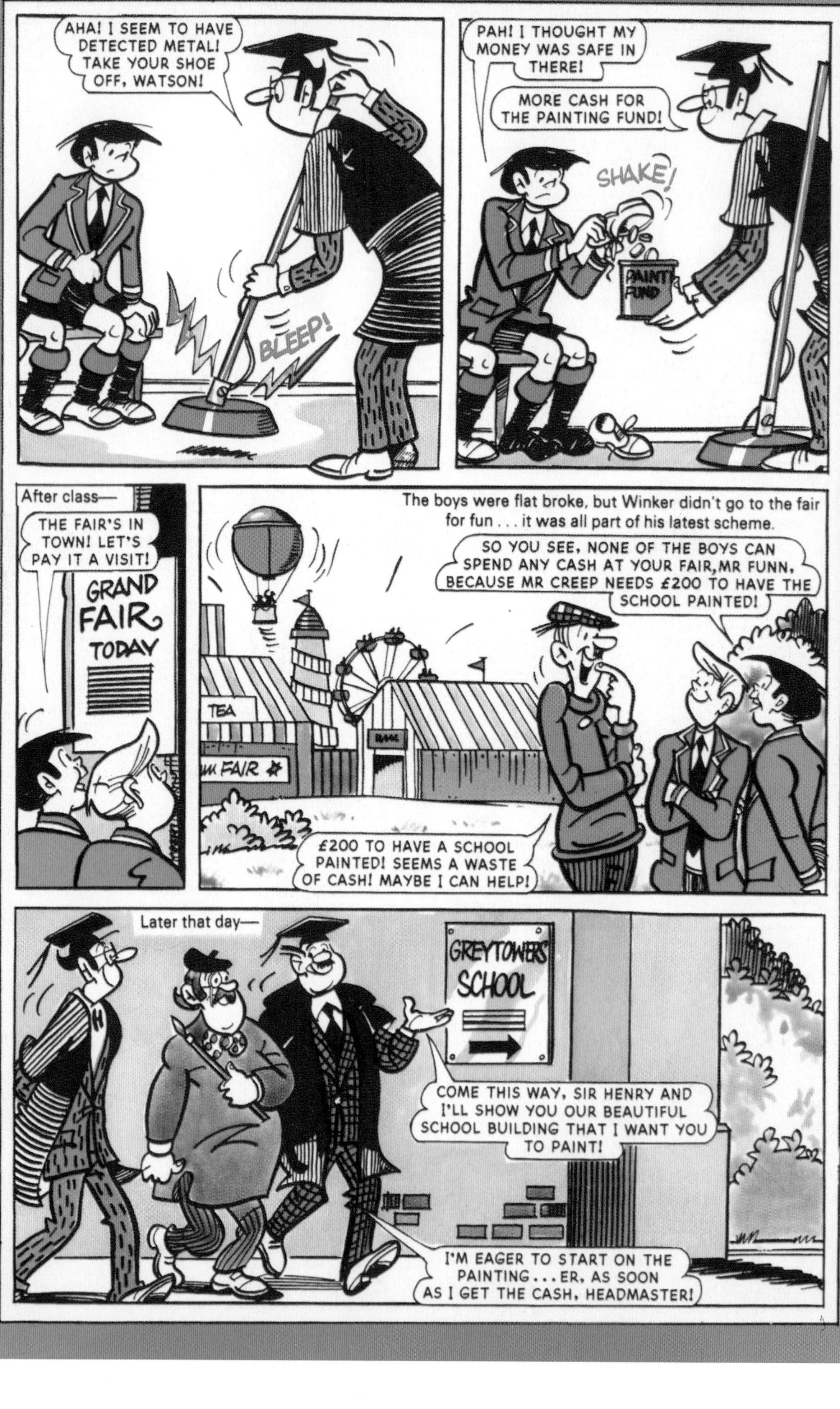
AHA! I SEEM TO HAVE DETECTED METAL! TAKE YOUR SHOE OFF, WATSON!
BLEEP!
PAH! I THOUGHT MY MONEY WAS SAFE IN THERE!
MORE CASH FOR THE PAINTING FUND!
SHAKE!
PAINT FUND
After class—
THE FAIR'S IN TOWN! LET'S PAY IT A VISIT!
GRAND FAIR TODAY
The boys were flat broke, but Winker didn't go to the fair for fun . . . it was all part of his latest scheme.
SO YOU SEE, NONE OF THE BOYS CAN SPEND ANY CASH AT YOUR FAIR, MR FUNN, BECAUSE MR CREEP NEEDS £200 TO HAVE THE SCHOOL PAINTED!
TEA
FAIR
£200 TO HAVE A SCHOOL PAINTED! SEEMS A WASTE OF CASH! MAYBE I CAN HELP!
Later that day—
GREYTOWERS' SCHOOL
COME THIS WAY, SIR HENRY AND I'LL SHOW YOU OUR BEAUTIFUL SCHOOL BUILDING THAT I WANT YOU TO PAINT!
I'M EAGER TO START ON THE PAINTING . . . ER, AS SOON AS I GET THE CASH, HEADMASTER!

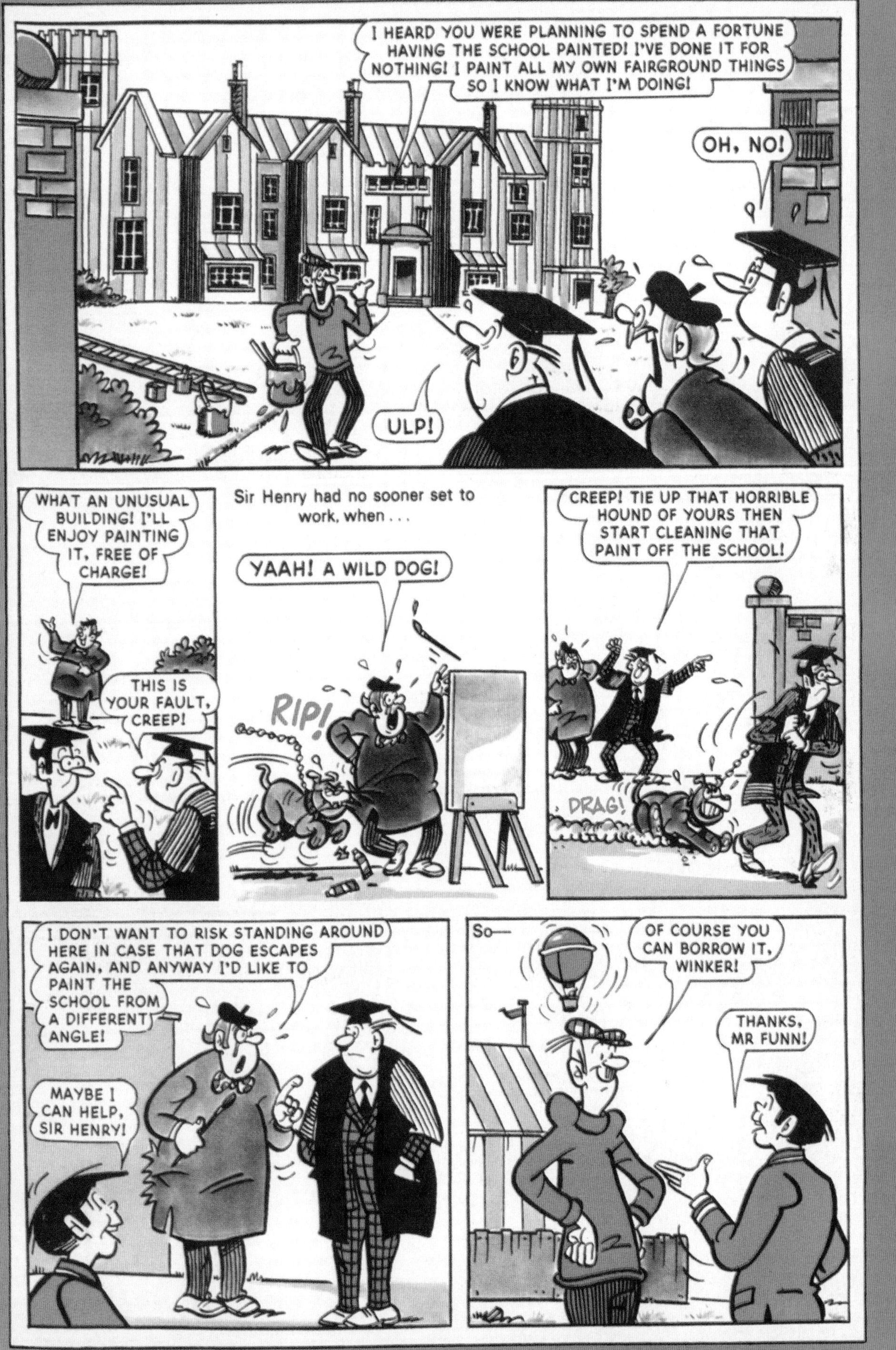
I HEARD YOU WERE PLANNING TO SPEND A FORTUNE HAVING THE SCHOOL PAINTED! I'VE DONE IT FOR NOTHING! I PAINT ALL MY OWN FAIRGROUND THINGS SO I KNOW WHAT I'M DOING!
OH, NO!
ULP!
WHAT AN UNUSUAL BUILDING! I'LL ENJOY PAINTING IT, FREE OF CHARGE!
THIS IS YOUR FAULT, CREEP!
Sir Henry had no sooner set to work, when . . .
YAAH! A WILD DOG!
RIP!
CREEP! TIE UP THAT HORRIBLE HOUND OF YOURS THEN START CLEANING THAT PAINT OFF THE SCHOOL!
DRAG!
I DON'T WANT TO RISK STANDING AROUND HERE IN CASE THAT DOG ESCAPES AGAIN, AND ANYWAY I'D LIKE TO PAINT THE SCHOOL FROM A DIFFERENT ANGLE!
MAYBE I CAN HELP, SIR HENRY!
So—
OF COURSE YOU CAN BORROW IT, WINKER!
THANKS, MR FUNN!

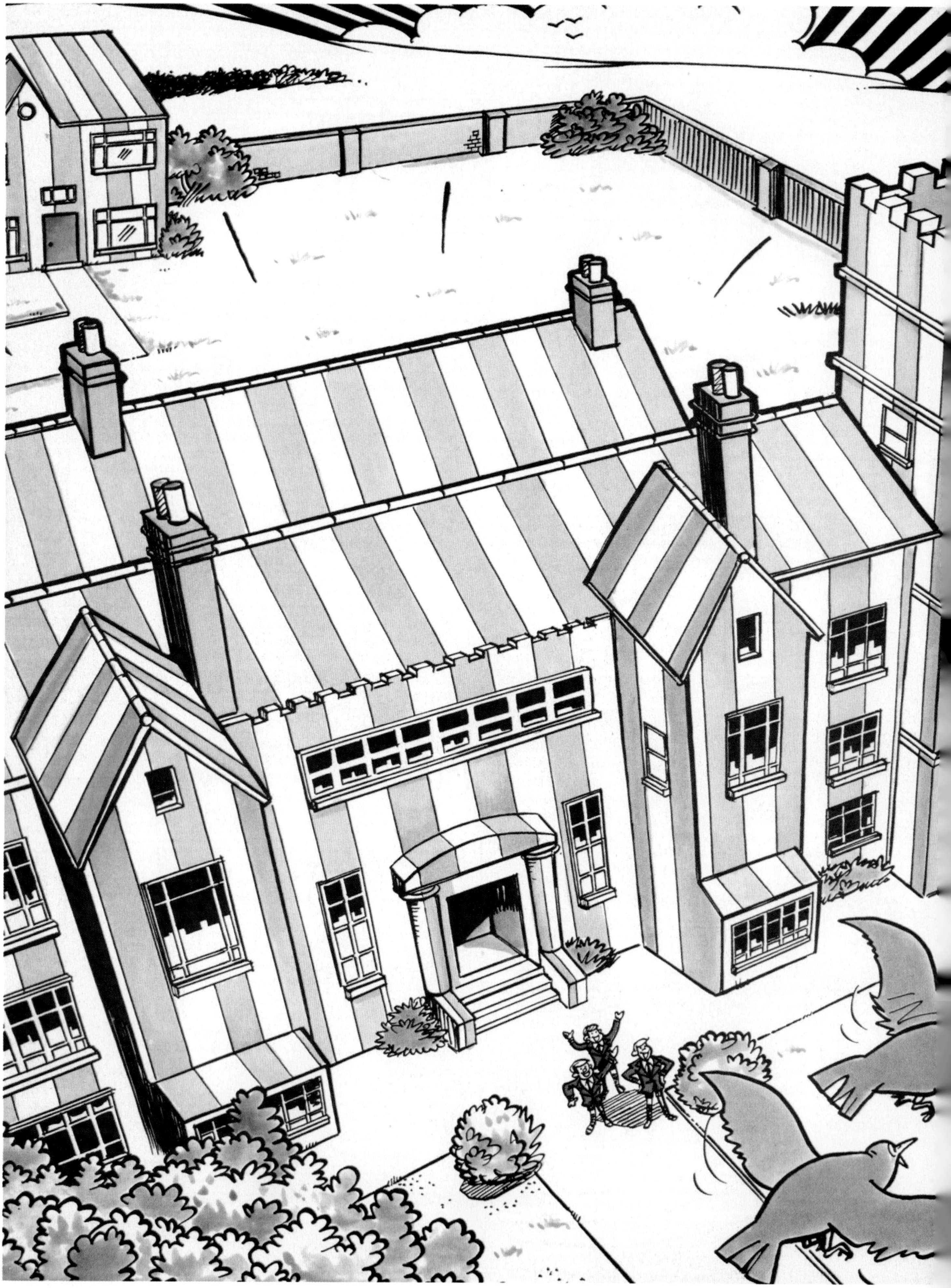

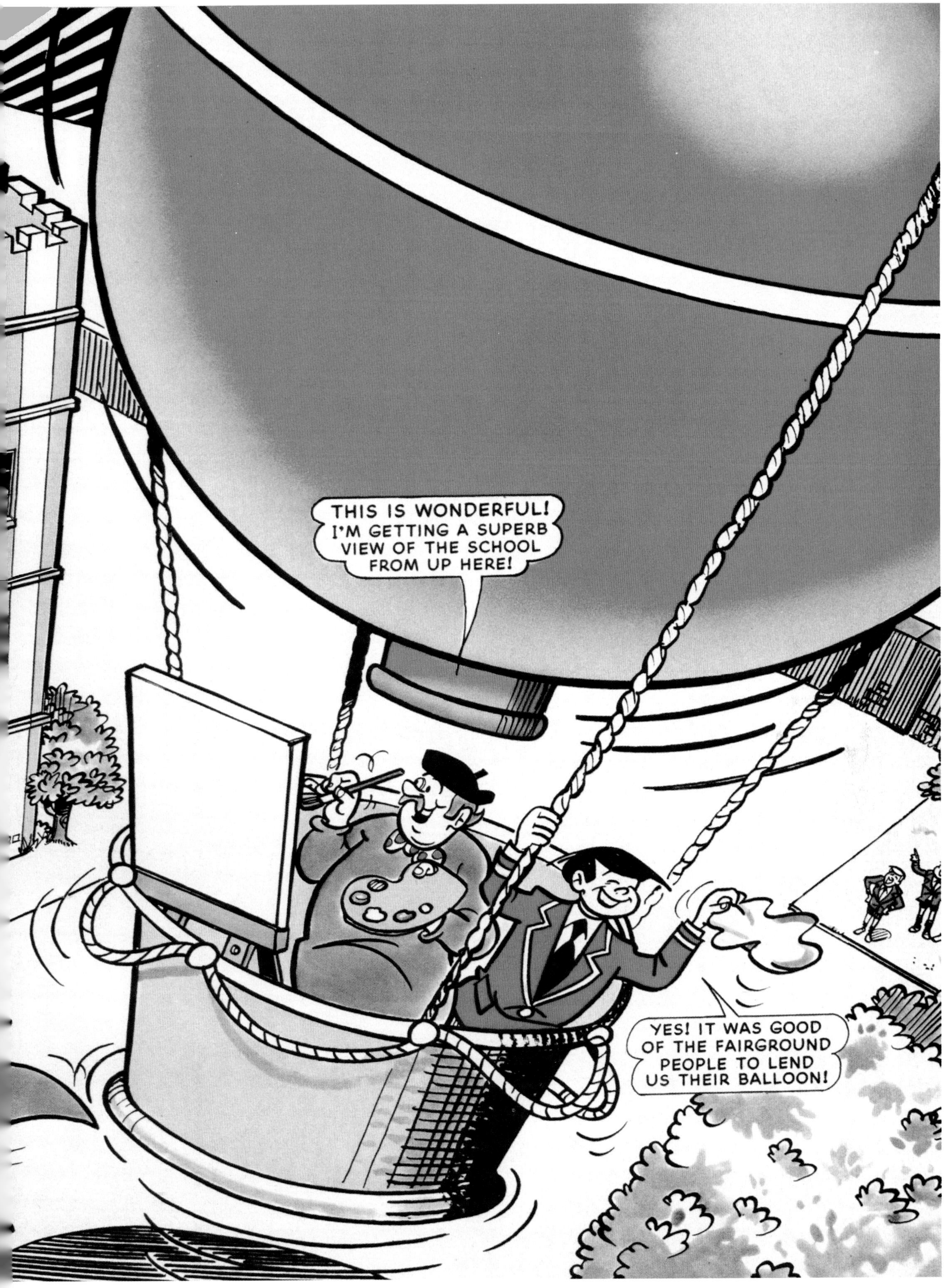
THIS IS WONDERFUL! I'M GETTING A SUPERB VIEW OF THE SCHOOL FROM UP HERE!
YES! IT WAS GOOD OF THE FAIRGROUND PEOPLE TO LEND US THEIR BALLOON!

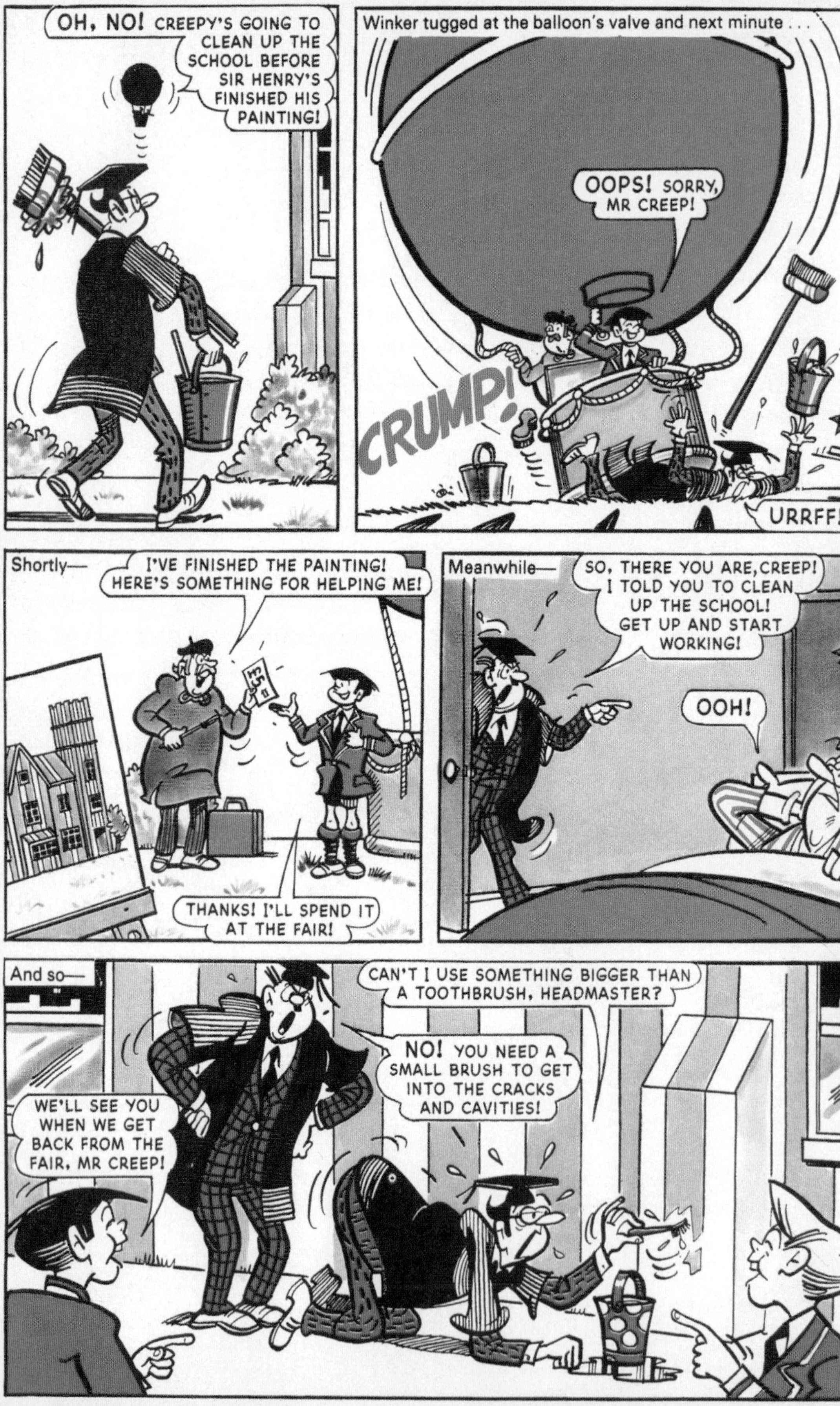
OH, NO! CREEPY'S GOING TO CLEAN UP THE SCHOOL BEFORE SIR HENRY'S FINISHED HIS PAINTING!
Winker tugged at the balloon's valve and next minute . . .
OOPS! SORRY, MR CREEP!
CRUMP!
URRFF!
Shortly—
I'VE FINISHED THE PAINTING! HERE'S SOMETHING FOR HELPING ME!
THANKS! I'LL SPEND IT AT THE FAIR!
Meanwhile—
SO, THERE YOU ARE, CREEP! I TOLD YOU TO CLEAN UP THE SCHOOL! GET UP AND START WORKING!
OOH!
And so—
CAN'T I USE SOMETHING BIGGER THAN A TOOTHBRUSH, HEADMASTER?
NO! YOU NEED A SMALL BRUSH TO GET INTO THE CRACKS AND CAVITIES!
WE'LL SEE YOU WHEN WE GET BACK FROM THE FAIR, MR CREEP!

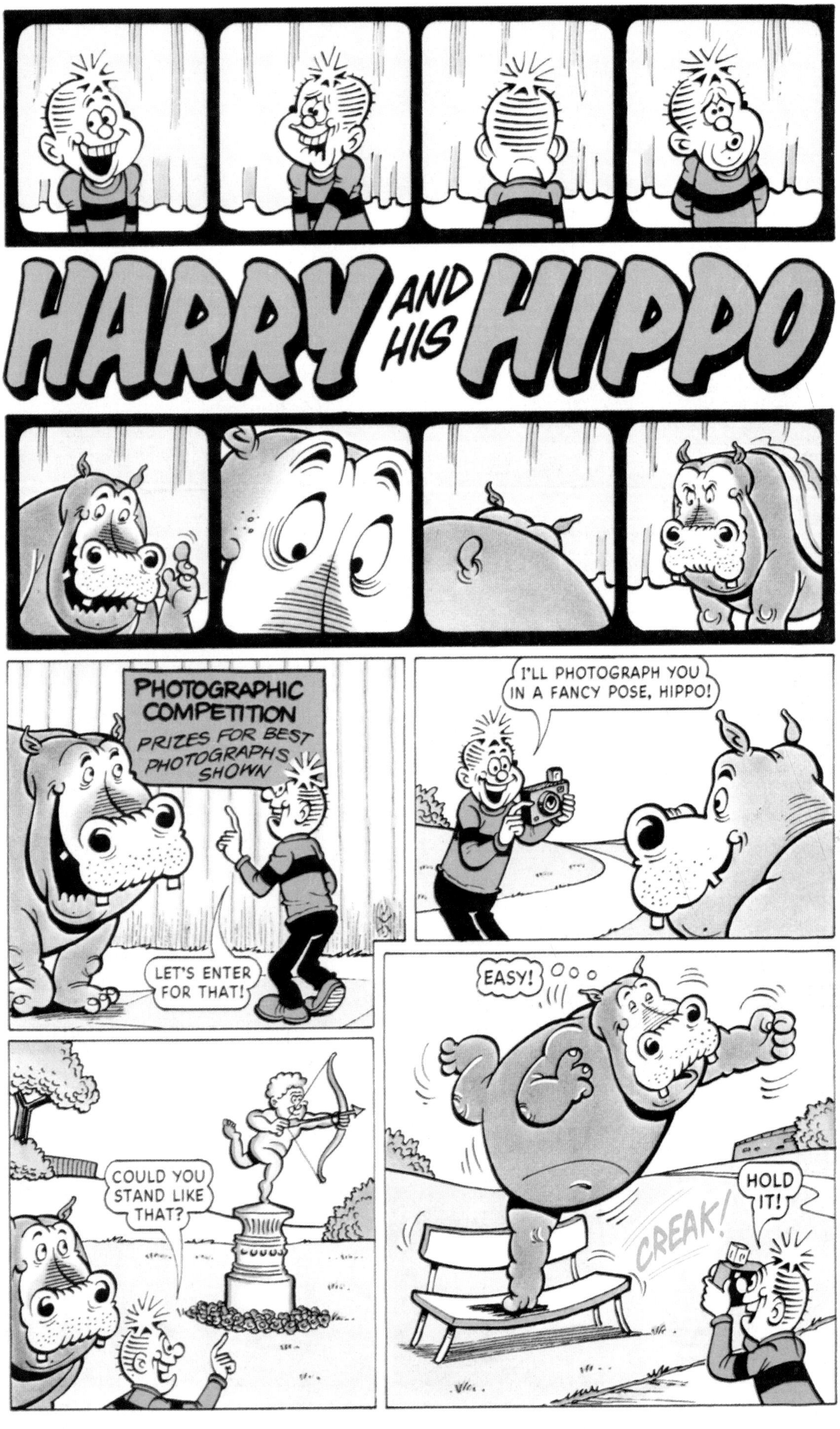
HARRY AND HIS HIPPO
PHOTOGRAPHIC COMPETITION
PRIZES FOR BEST PHOTOGRAPHS SHOWN
LET'S ENTER FOR THAT!
I'LL PHOTOGRAPH YOU IN A FANCY POSE, HIPPO!
COULD YOU STAND LIKE THAT?
EASY!
CREAK!
HOLD IT!

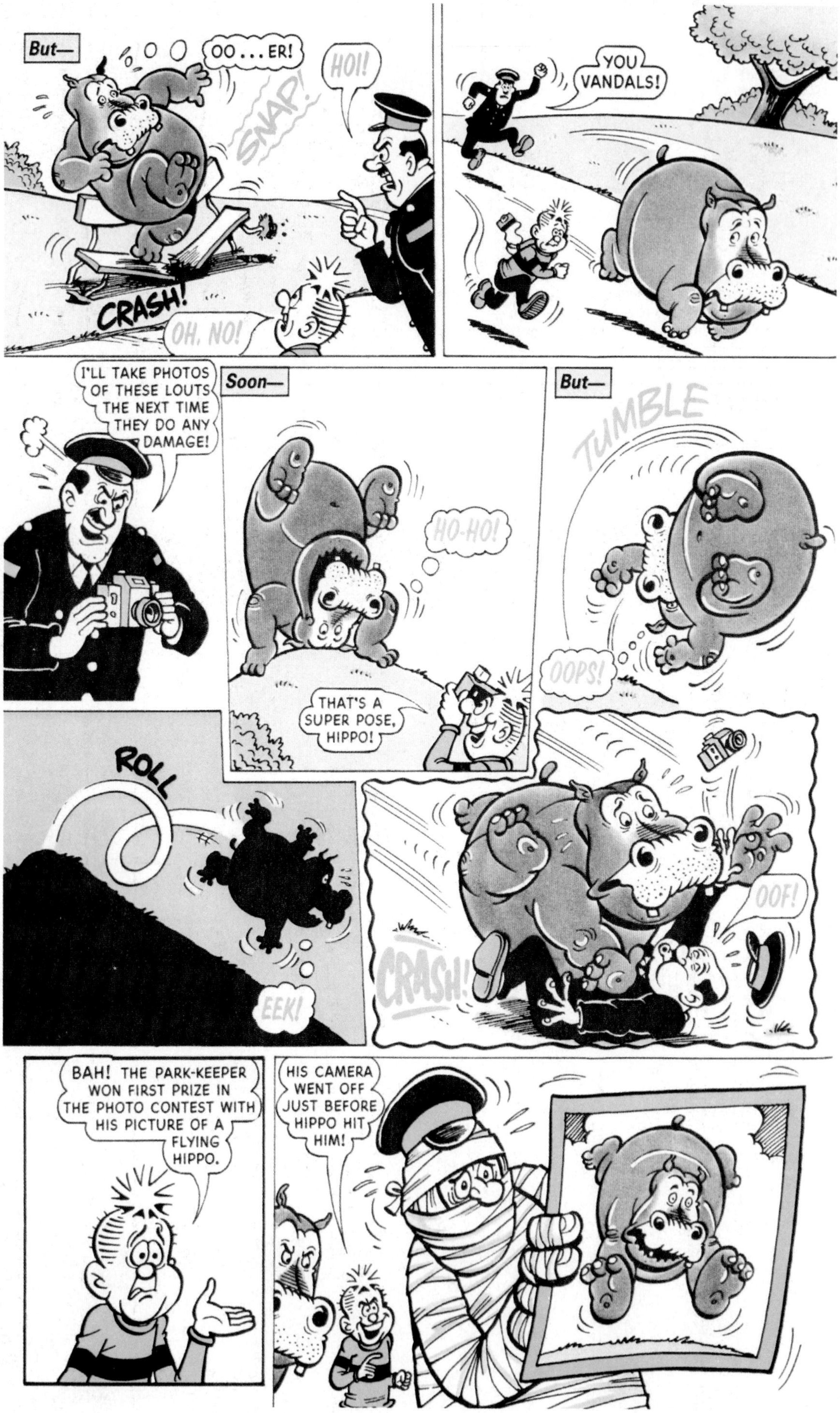

But—
OO ... ER!
HOI!
SNAP!
CRASH!
OH, NO!
YOU VANDALS!
I'LL TAKE PHOTOS OF THESE LOUTS THE NEXT TIME THEY DO ANY DAMAGE!
Soon—
HO-HO!
THAT'S A SUPER POSE, HIPPO!
But—
TUMBLE
OOPS!
ROLL
EEK!
CRASH!
OOF!
BAH! THE PARK-KEEPER WON FIRST PRIZE IN THE PHOTO CONTEST WITH HIS PICTURE OF A FLYING HIPPO.
HIS CAMERA WENT OFF JUST BEFORE HIPPO HIT HIM!

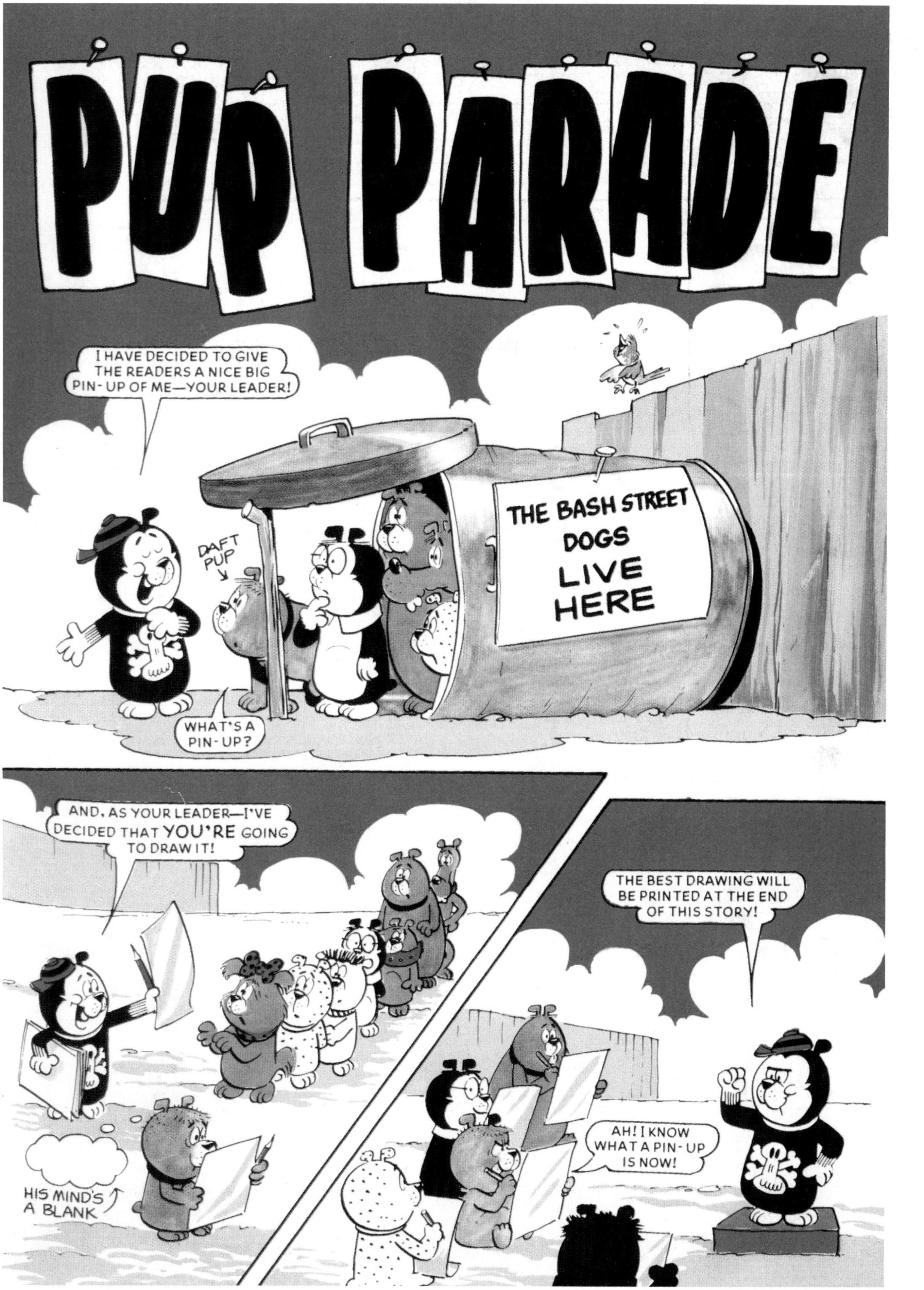
PUP PARADE
I HAVE DECIDED TO GIVE THE READERS A NICE BIG PIN-UP OF ME—YOUR LEADER!
DAFT PUP
THE BASH STREET DOGS LIVE HERE
WHAT'S A PIN-UP?
AND, AS YOUR LEADER—I'VE DECIDED THAT YOU'RE GOING TO DRAW IT!
HIS MIND'S A BLANK
THE BEST DRAWING WILL BE PRINTED AT THE END OF THIS STORY!
AH! I KNOW WHAT A PIN-UP IS NOW!

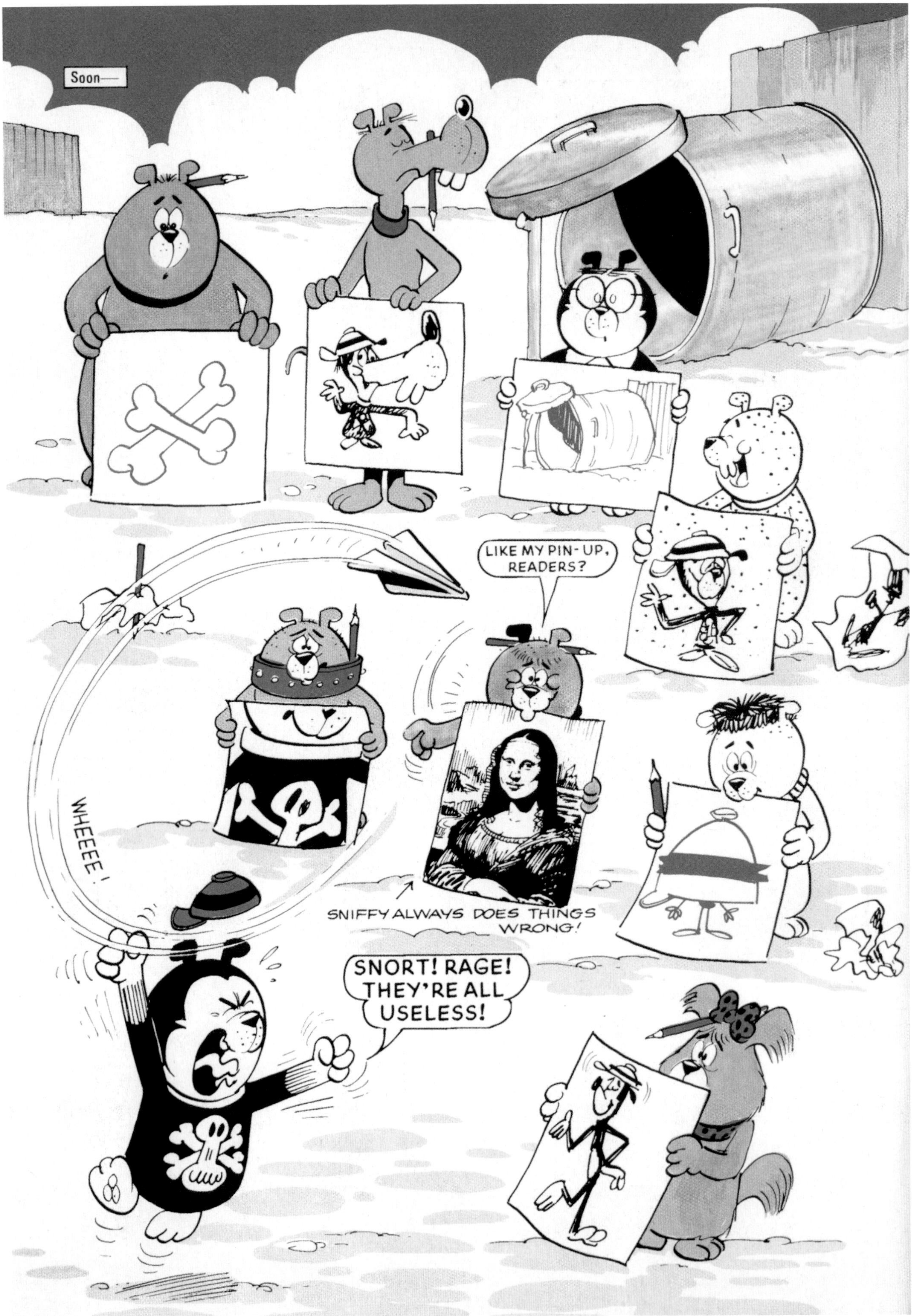
Soon—
LIKE MY PIN-UP, READERS?
WHEEEEE!
SNIFFY ALWAYS DOES THINGS WRONG!
SNORT! RAGE! THEY'RE ALL USELESS!

Never fear, the artist's here!

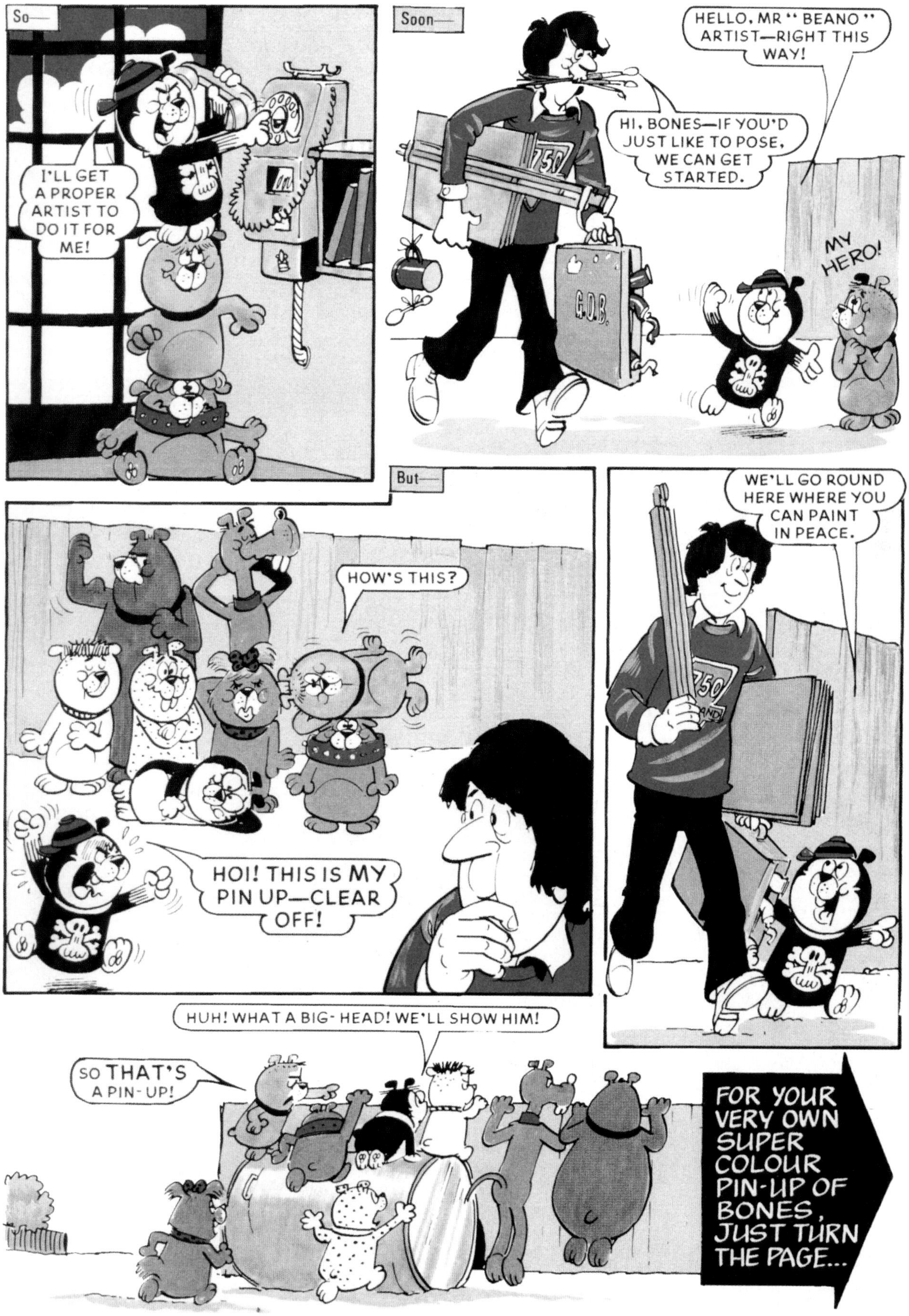
So—
I'LL GET A PROPER ARTIST TO DO IT FOR ME!
Soon—
HELLO, MR "BEANO" ARTIST—RIGHT THIS WAY!
HI, BONES—IF YOU'D JUST LIKE TO POSE, WE CAN GET STARTED.
MY HERO!
But—
HOW'S THIS?
HOI! THIS IS MY PIN UP—CLEAR OFF!
WE'LL GO ROUND HERE WHERE YOU CAN PAINT IN PEACE.
HUH! WHAT A BIG-HEAD! WE'LL SHOW HIM!
SO THAT'S A PIN-UP!
FOR YOUR VERY OWN SUPER COLOUR PIN-UP OF BONES, JUST TURN THE PAGE...

Bones doesn't know his pals are on show!

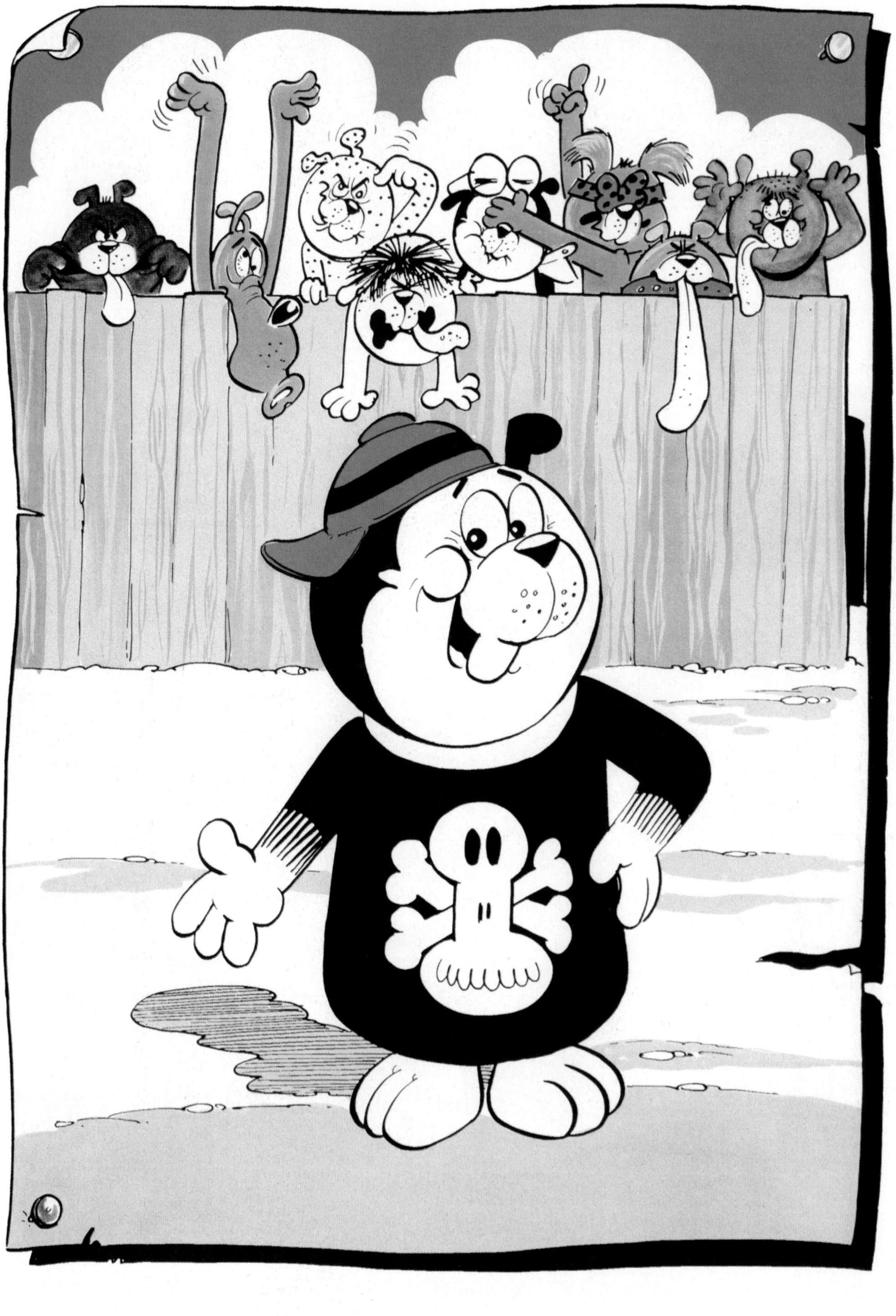

BRASSNECK

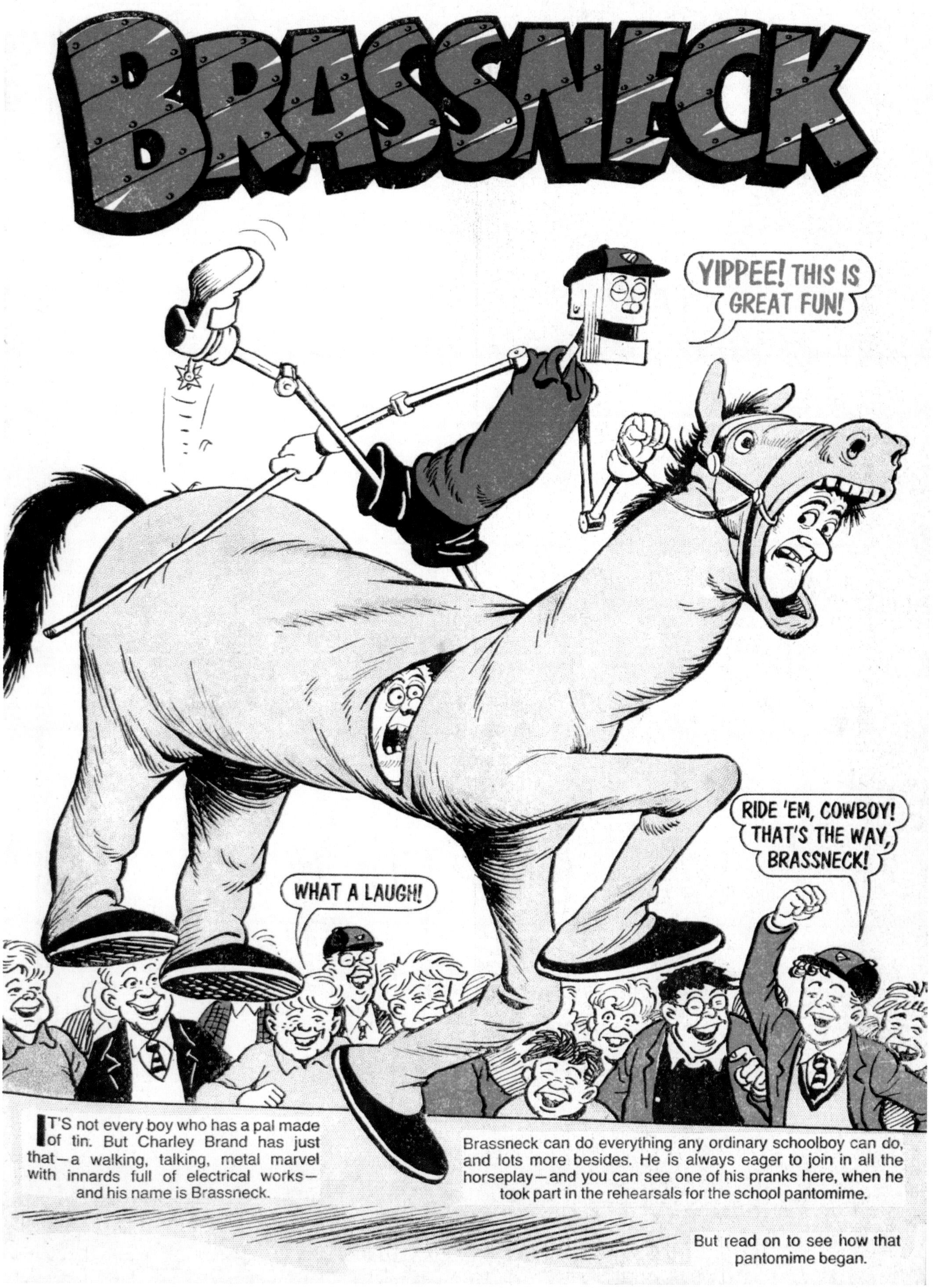
YIPPEE! THIS IS GREAT FUN!
RIDE 'EM, COWBOY! THAT'S THE WAY, BRASSNECK!
WHAT A LAUGH!
IT'S not every boy who has a pal made of tin. But Charley Brand has just that—a walking, talking, metal marvel with innards full of electrical works—and his name is Brassneck.
Brassneck can do everything any ordinary schoolboy can do, and lots more besides. He is always eager to join in all the horseplay—and you can see one of his pranks here, when he took part in the rehearsals for the school pantomime.

But read on to see how that pantomime began.

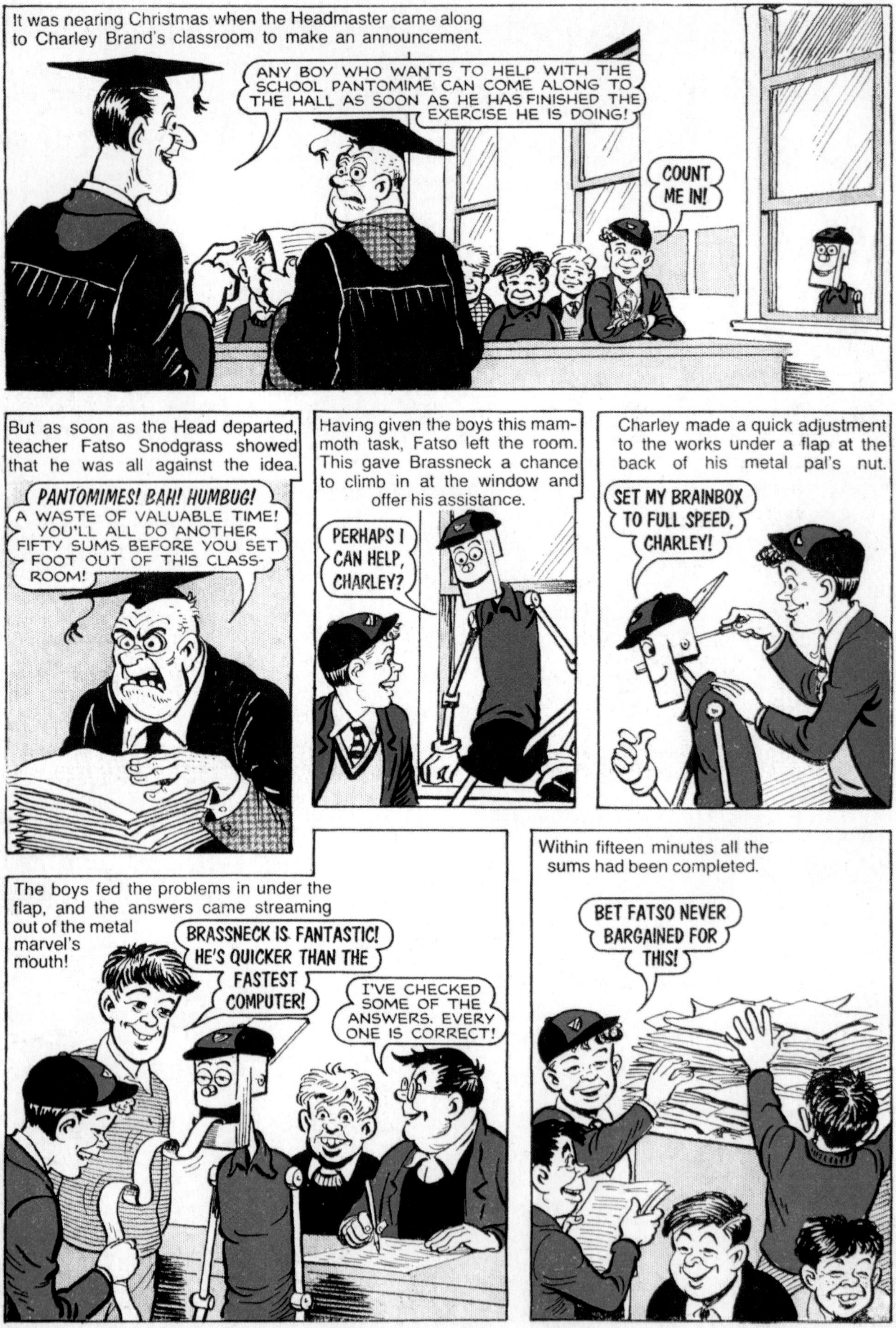
It was nearing Christmas when the Headmaster came along to Charley Brand's classroom to make an announcement.
ANY BOY WHO WANTS TO HELP WITH THE SCHOOL PANTOMIME CAN COME ALONG TO THE HALL AS SOON AS HE HAS FINISHED THE EXERCISE HE IS DOING!
COUNT ME IN!
But as soon as the Head departed, teacher Fatso Snodgrass showed that he was all against the idea.
PANTOMIMES! BAH! HUMBUG! A WASTE OF VALUABLE TIME! YOU'LL ALL DO ANOTHER FIFTY SUMS BEFORE YOU SET FOOT OUT OF THIS CLASS-ROOM!
Having given the boys this mammoth task, Fatso left the room. This gave Brassneck a chance to climb in at the window and offer his assistance.
PERHAPS I CAN HELP, CHARLEY?
Charley made a quick adjustment to the works under a flap at the back of his metal pal's nut.
SET MY BRAINBOX TO FULL SPEED, CHARLEY!
The boys fed the problems in under the flap, and the answers came streaming out of the metal marvel's mouth!
BRASSNECK IS FANTASTIC! HE'S QUICKER THAN THE FASTEST COMPUTER!
I'VE CHECKED SOME OF THE ANSWERS. EVERY ONE IS CORRECT!
Within fifteen minutes all the sums had been completed.
BET FATSO NEVER BARGAINED FOR THIS!

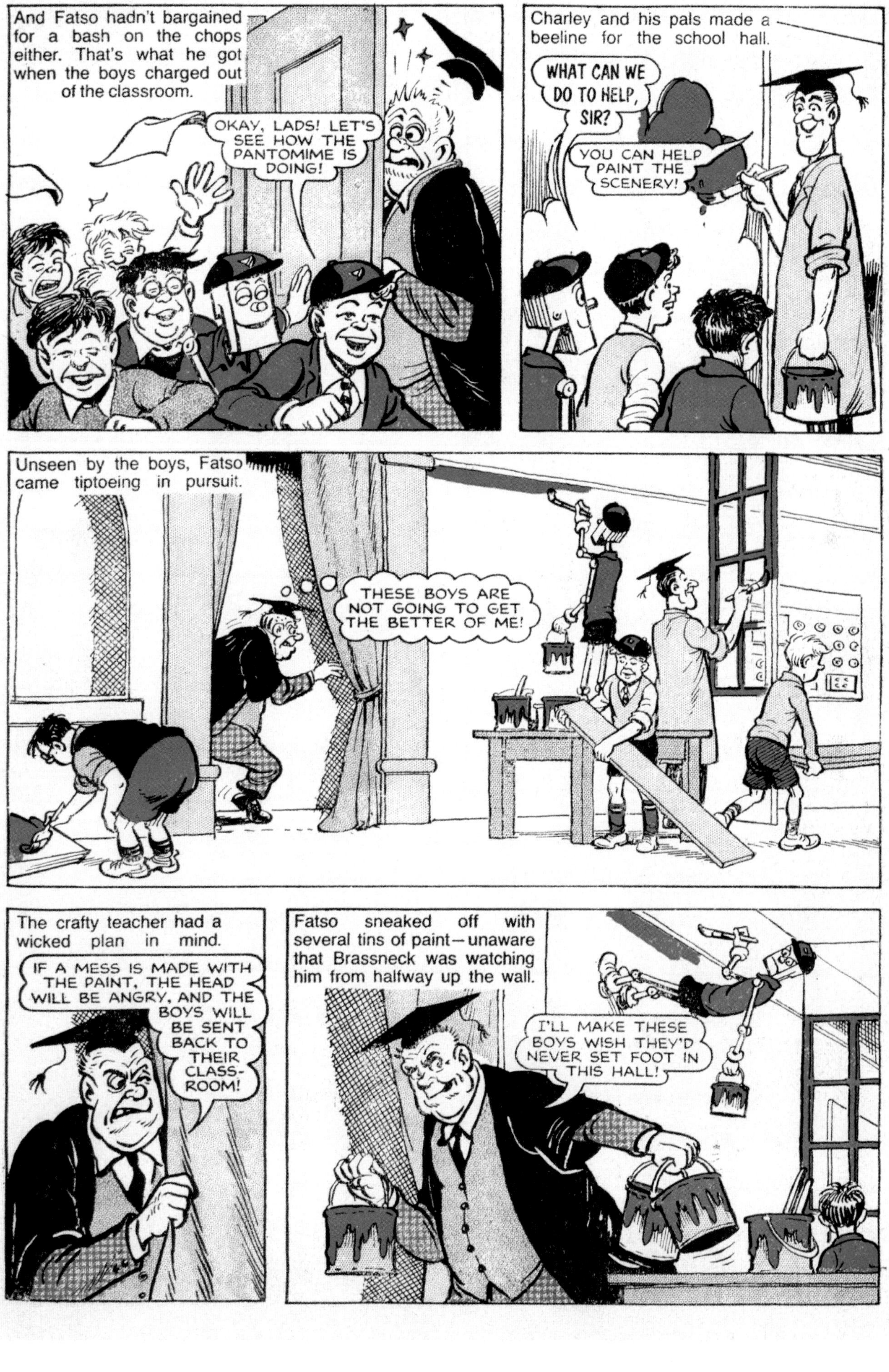
And Fatso hadn't bargained for a bash on the chops either. That's what he got when the boys charged out of the classroom.
OKAY, LADS! LET'S SEE HOW THE PANTOMIME IS DOING!
Charley and his pals made a beeline for the school hall.
WHAT CAN WE DO TO HELP, SIR?
YOU CAN HELP PAINT THE SCENERY!
Unseen by the boys, Fatso came tiptoeing in pursuit.
THESE BOYS ARE NOT GOING TO GET THE BETTER OF ME!
The crafty teacher had a wicked plan in mind.
IF A MESS IS MADE WITH THE PAINT, THE HEAD WILL BE ANGRY, AND THE BOYS WILL BE SENT BACK TO THEIR CLASS-ROOM!
Fatso sneaked off with several tins of paint—unaware that Brassneck was watching him from halfway up the wall.
I'LL MAKE THESE BOYS WISH THEY'D NEVER SET FOOT IN THIS HALL!

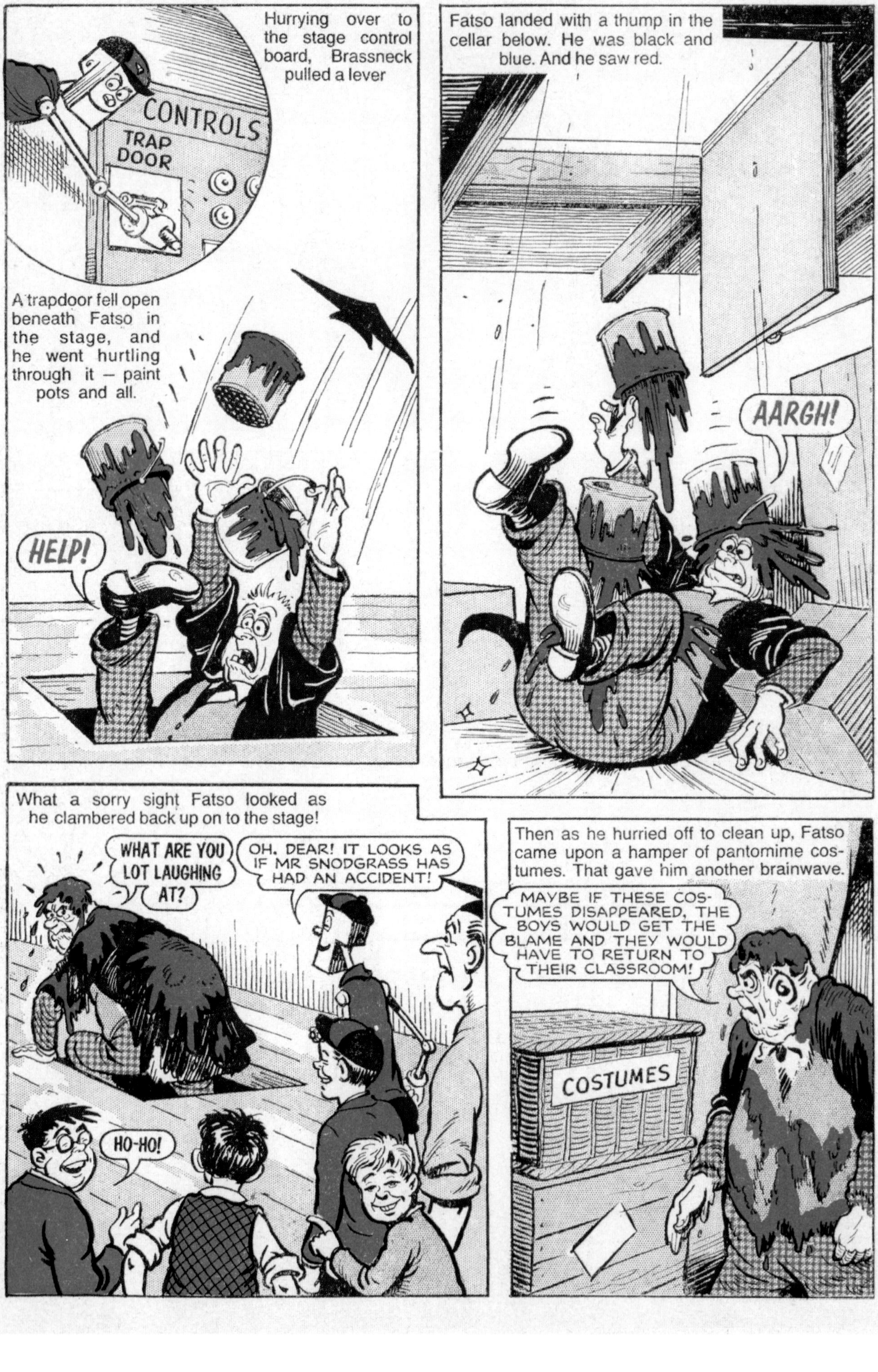
Hurrying over to the stage control board, Brassneck pulled a lever
CONTROLS
TRAP DOOR
A trapdoor fell open beneath Fatso in the stage, and he went hurtling through it – paint pots and all.
HELP!
Fatso landed with a thump in the cellar below. He was black and blue. And he saw red.
AARGH!
What a sorry sight Fatso looked as he clambered back up on to the stage!
WHAT ARE YOU LOT LAUGHING AT?
OH, DEAR! IT LOOKS AS IF MR SNODGRASS HAS HAD AN ACCIDENT!
HO-HO!
Then as he hurried off to clean up, Fatso came upon a hamper of pantomime costumes. That gave him another brainwave.
MAYBE IF THESE COSTUMES DISAPPEARED, THE BOYS WOULD GET THE BLAME AND THEY WOULD HAVE TO RETURN TO THEIR CLASSROOM!
COSTUMES

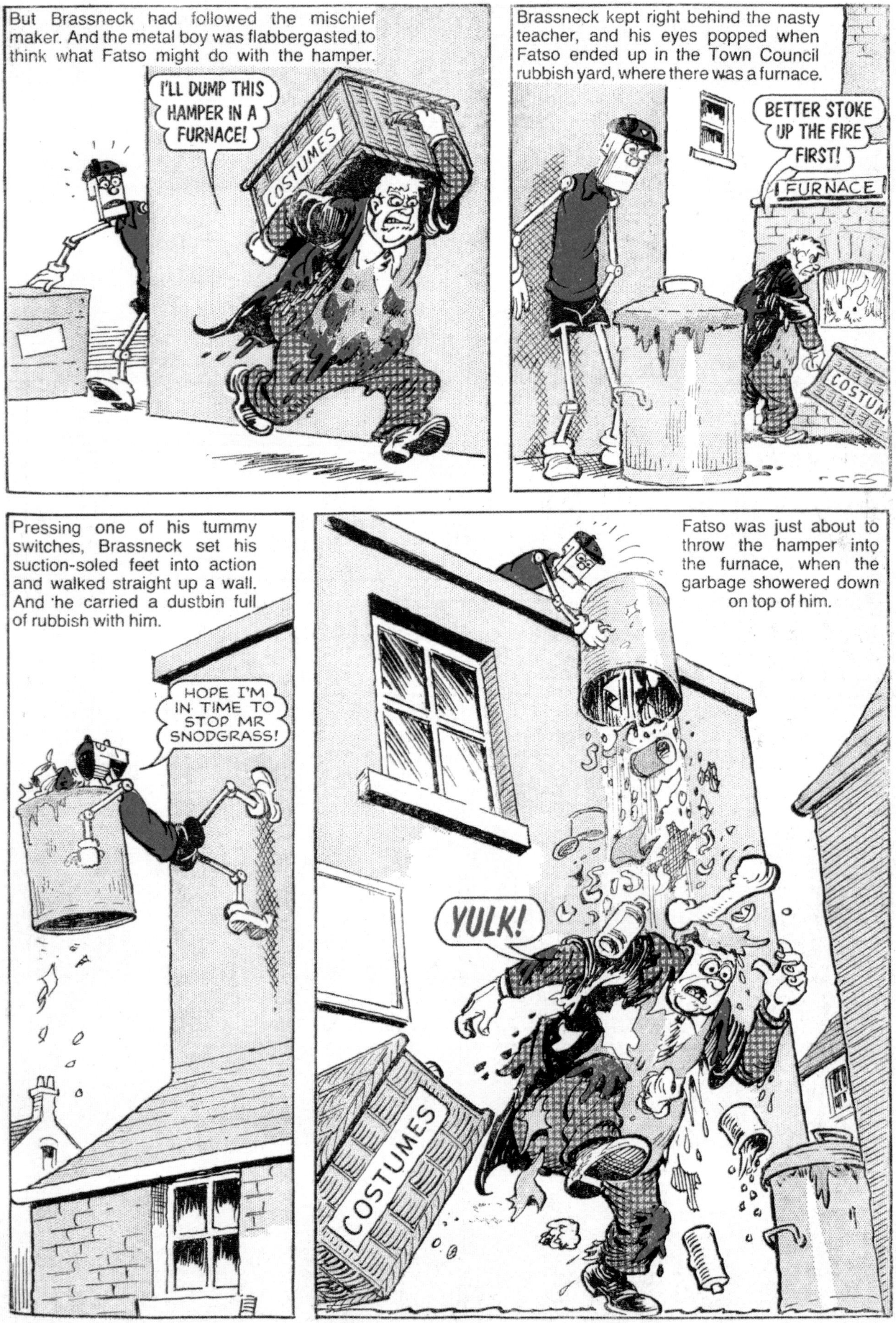
But Brassneck had followed the mischief maker. And the metal boy was flabbergasted to think what Fatso might do with the hamper.
I'LL DUMP THIS HAMPER IN A FURNACE!
COSTUMES
Brassneck kept right behind the nasty teacher, and his eyes popped when Fatso ended up in the Town Council rubbish yard, where there was a furnace.
BETTER STOKE UP THE FIRE FIRST!
FURNACE
Pressing one of his tummy switches, Brassneck set his suction-soled feet into action and walked straight up a wall. And he carried a dustbin full of rubbish with him.
HOPE I'M IN TIME TO STOP MR SNODGRASS!
Fatso was just about to throw the hamper into the furnace, when the garbage showered down on top of him.
YULK!
COSTUMES

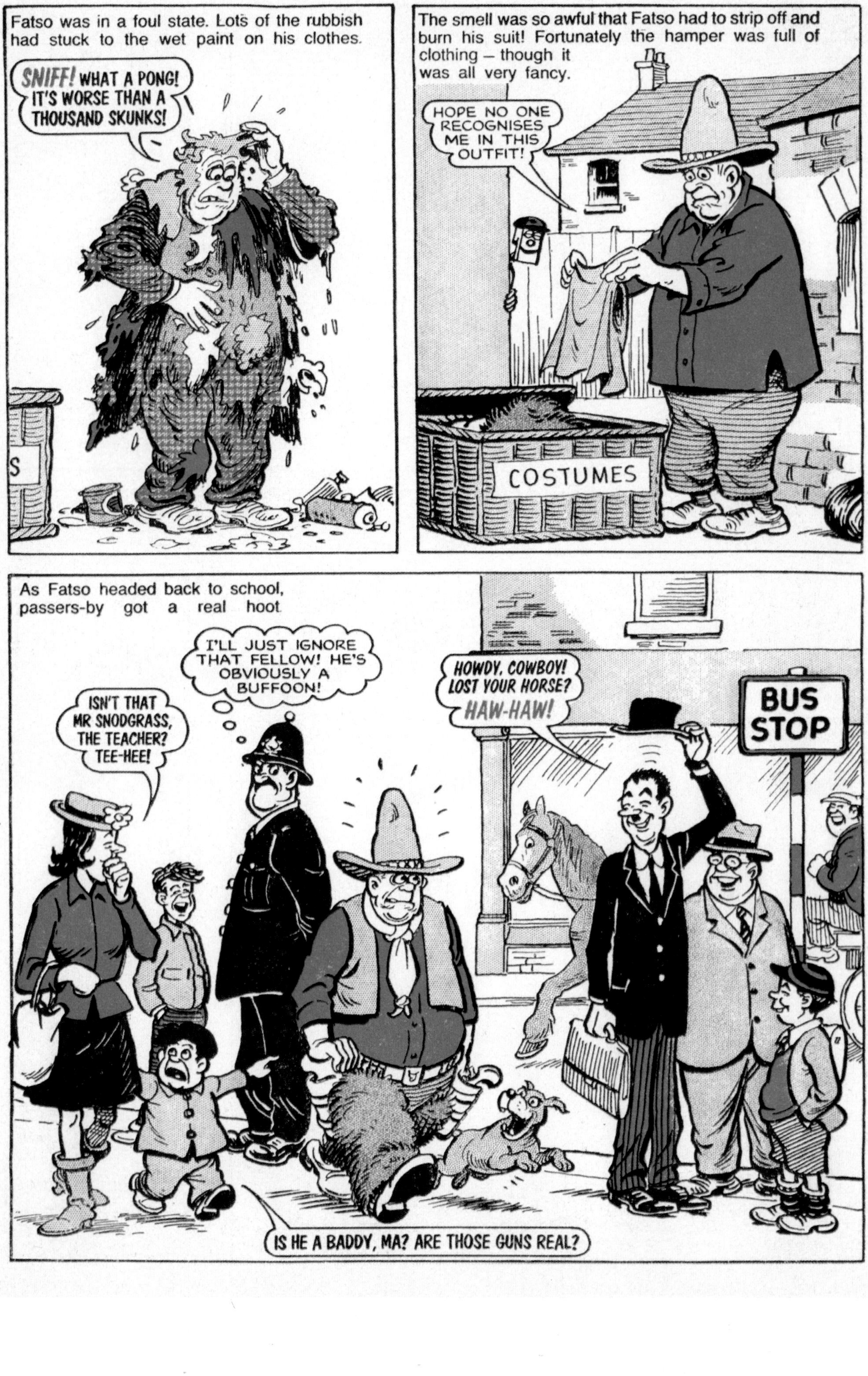

Fatso was in a foul state. Lots of the rubbish had stuck to the wet paint on his clothes.
SNIFF! WHAT A PONG! IT'S WORSE THAN A THOUSAND SKUNKS!
The smell was so awful that Fatso had to strip off and burn his suit! Fortunately the hamper was full of clothing – though it was all very fancy.
HOPE NO ONE RECOGNISES ME IN THIS OUTFIT!
COSTUMES
As Fatso headed back to school, passers-by got a real hoot.
ISN'T THAT MR SNODGRASS, THE TEACHER? TEE-HEE!
I'LL JUST IGNORE THAT FELLOW! HE'S OBVIOUSLY A BUFFOON!
HOWDY, COWBOY! LOST YOUR HORSE? HAW-HAW!
BUS STOP
IS HE A BADDY, MA? ARE THOSE GUNS REAL?

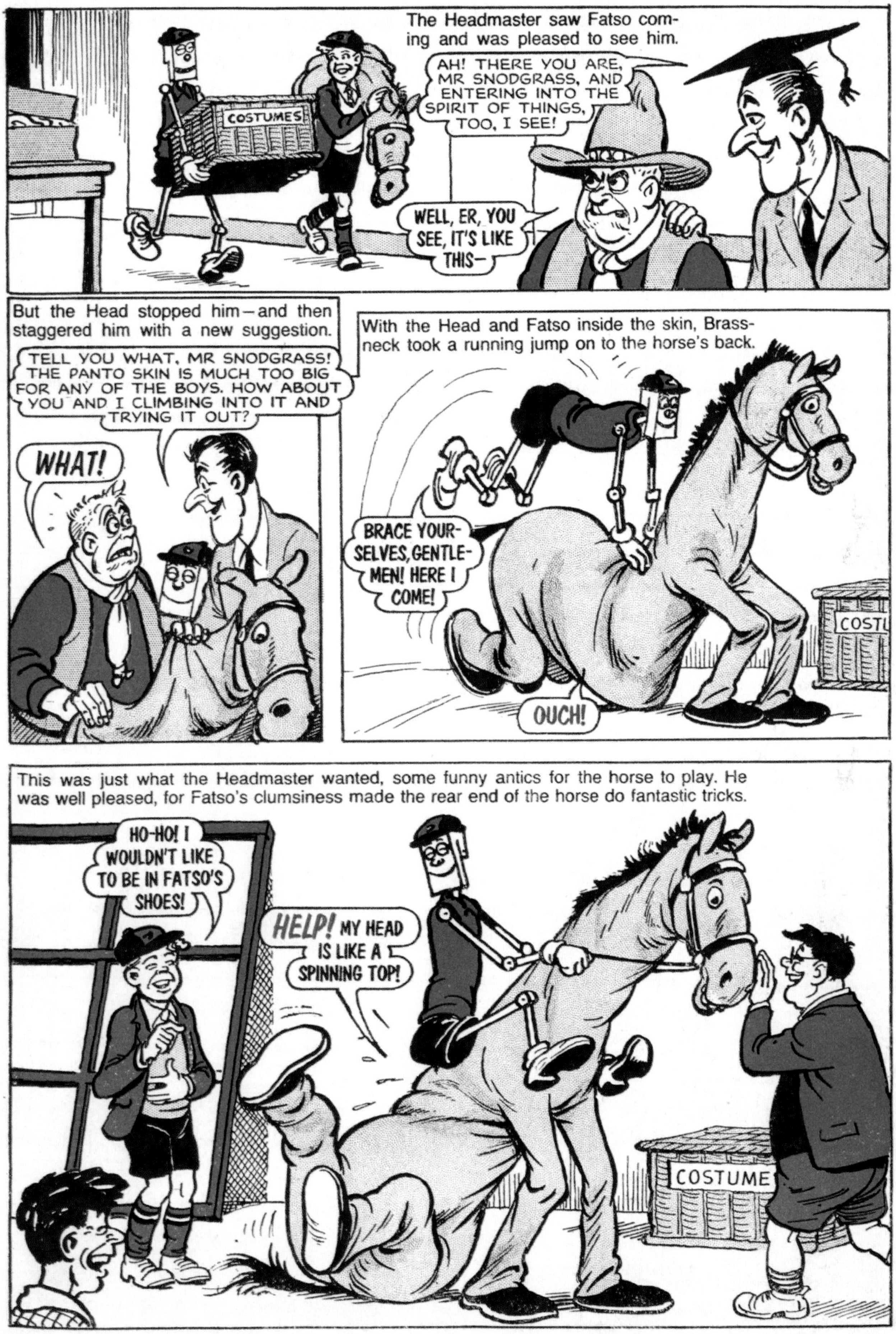
The Headmaster saw Fatso coming and was pleased to see him.
COSTUMES
AH! THERE YOU ARE, MR SNODGRASS, AND ENTERING INTO THE SPIRIT OF THINGS, TOO, I SEE!
WELL, ER, YOU SEE, IT'S LIKE THIS—
But the Head stopped him—and then staggered him with a new suggestion.
TELL YOU WHAT, MR SNODGRASS! THE PANTO SKIN IS MUCH TOO BIG FOR ANY OF THE BOYS. HOW ABOUT YOU AND I CLIMBING INTO IT AND TRYING IT OUT?
WHAT!
With the Head and Fatso inside the skin, Brassneck took a running jump on to the horse's back.
BRACE YOURSELVES, GENTLEMEN! HERE I COME!
OUCH!
COSTU
This was just what the Headmaster wanted, some funny antics for the horse to play. He was well pleased, for Fatso's clumsiness made the rear end of the horse do fantastic tricks.
HO-HO! I WOULDN'T LIKE TO BE IN FATSO'S SHOES!
HELP! MY HEAD IS LIKE A SPINNING TOP!
COSTUME

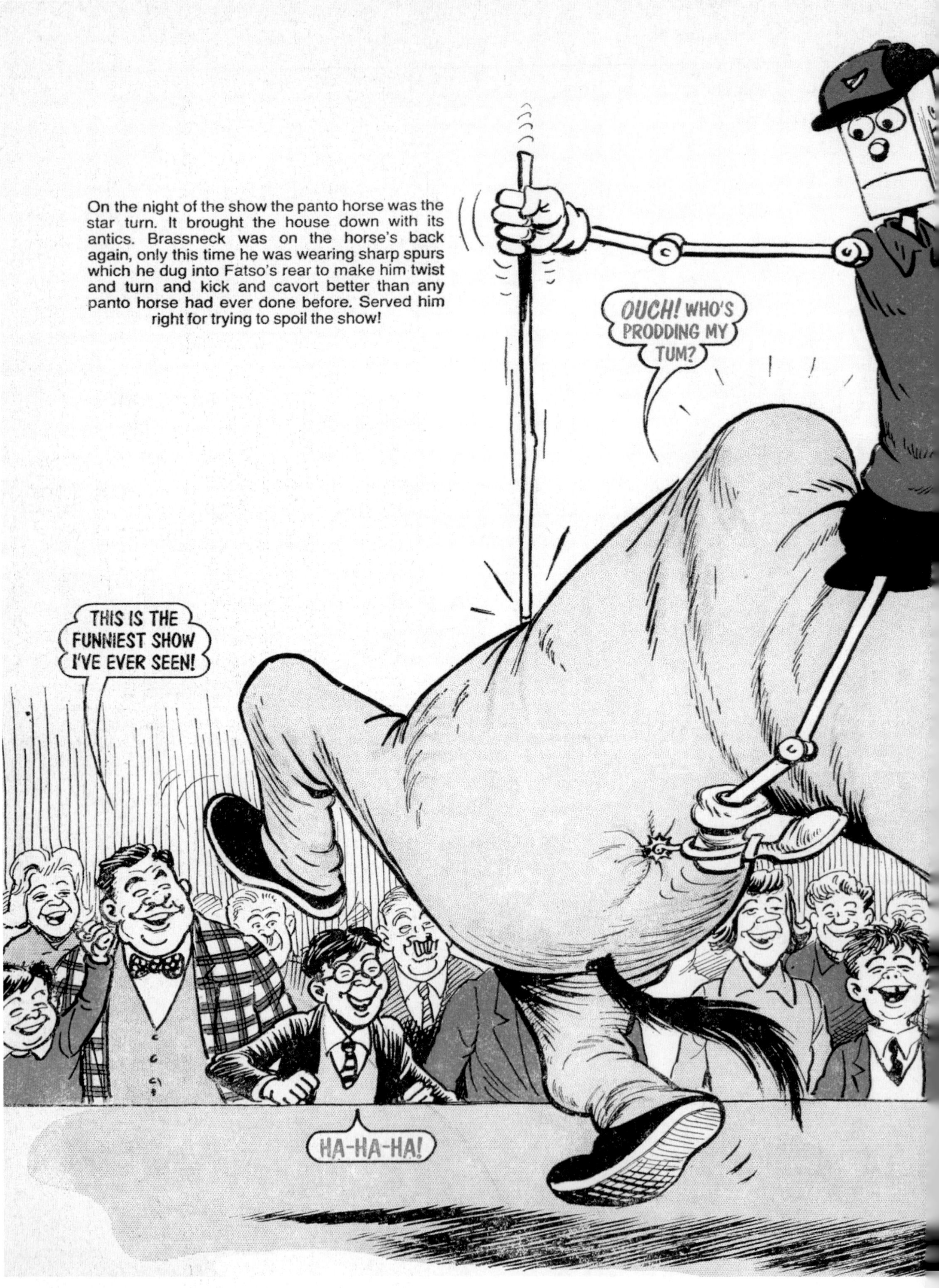
On the night of the show the panto horse was the star turn. It brought the house down with its antics. Brassneck was on the horse's back again, only this time he was wearing sharp spurs which he dug into Fatso's rear to make him twist and turn and kick and cavort better than any panto horse had ever done before. Served him right for trying to spoil the show!
OUCH! WHO'S PRODDING MY TUM?
THIS IS THE FUNNIEST SHOW I'VE EVER SEEN!
HA-HA-HA!

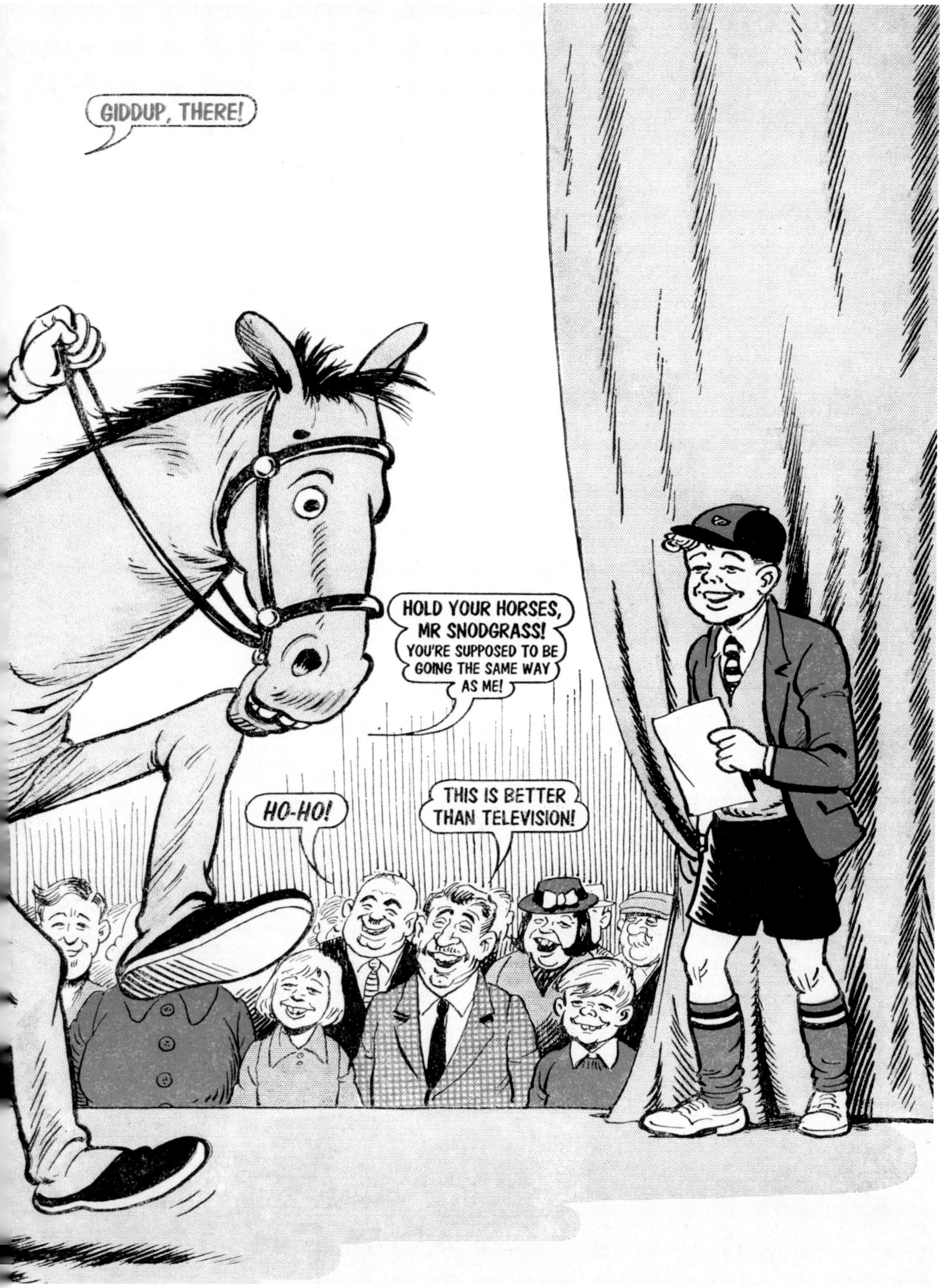
GIDDUP, THERE!
HOLD YOUR HORSES, MR SNODGRASS! YOU'RE SUPPOSED TO BE GOING THE SAME WAY AS ME!
HO-HO!
THIS IS BETTER THAN TELEVISION!

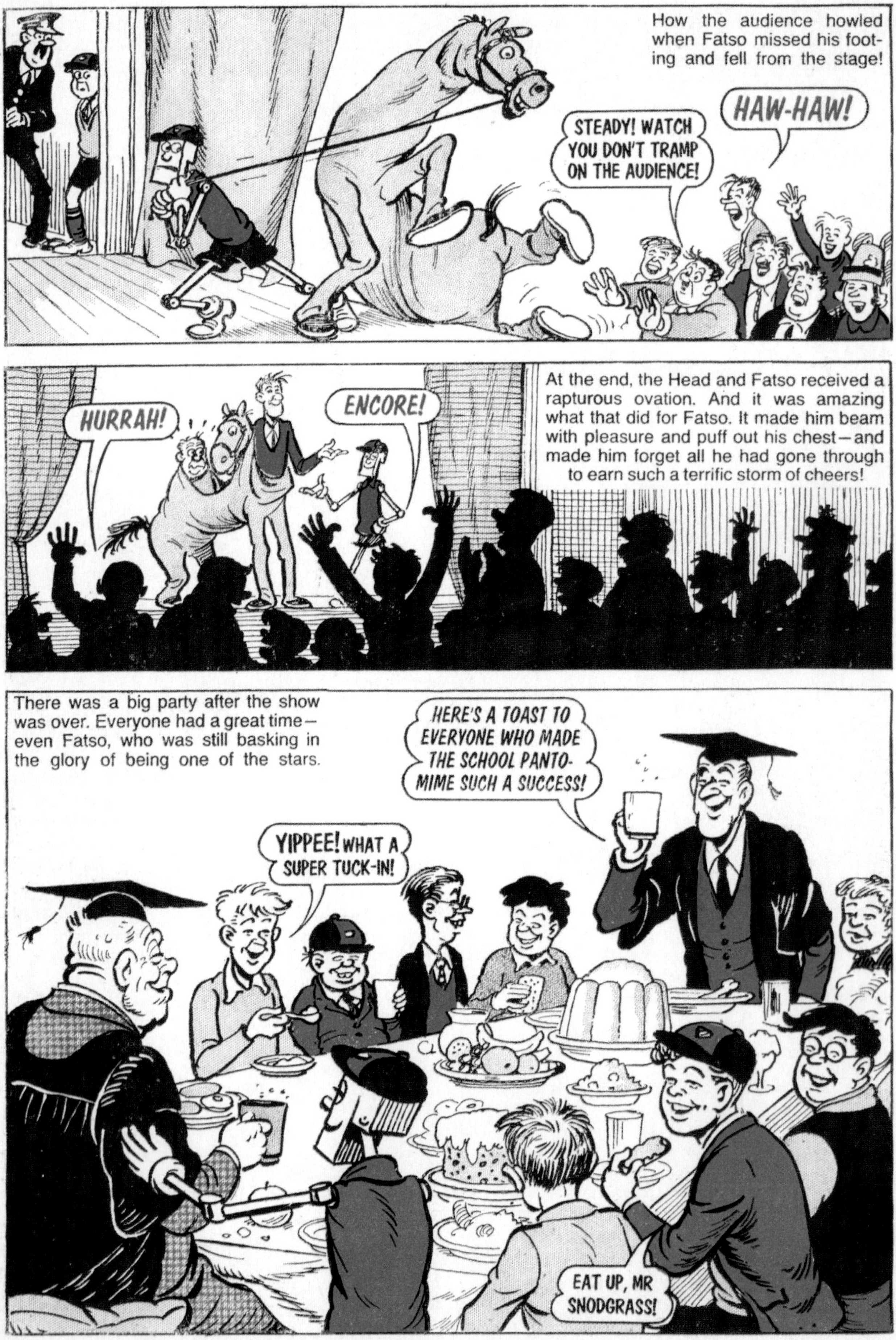
How the audience howled when Fatso missed his footing and fell from the stage!
STEADY! WATCH YOU DON'T TRAMP ON THE AUDIENCE!
HAW-HAW!
At the end, the Head and Fatso received a rapturous ovation. And it was amazing what that did for Fatso. It made him beam with pleasure and puff out his chest—and made him forget all he had gone through to earn such a terrific storm of cheers!
HURRAH!
ENCORE!
There was a big party after the show was over. Everyone had a great time—even Fatso, who was still basking in the glory of being one of the stars.
HERE'S A TOAST TO EVERYONE WHO MADE THE SCHOOL PANTOMIME SUCH A SUCCESS!
YIPPEE! WHAT A SUPER TUCK-IN!
EAT UP, MR SNODGRASS!

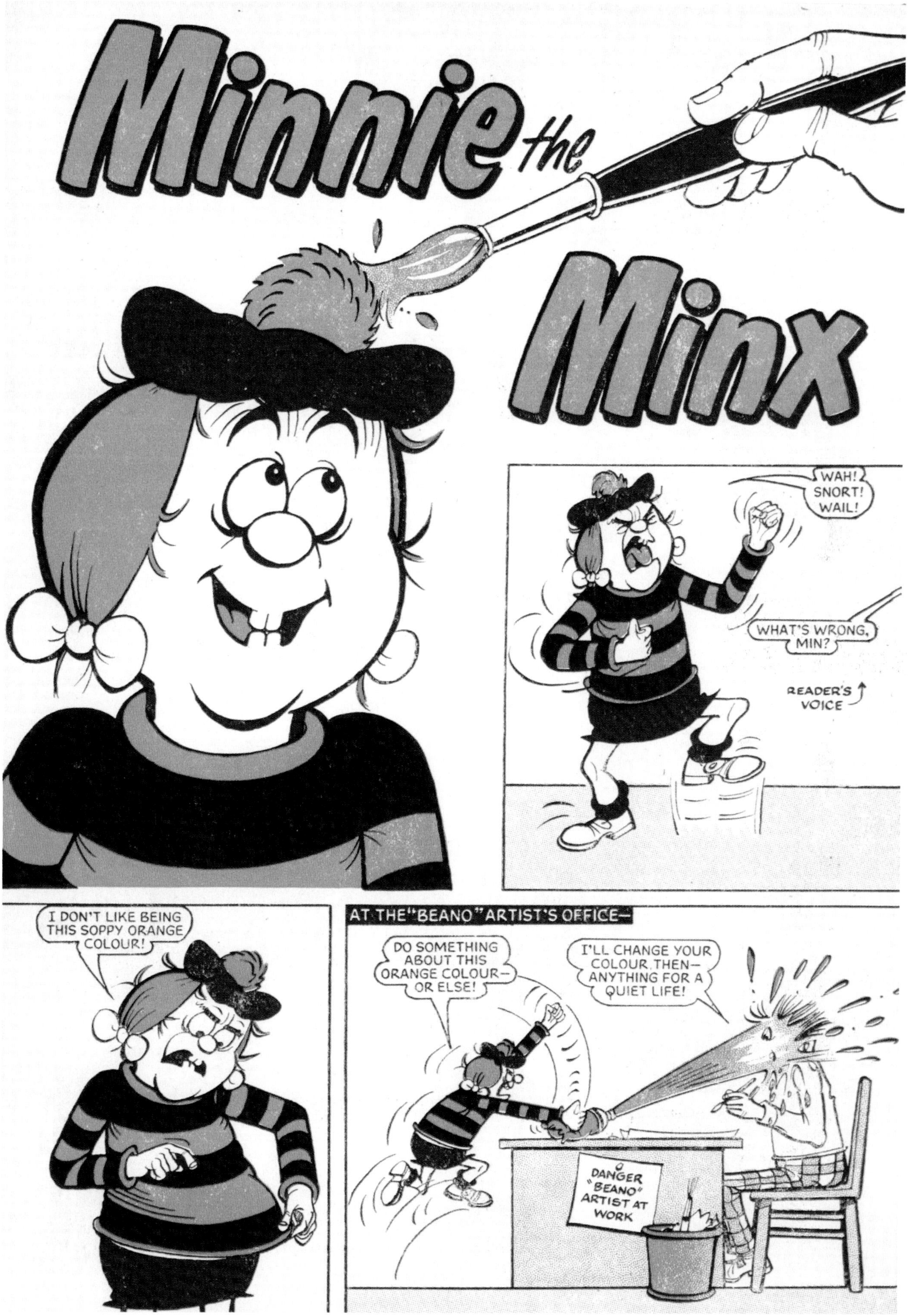
Minnie the Minx
WAH! SNORT! WAIL!
WHAT'S WRONG, MIN?
READER'S VOICE
I DON'T LIKE BEING THIS SOPPY ORANGE COLOUR!
AT THE "BEANO" ARTIST'S OFFICE—
DO SOMETHING ABOUT THIS ORANGE COLOUR— OR ELSE!
I'LL CHANGE YOUR COLOUR, THEN— ANYTHING FOR A QUIET LIFE!
DANGER "BEANO" ARTIST AT WORK

Min's wish comes true—she's changed to blue!

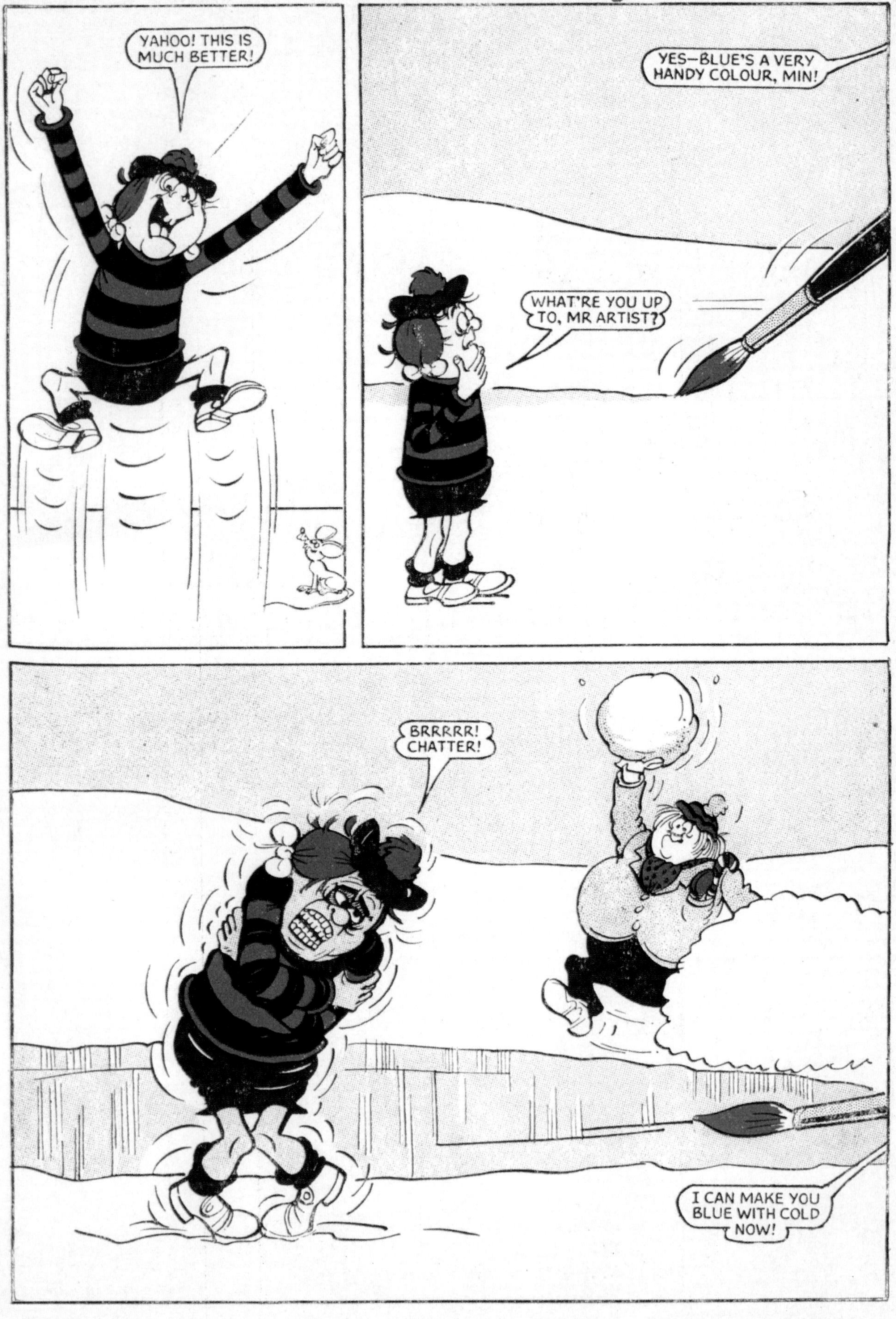
YAHOO! THIS IS MUCH BETTER!
YES—BLUE'S A VERY HANDY COLOUR, MIN!
WHAT'RE YOU UP TO, MR ARTIST?
BRRRRR! CHATTER!
I CAN MAKE YOU BLUE WITH COLD NOW!

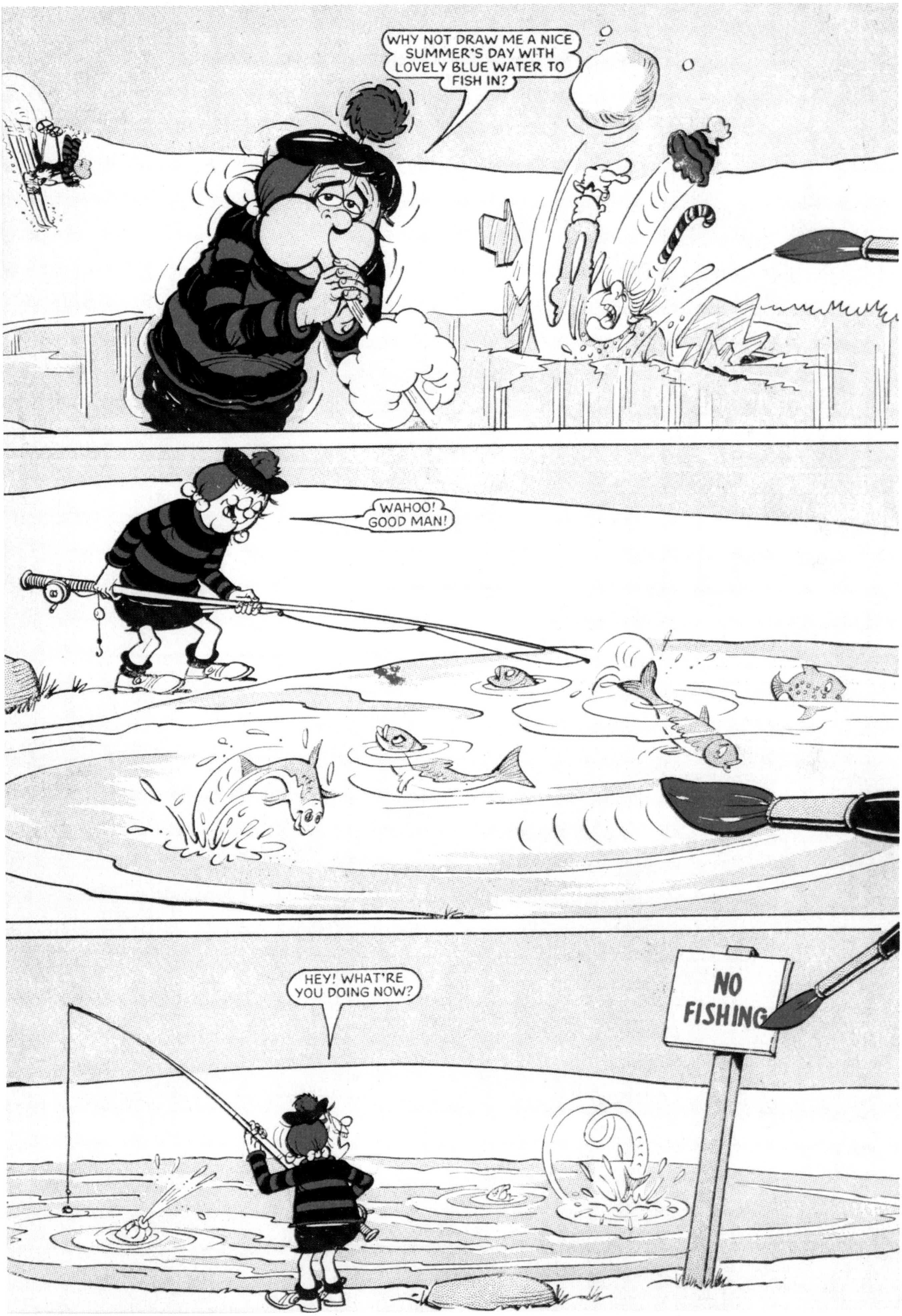
WHY NOT DRAW ME A NICE SUMMER'S DAY WITH LOVELY BLUE WATER TO FISH IN?
WAHOO! GOOD MAN!
HEY! WHAT'RE YOU DOING NOW?
NO FISHING

What a "to-do" with the man in blue!

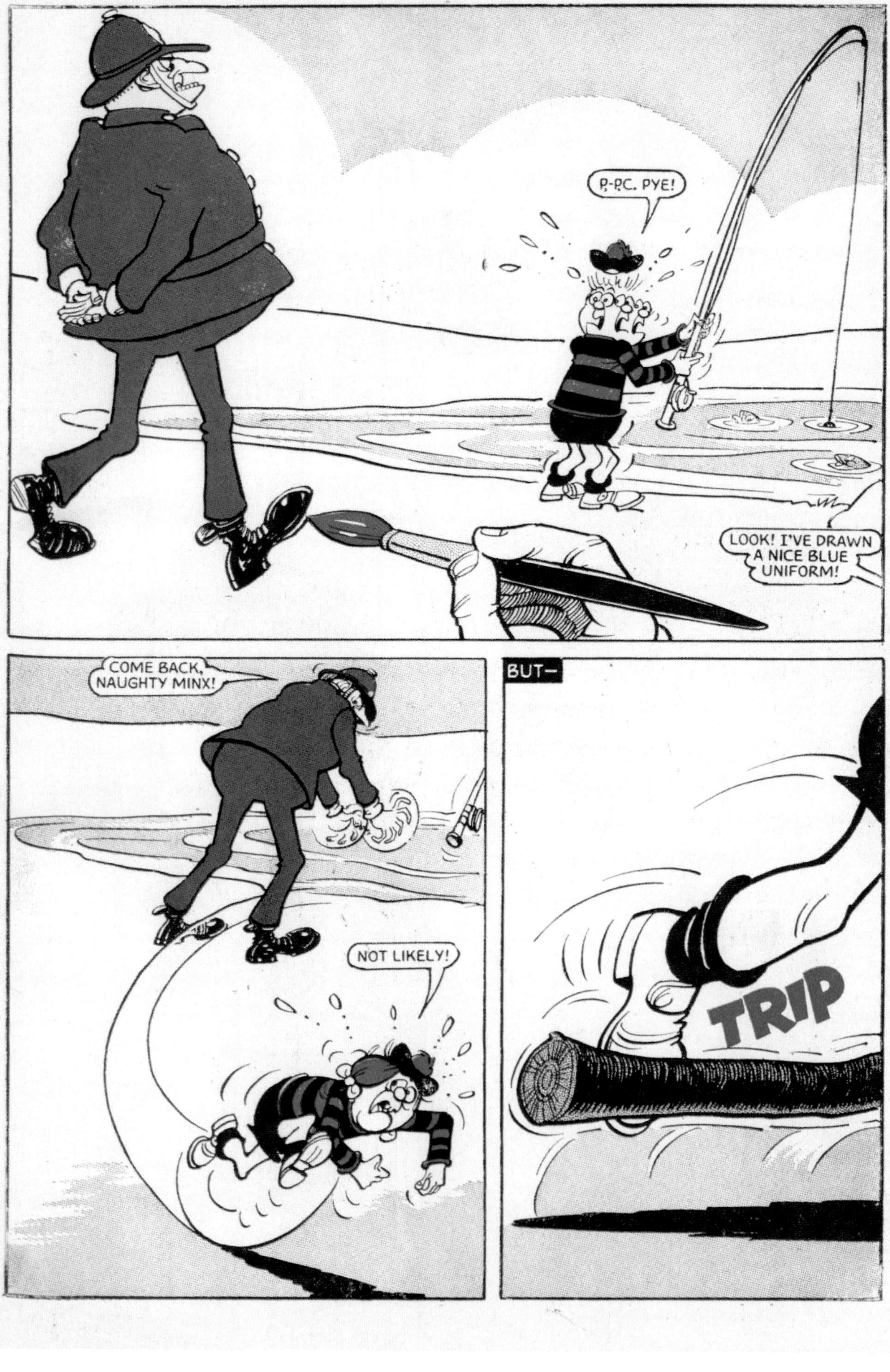
P-P.C. PYE!
LOOK! I'VE DRAWN A NICE BLUE UNIFORM!
COME BACK, NAUGHTY MINX!
NOT LIKELY!
BUT—
TRIP

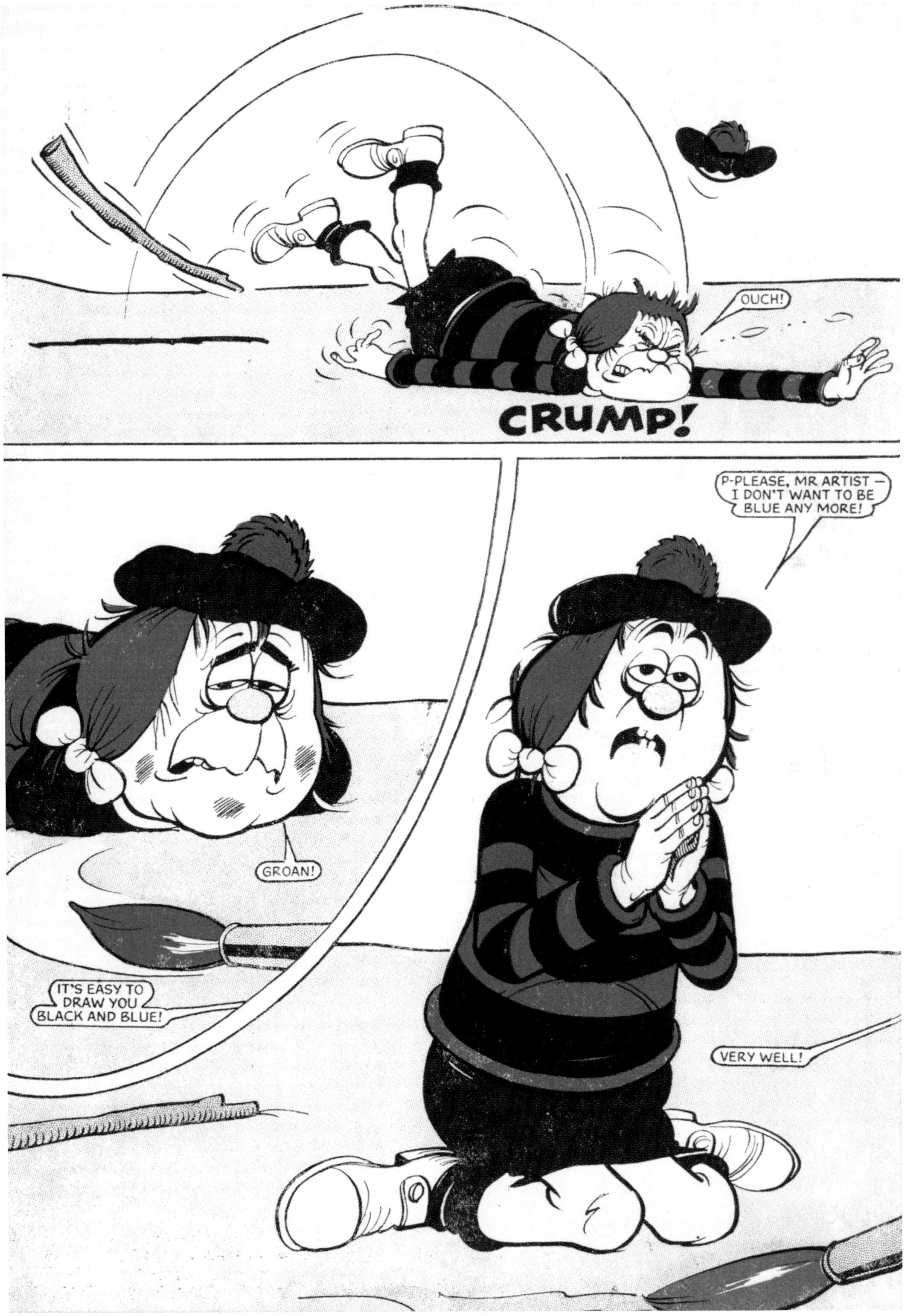
OUCH!
CRUMP!
GROAN!
IT'S EASY TO DRAW YOU BLACK AND BLUE!
P-PLEASE, MR ARTIST — I DON'T WANT TO BE BLUE ANY MORE!
VERY WELL!

Oh, gosh! Look what's in the wash!

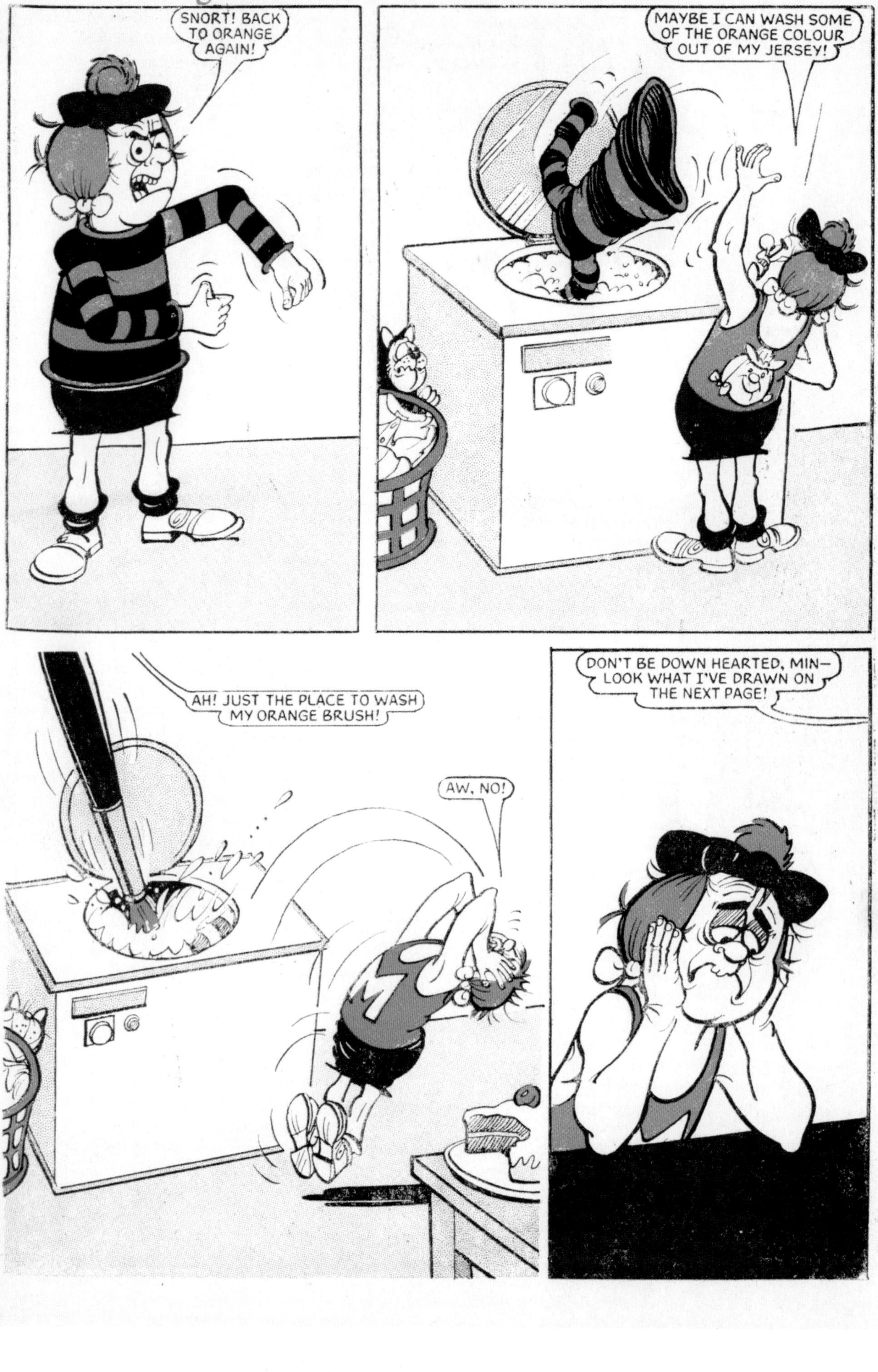

SNORT! BACK TO ORANGE AGAIN!
MAYBE I CAN WASH SOME OF THE ORANGE COLOUR OUT OF MY JERSEY!
AH! JUST THE PLACE TO WASH MY ORANGE BRUSH!
AW, NO!
DON'T BE DOWN HEARTED, MIN— LOOK WHAT I'VE DRAWN ON THE NEXT PAGE!

What do you think of this orange drink?

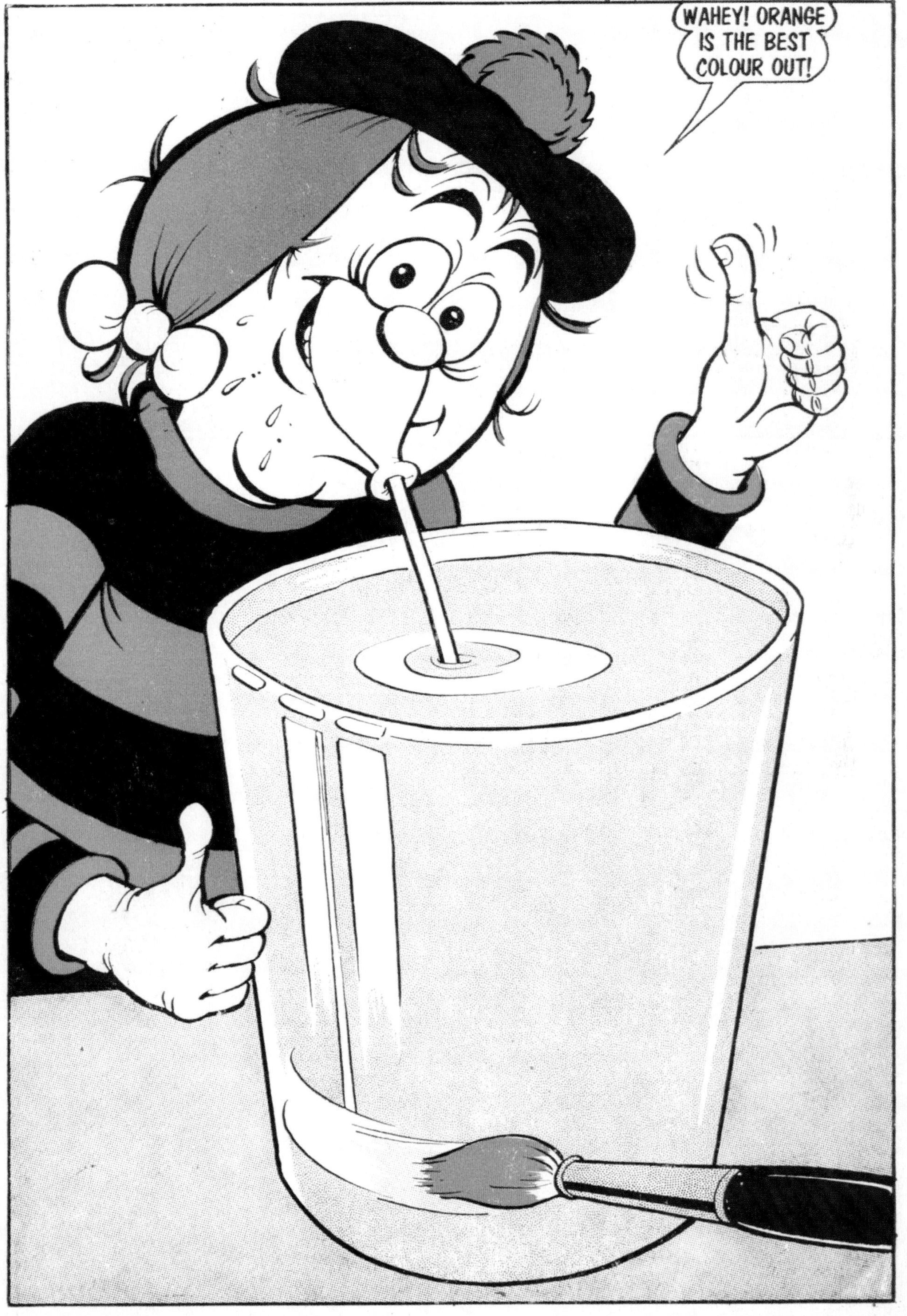
WAHEY! ORANGE IS THE BEST COLOUR OUT!

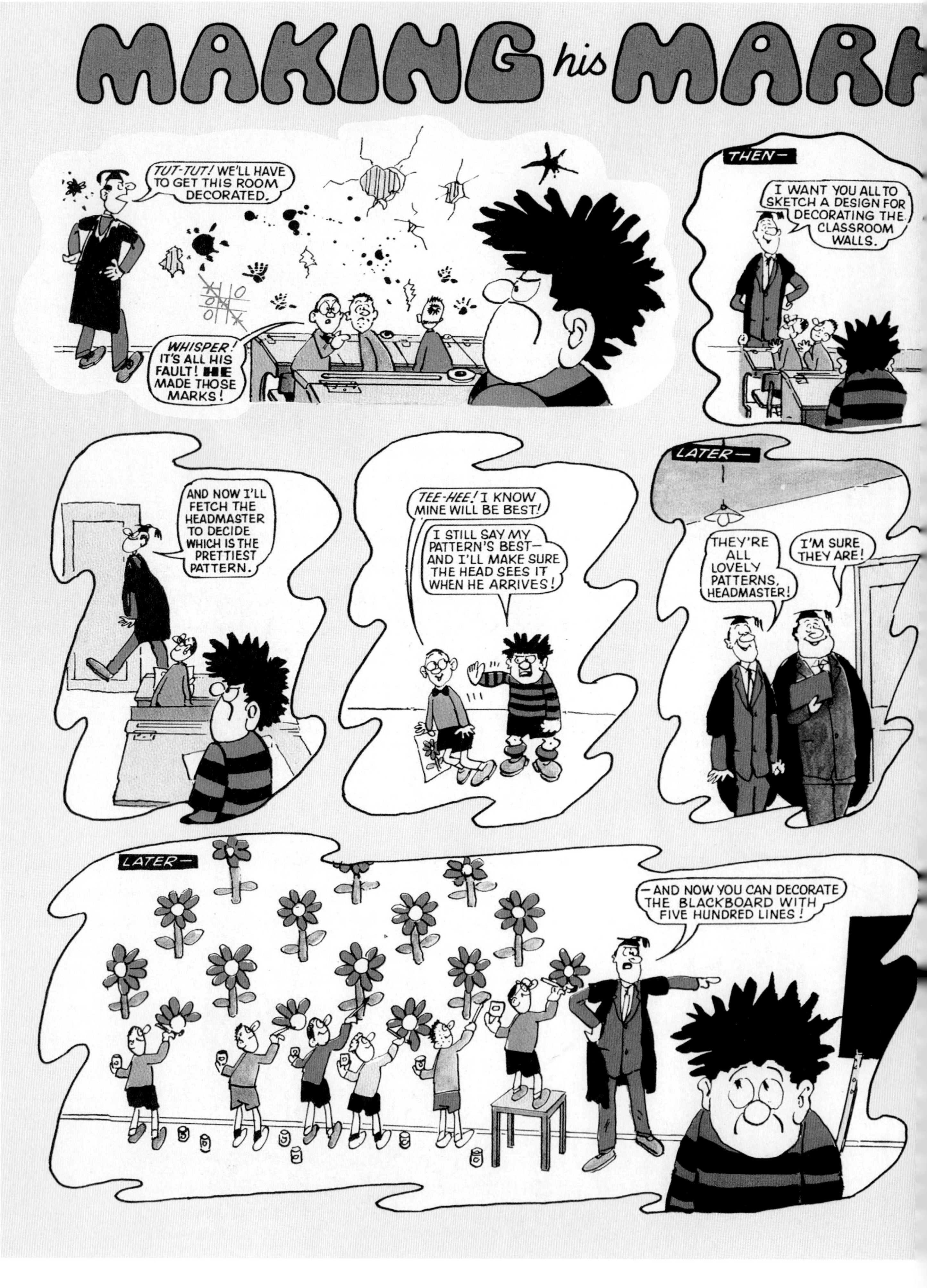

MAKING his MARK
TUT-TUT! WE'LL HAVE TO GET THIS ROOM DECORATED.
WHISPER! IT'S ALL HIS FAULT! HE MADE THOSE MARKS!
THEN—
I WANT YOU ALL TO SKETCH A DESIGN FOR DECORATING THE CLASSROOM WALLS.
AND NOW I'LL FETCH THE HEADMASTER TO DECIDE WHICH IS THE PRETTIEST PATTERN.
TEE-HEE! I KNOW MINE WILL BE BEST!
I STILL SAY MY PATTERN'S BEST— AND I'LL MAKE SURE THE HEAD SEES IT WHEN HE ARRIVES!
LATER—
THEY'RE ALL LOVELY PATTERNS, HEADMASTER!
I'M SURE THEY ARE!
LATER—
—AND NOW YOU CAN DECORATE THE BLACKBOARD WITH FIVE HUNDRED LINES!

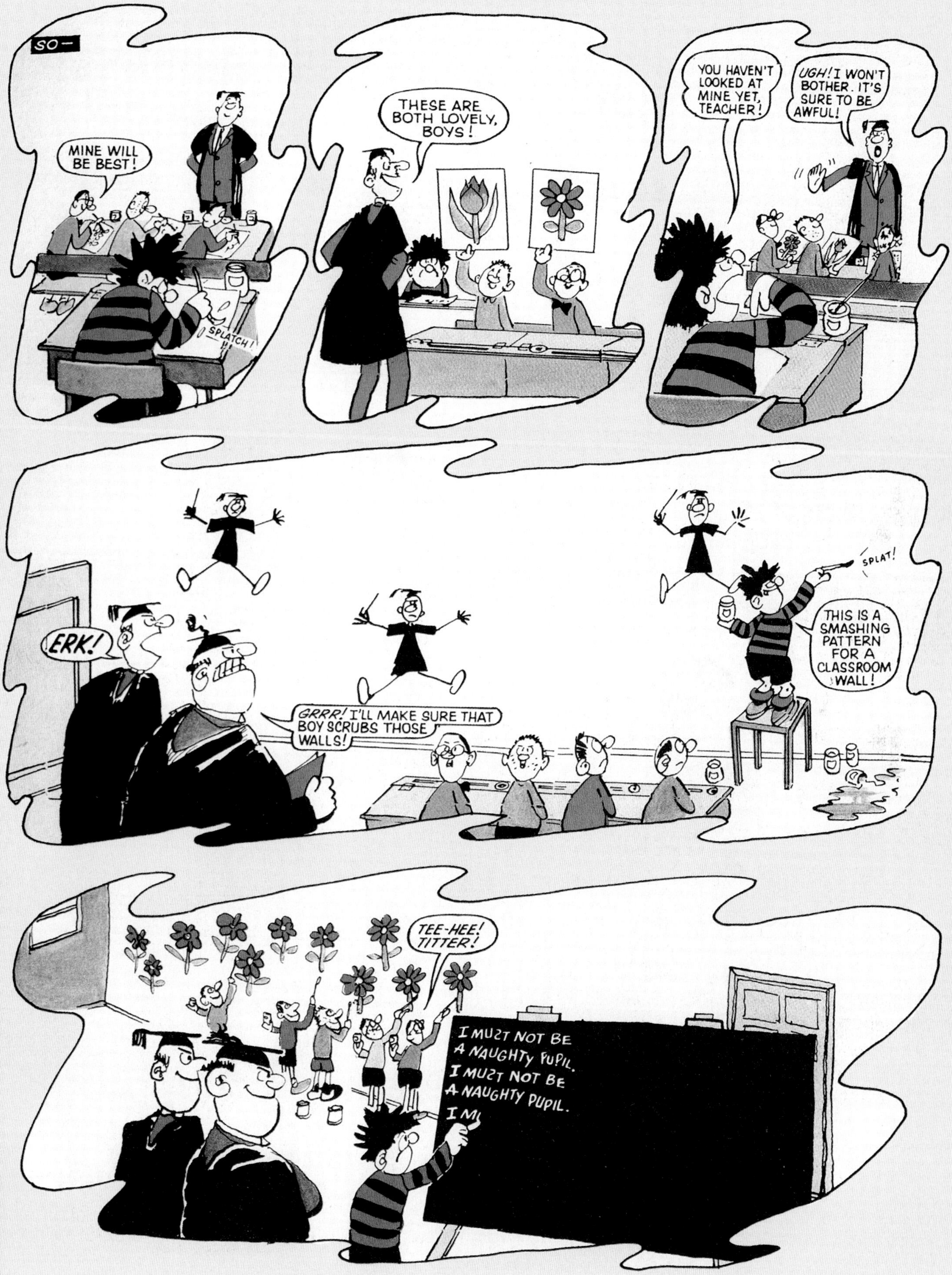
SO—
MINE WILL BE BEST!
SPLATCH!
THESE ARE BOTH LOVELY, BOYS!
YOU HAVEN'T LOOKED AT MINE YET, TEACHER!
UGH! I WON'T BOTHER. IT'S SURE TO BE AWFUL!
ERK!
GRRR! I'LL MAKE SURE THAT BOY SCRUBS THOSE WALLS!
SPLAT!
THIS IS A SMASHING PATTERN FOR A CLASSROOM WALL!
TEE-HEE! TITTER!
I MUZT NOT BE A NAUGHTY PUPIL.
I MUZT NOT BE A NAUGHTY PUPIL.
I M

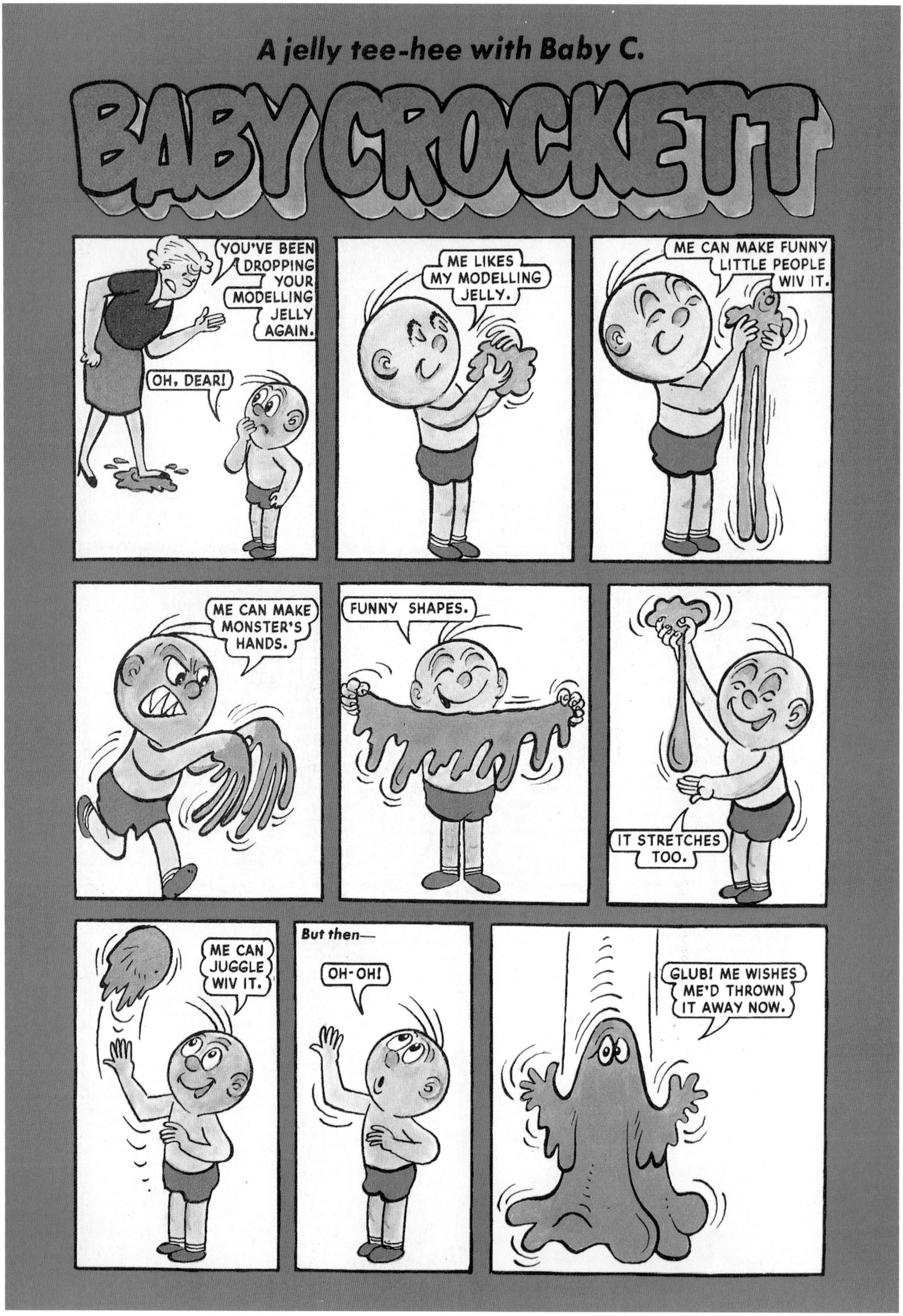
A jelly tee-hee with Baby C.
BABY CROCKETT
YOU'VE BEEN DROPPING YOUR MODELLING JELLY AGAIN.
OH, DEAR!
ME LIKES MY MODELLING JELLY.
ME CAN MAKE FUNNY LITTLE PEOPLE WIV IT.
ME CAN MAKE MONSTER'S HANDS.
FUNNY SHAPES.
IT STRETCHES TOO.
ME CAN JUGGLE WIV IT.
But then—
OH-OH!
GLUB! ME WISHES ME'D THROWN IT AWAY NOW.

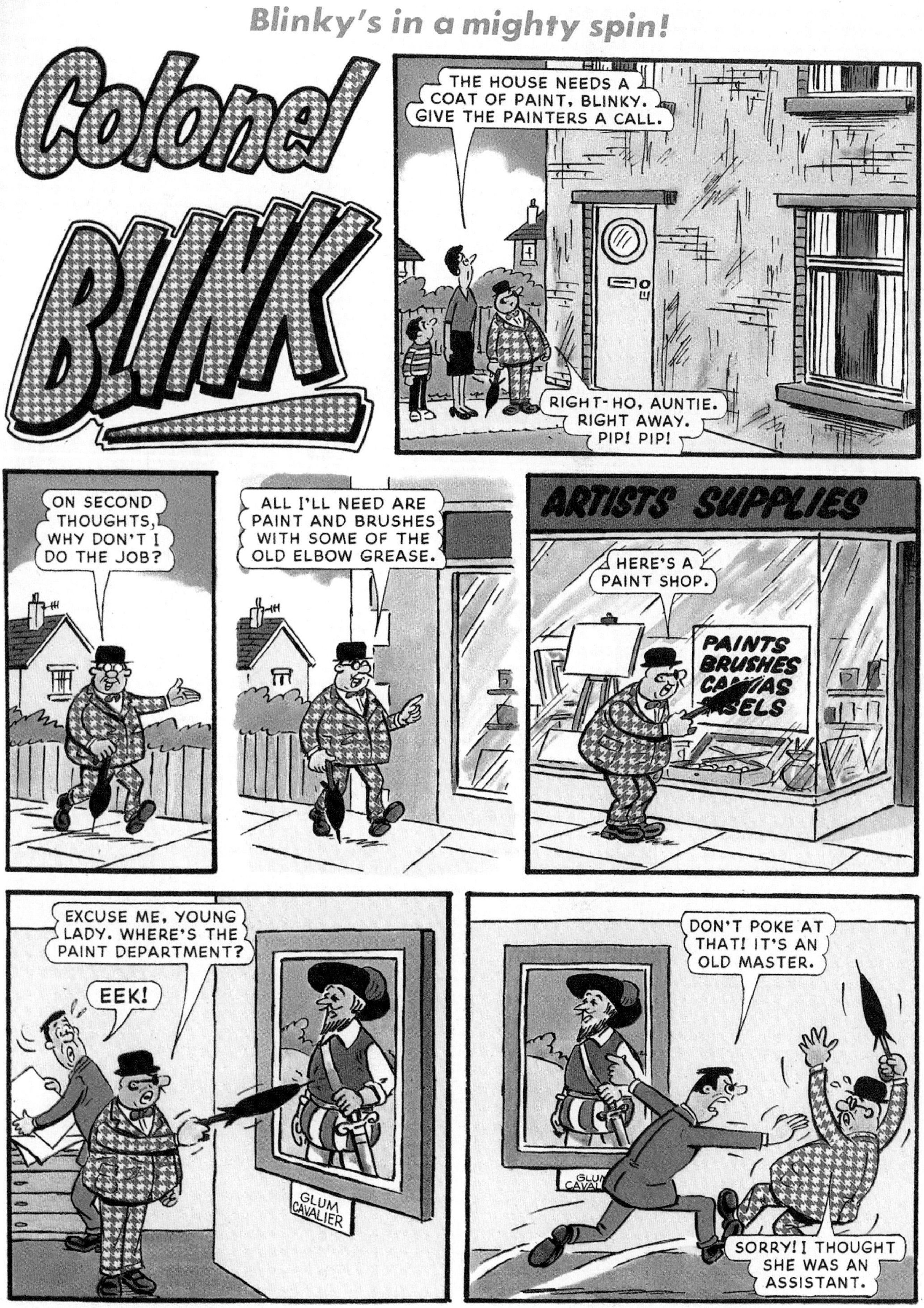
Blinky's in a mighty spin!
Colonel BLINK
THE HOUSE NEEDS A COAT OF PAINT, BLINKY. GIVE THE PAINTERS A CALL.
RIGHT-HO, AUNTIE. RIGHT AWAY. PIP! PIP!
ON SECOND THOUGHTS, WHY DON'T I DO THE JOB?
ALL I'LL NEED ARE PAINT AND BRUSHES WITH SOME OF THE OLD ELBOW GREASE.
ARTISTS SUPPLIES
HERE'S A PAINT SHOP.
PAINTS
BRUSHES
EXCUSE ME, YOUNG LADY. WHERE'S THE PAINT DEPARTMENT?
EEK!
GLUM CAVALIER
DON'T POKE AT THAT! IT'S AN OLD MASTER.
SORRY! I THOUGHT SHE WAS AN ASSISTANT.

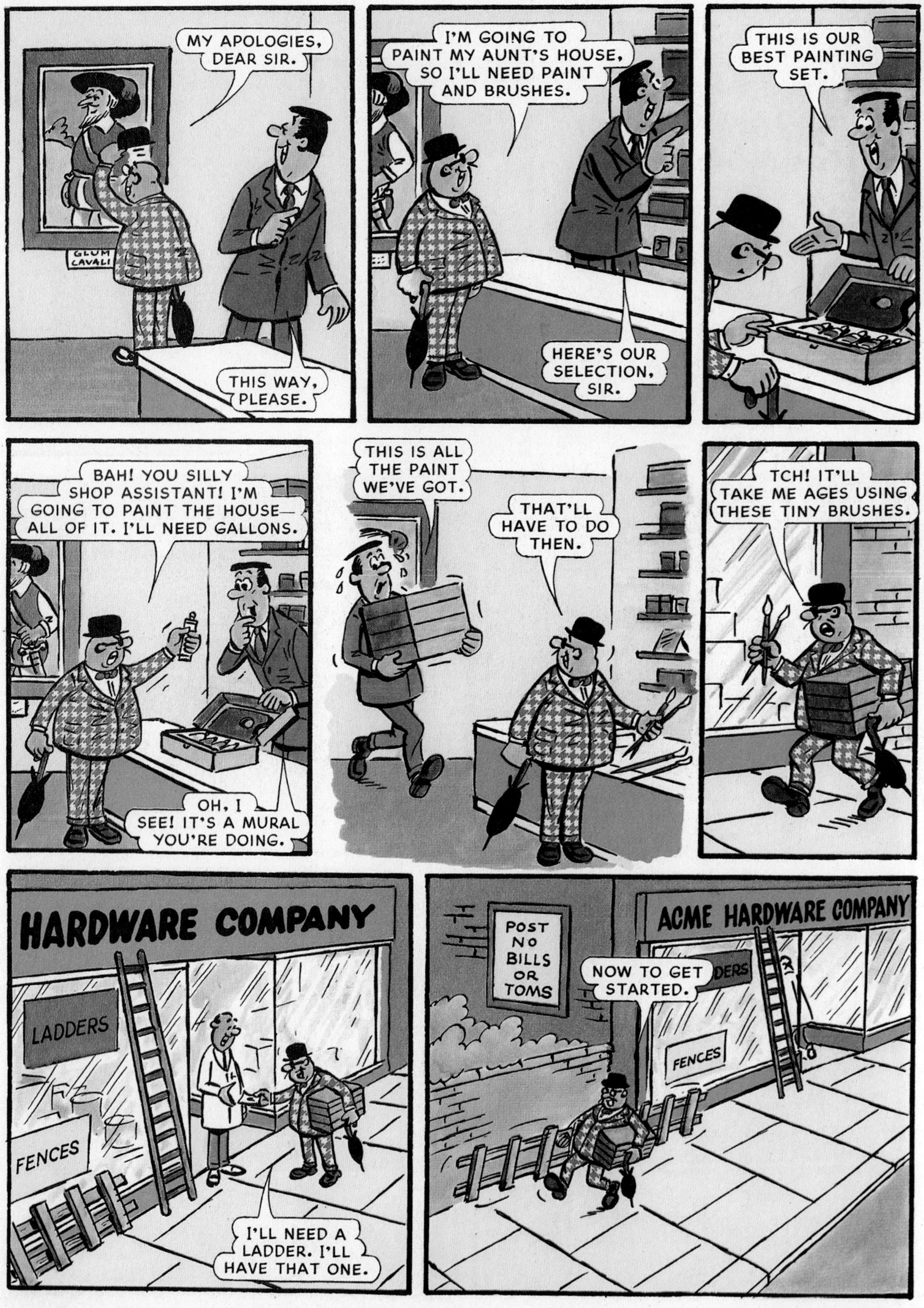
GLUM CAVALI
MY APOLOGIES, DEAR SIR.
THIS WAY, PLEASE.
I'M GOING TO PAINT MY AUNT'S HOUSE, SO I'LL NEED PAINT AND BRUSHES.
HERE'S OUR SELECTION, SIR.
THIS IS OUR BEST PAINTING SET.
BAH! YOU SILLY SHOP ASSISTANT! I'M GOING TO PAINT THE HOUSE— ALL OF IT. I'LL NEED GALLONS.
OH, I SEE! IT'S A MURAL YOU'RE DOING.
THIS IS ALL THE PAINT WE'VE GOT.
THAT'LL HAVE TO DO THEN.
TCH! IT'LL TAKE ME AGES USING THESE TINY BRUSHES.
HARDWARE COMPANY
LADDERS
FENCES
I'LL NEED A LADDER. I'LL HAVE THAT ONE.
POST NO BILLS OR TOMS
ACME HARDWARE COMPANY
NOW TO GET STARTED.
FENCES

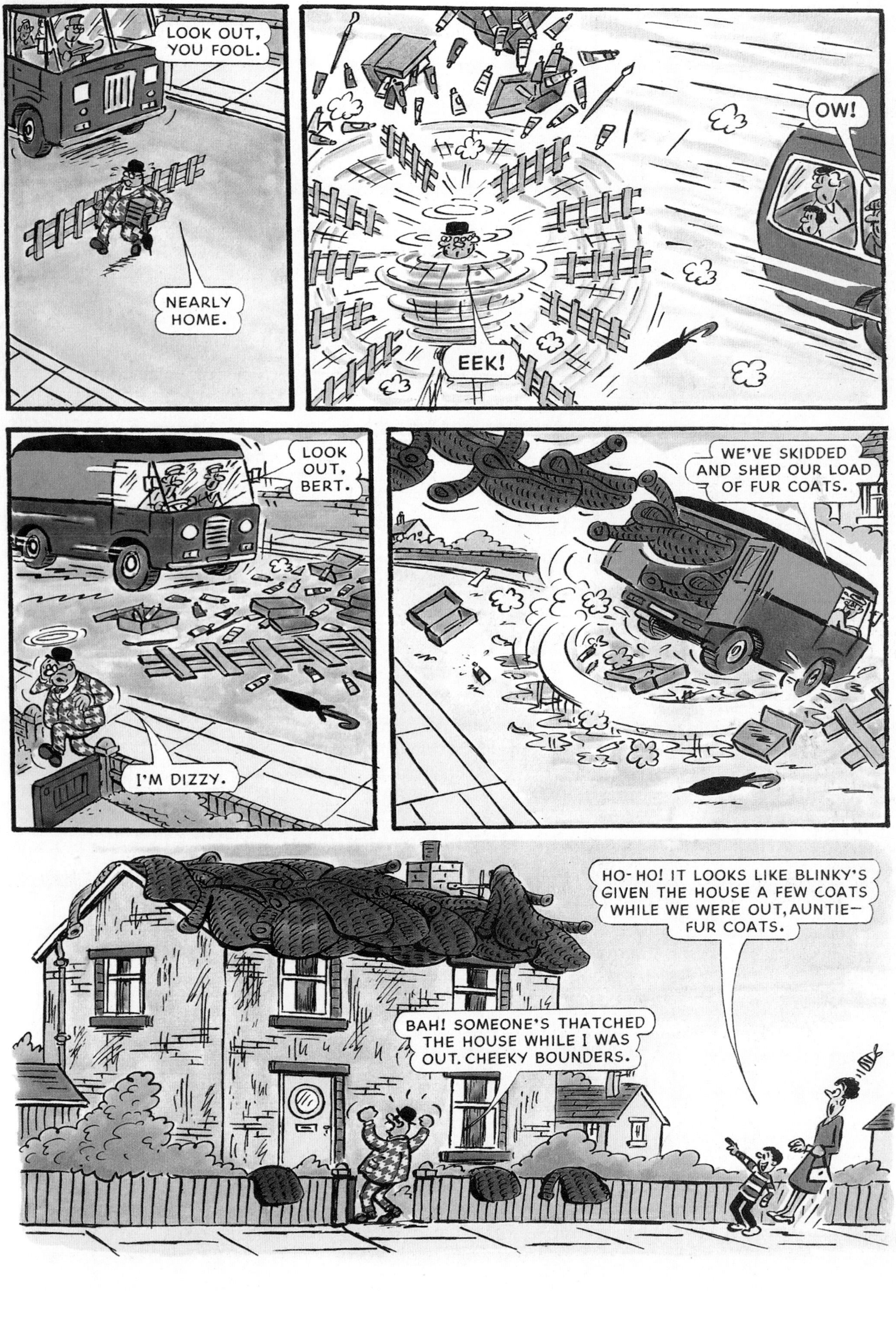
LOOK OUT, YOU FOOL.
NEARLY HOME.
OW!
EEK!
LOOK OUT, BERT.
I'M DIZZY.
WE'VE SKIDDED AND SHED OUR LOAD OF FUR COATS.
HO-HO! IT LOOKS LIKE BLINKY'S GIVEN THE HOUSE A FEW COATS WHILE WE WERE OUT, AUNTIE— FUR COATS.
BAH! SOMEONE'S THATCHED THE HOUSE WHILE I WAS OUT. CHEEKY BOUNDERS.

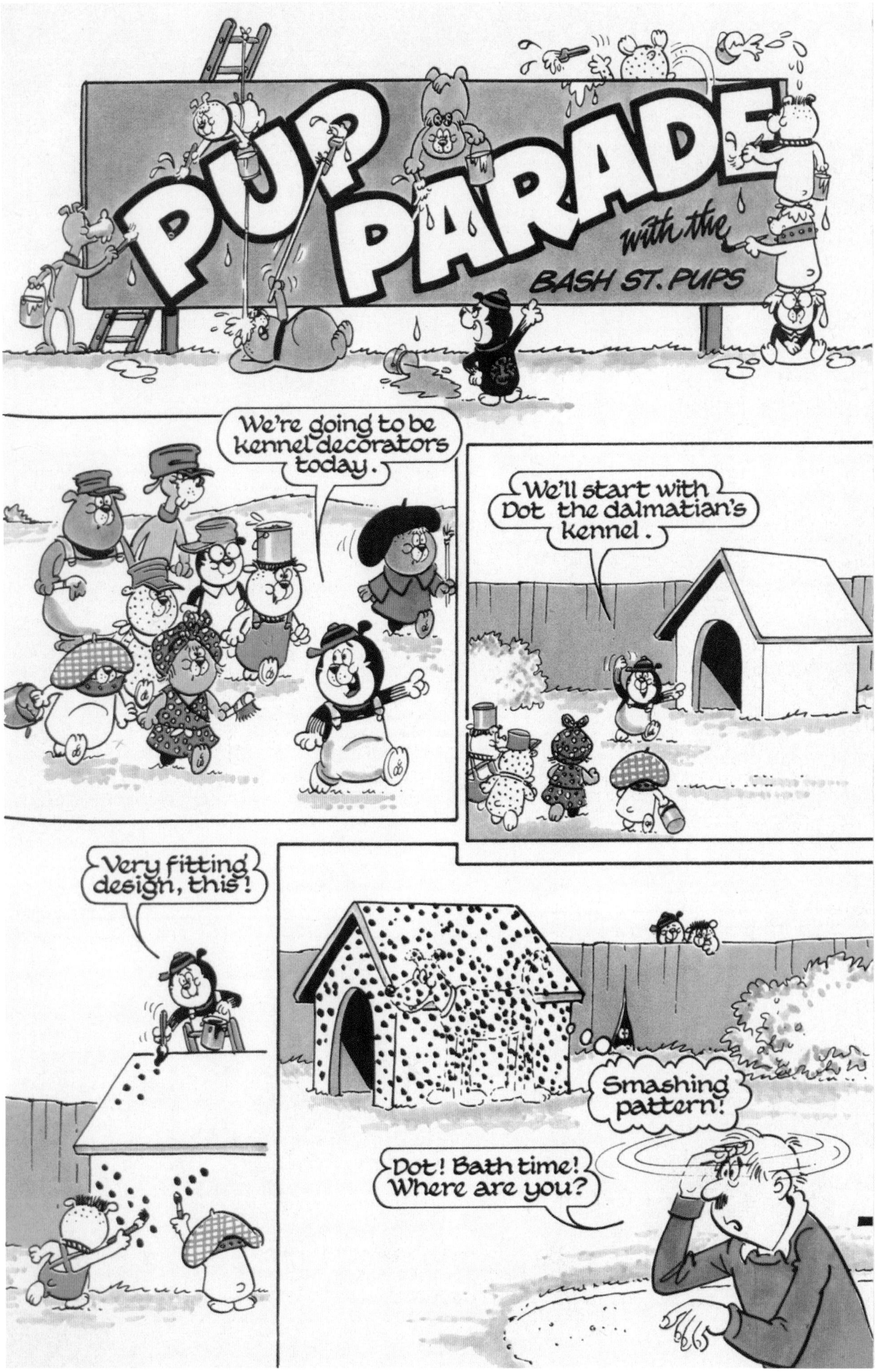
PUP PARADE
with the
BASH ST. PUPS
We're going to be kennel decorators today.
We'll start with Dot the dalmatian's kennel.
Very fitting design, this!
Smashing pattern!
Dot! Bath time! Where are you?

Here's a fine Scottish design.

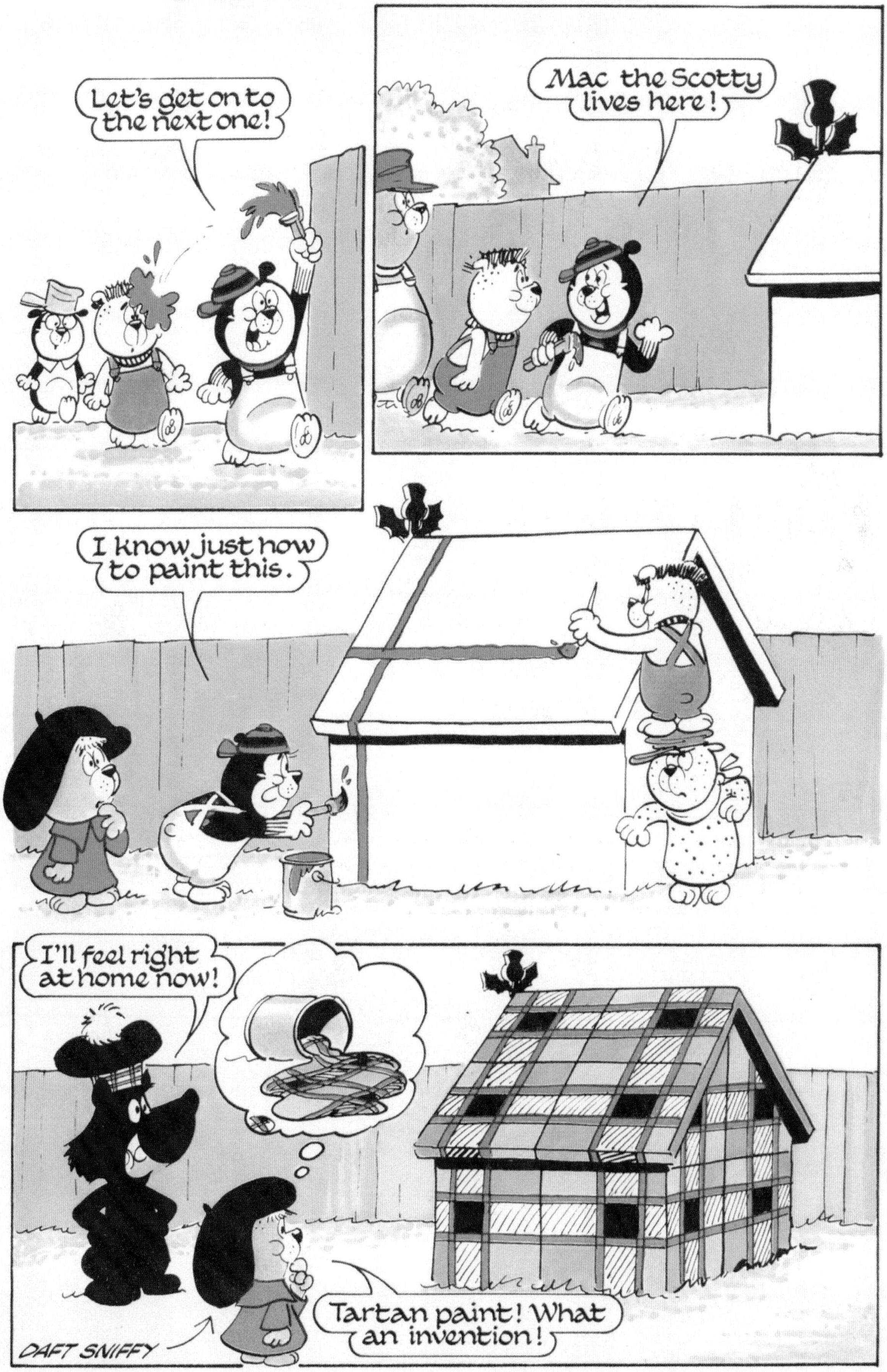

Let's get on to the next one!
Mac the Scotty lives here!
I know just how to paint this.
I'll feel right at home now!
Tartan paint! What an invention!
DAFT SNIFFY

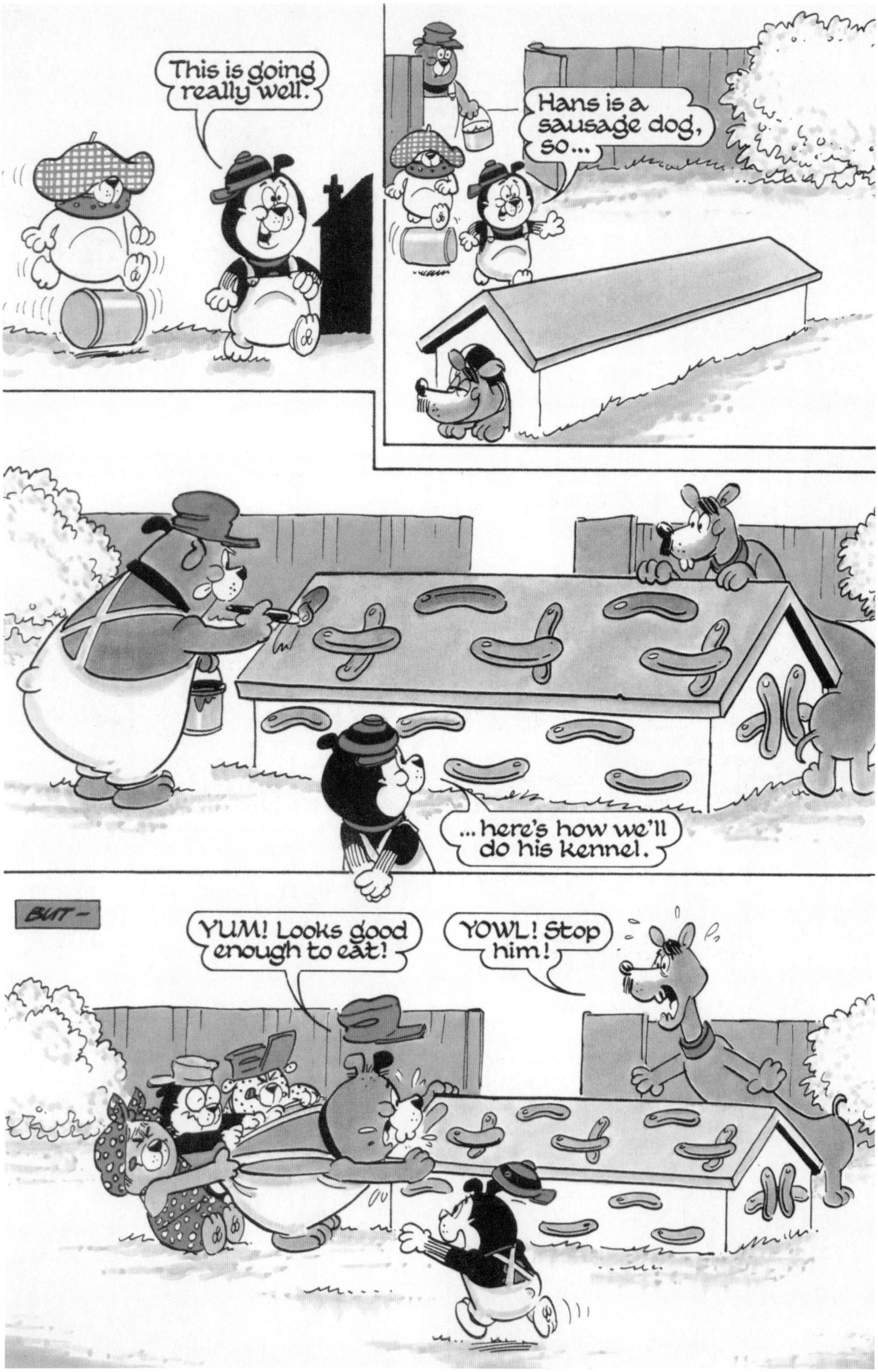
This is going really well.
Hans is a sausage dog, so...
...here's how we'll do his kennel.
BUT –
YUM! Looks good enough to eat!
YOWL! Stop him!

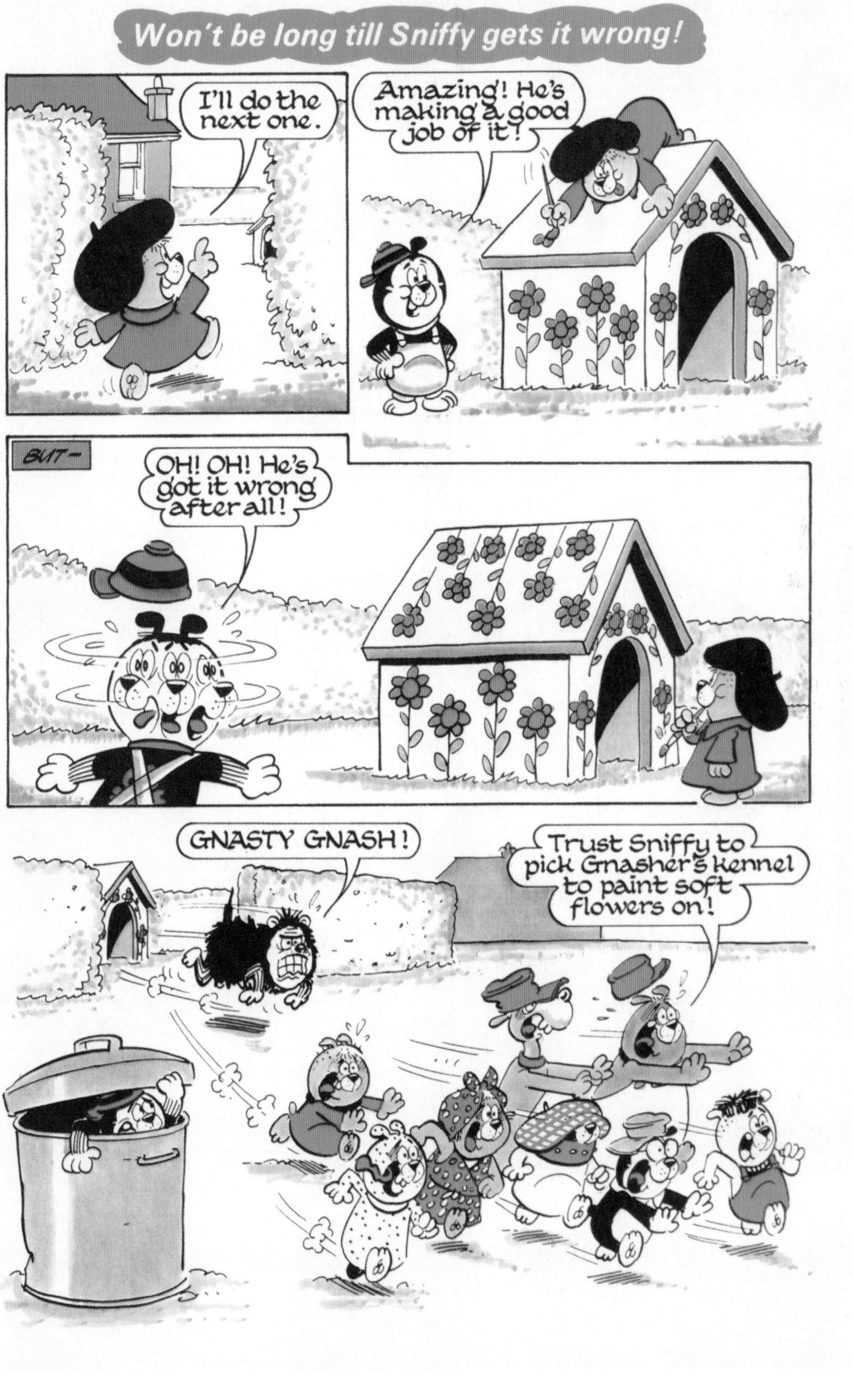
Won't be long till Sniffy gets it wrong!
I'll do the next one.
Amazing! He's making a good job of it!
BUT—
OH! OH! He's got it wrong after all!
GNASTY GNASH!
Trust Sniffy to pick Gnasher's kennel to paint soft flowers on!

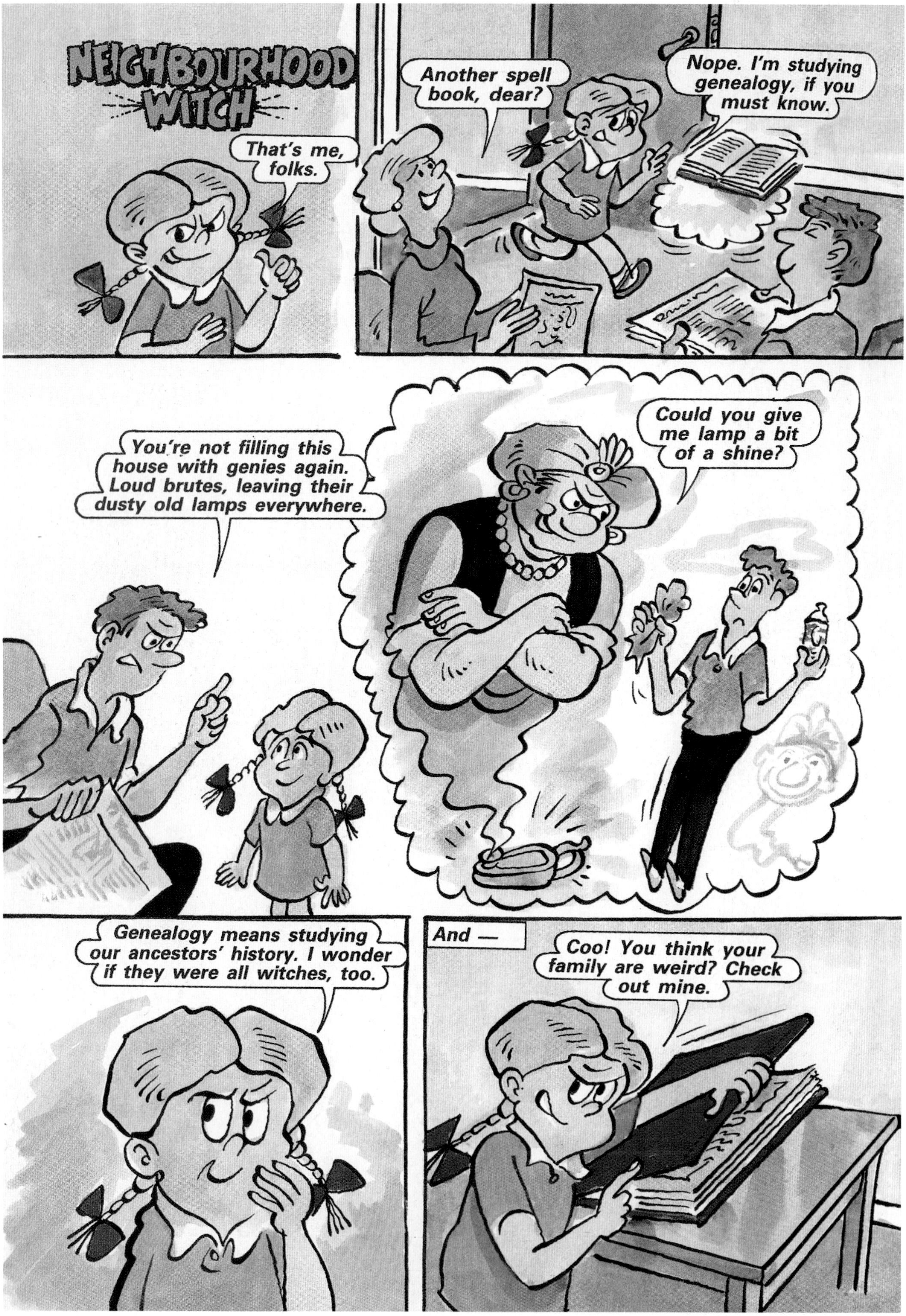
NEIGHBOURHOOD WITCH
That's me, folks.
Another spell book, dear?
Nope. I'm studying genealogy, if you must know.
You're not filling this house with genies again. Loud brutes, leaving their dusty old lamps everywhere.
Could you give me lamp a bit of a shine?
Genealogy means studying our ancestors' history. I wonder if they were all witches, too.
And —
Coo! You think your family are weird? Check out mine.

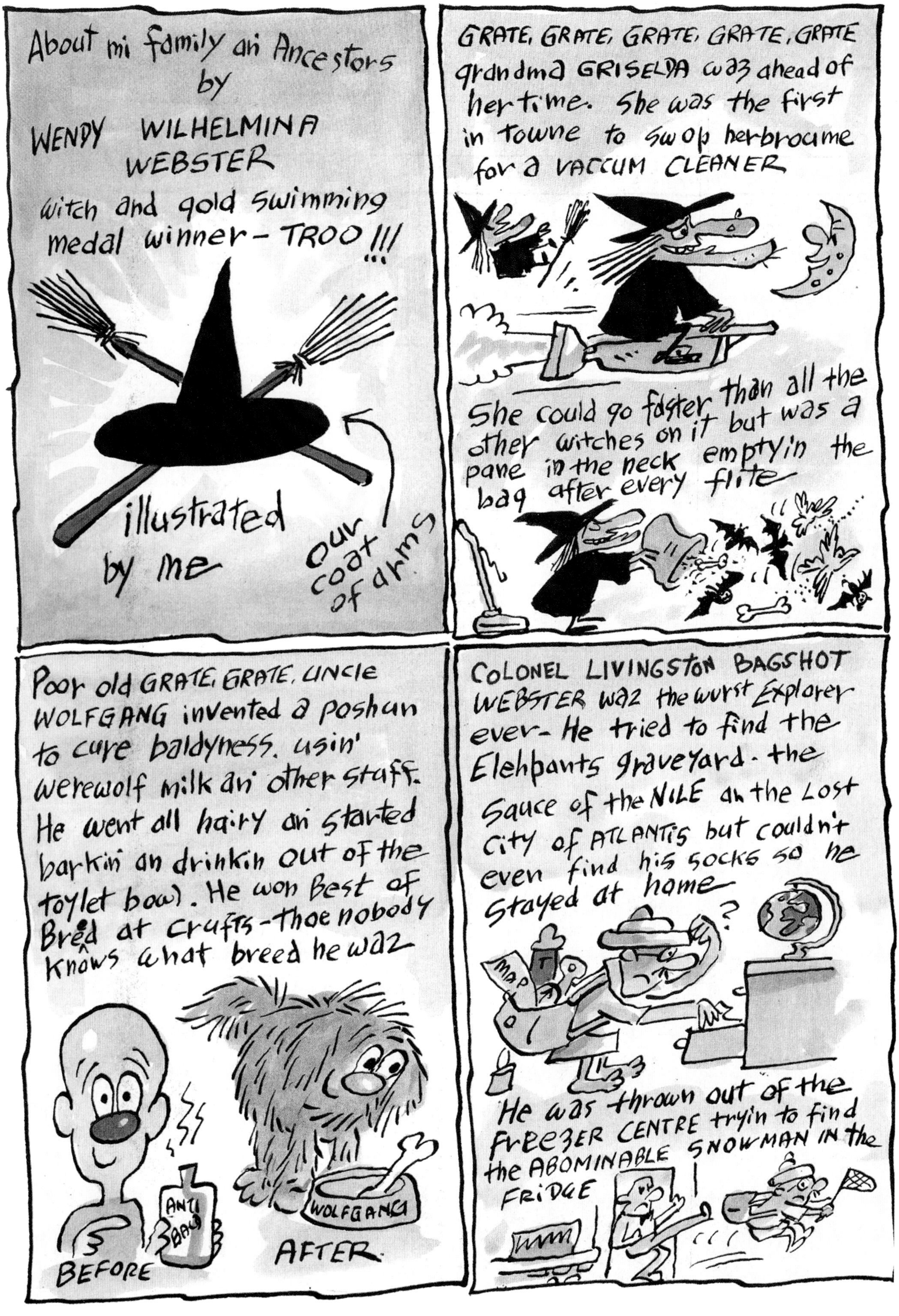
About mi family an Ancestors
by
WENDY WILHELMINA WEBSTER
witch and gold swimming medal winner - TROO!!!
illustrated by me
our coat of arms
GRATE, GRATE, GRATE, GRATE, GRATE grandma GRISELDA waz ahead of her time. She was the first in towne to swop herbroome for a VACCUM CLEANER
She could go faster than all the other witches on it but was a pane in the neck emptyin the bag after every flite
Poor old GRATE, GRATE, UNCLE WOLFGANG invented a poshun to cure baldyness. usin' werewolf milk an other stuff. He went all hairy an started barkin an drinkin out of the toylet bowl. He won Best of Breed at Crufts - thoe nobody knows what breed he waz
ANTI BALD
WOLFGANG
BEFORE
AFTER
COLONEL LIVINGSTON BAGSHOT WEBSTER waz the wurst Explorer ever - He tried to find the Elehpants graveyard - the Sauce of the NILE an the Lost City of ATLANTIS but couldn't even find his socks so he stayed at home
?
MAP
He was thrown out of the FREEZER CENTRE tryin to find the ABOMINABLE SNOWMAN in the FRIDGE

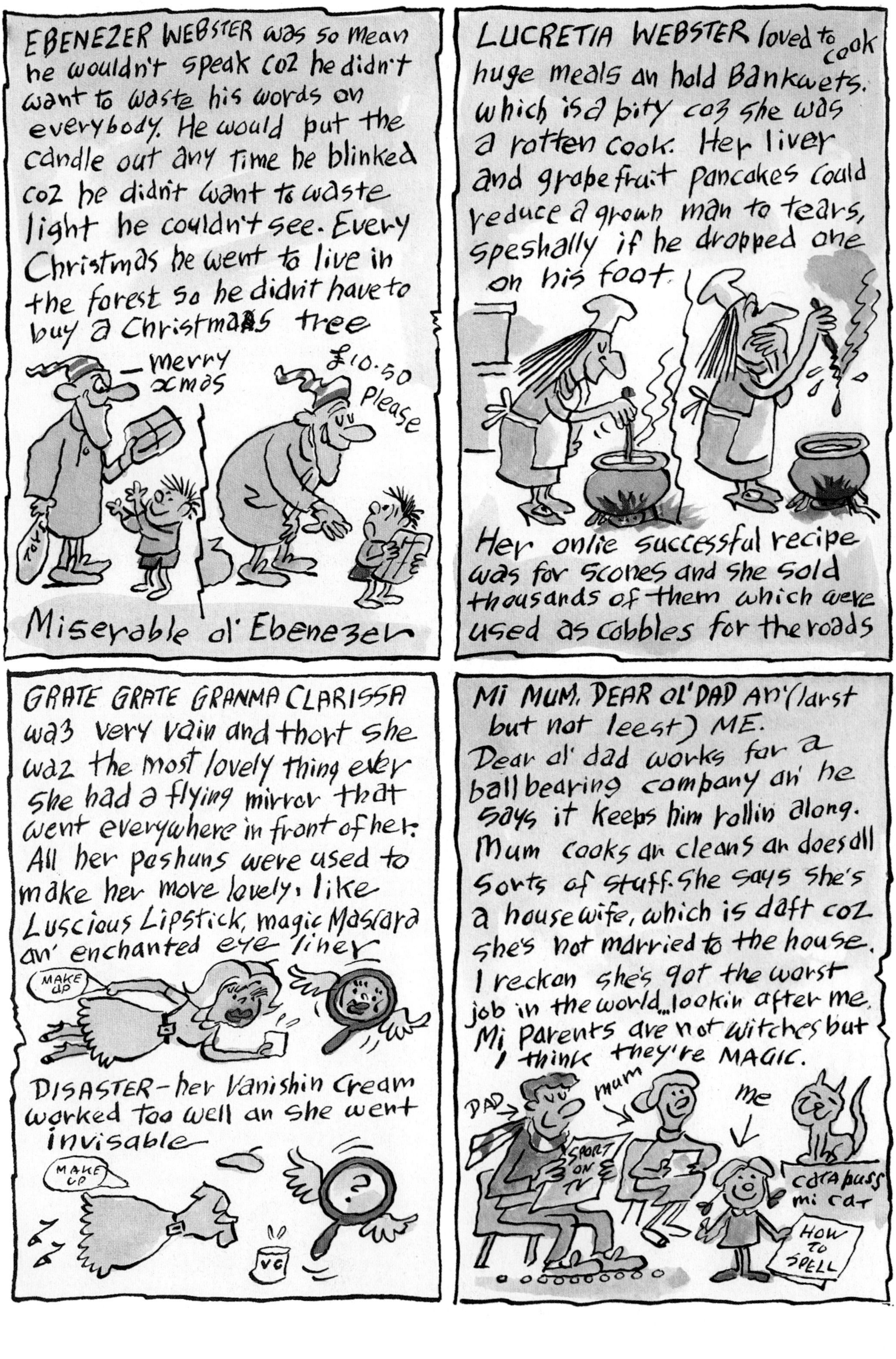
EBENEZER WEBSTER was so mean he wouldn't speak coz he didn't want to waste his words on everybody. He would put the candle out any time he blinked coz he didn't want to waste light he couldn't see. Every Christmas he went to live in the forest so he didn't have to buy a Christmas tree
Merry xmas
TOYS
£10.50 Please
Miserable ol' Ebenezer
LUCRETIA WEBSTER loved to cook huge meals an hold Bankwets. which is a pity coz she was a rotten cook. Her liver and grapefruit pancakes could reduce a grown man to tears, speshally if he dropped one on his foot.
Her onlie successful recipe was for scones and she sold thousands of them which were used as cobbles for the roads
GRATE GRATE GRANMA CLARISSA waz very vain and thort she waz the most lovely thing ever She had a flying mirror that went everywhere in front of her. All her poshuns were used to make her more lovely, like Luscious Lipstick, magic Mascara an' enchanted eye liner
MAKE UP
DISASTER—her Vanishin Cream worked too well an she went invisable
MAKE UP
?
VC
MI MUM, DEAR OL' DAD AN' (larst but not leest) ME.
Dear ol' dad works for a ball bearing company an' he says it keeps him rollin along. Mum cooks an cleans an does all sorts of stuff. She says she's a house wife, which is daft coz she's not married to the house. I reckon she's got the worst job in the world...lookin after me. Mi parents are not witches but I think they're MAGIC.
DAD
mum
me
SPORT ON TV
carapuss mi cat
HOW TO SPELL

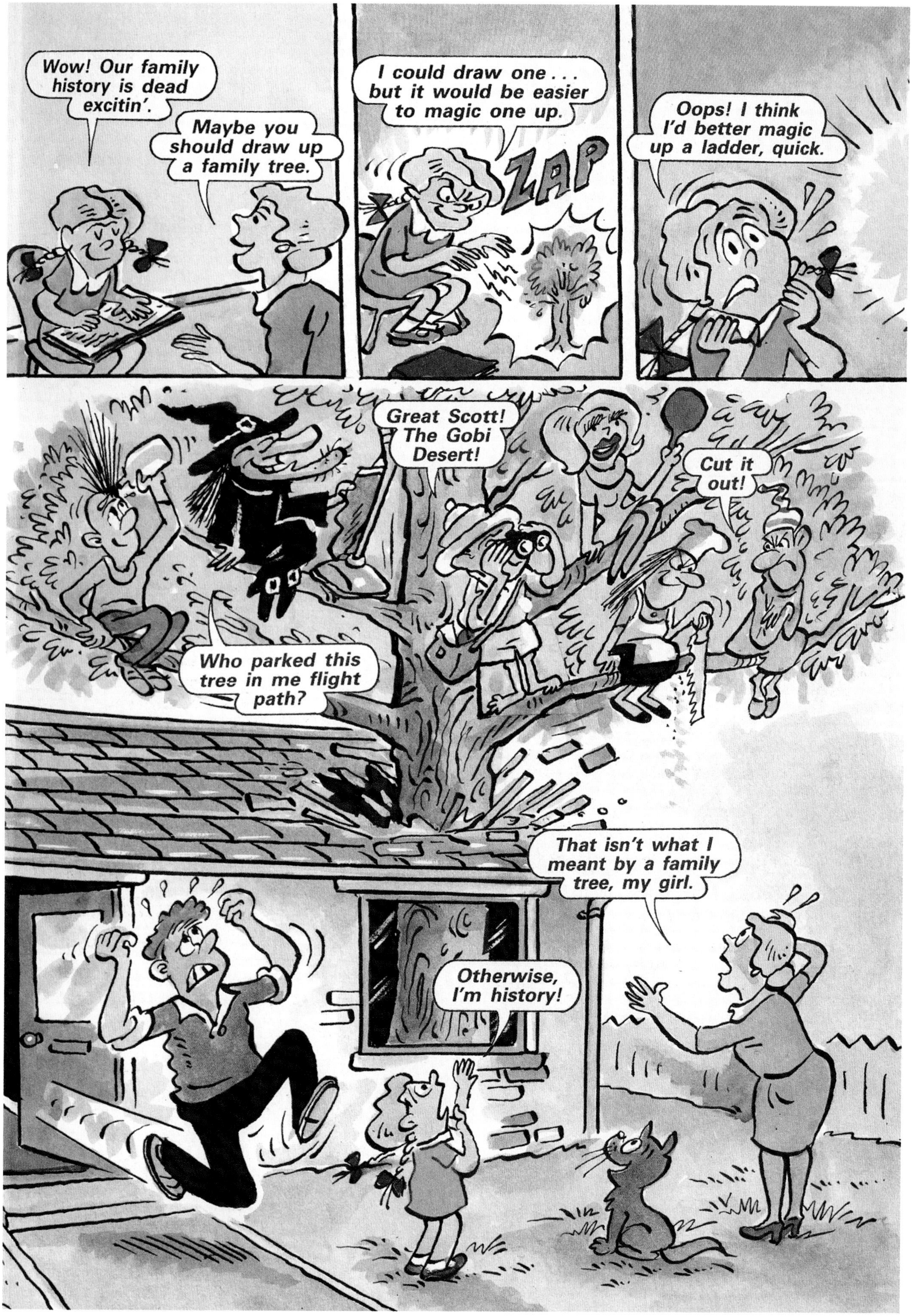
Wow! Our family history is dead excitin'.
Maybe you should draw up a family tree.
I could draw one . . . but it would be easier to magic one up.
ZAP
Oops! I think I'd better magic up a ladder, quick.
Great Scott! The Gobi Desert!
Cut it out!
Who parked this tree in me flight path?
That isn't what I meant by a family tree, my girl.
Otherwise, I'm history!

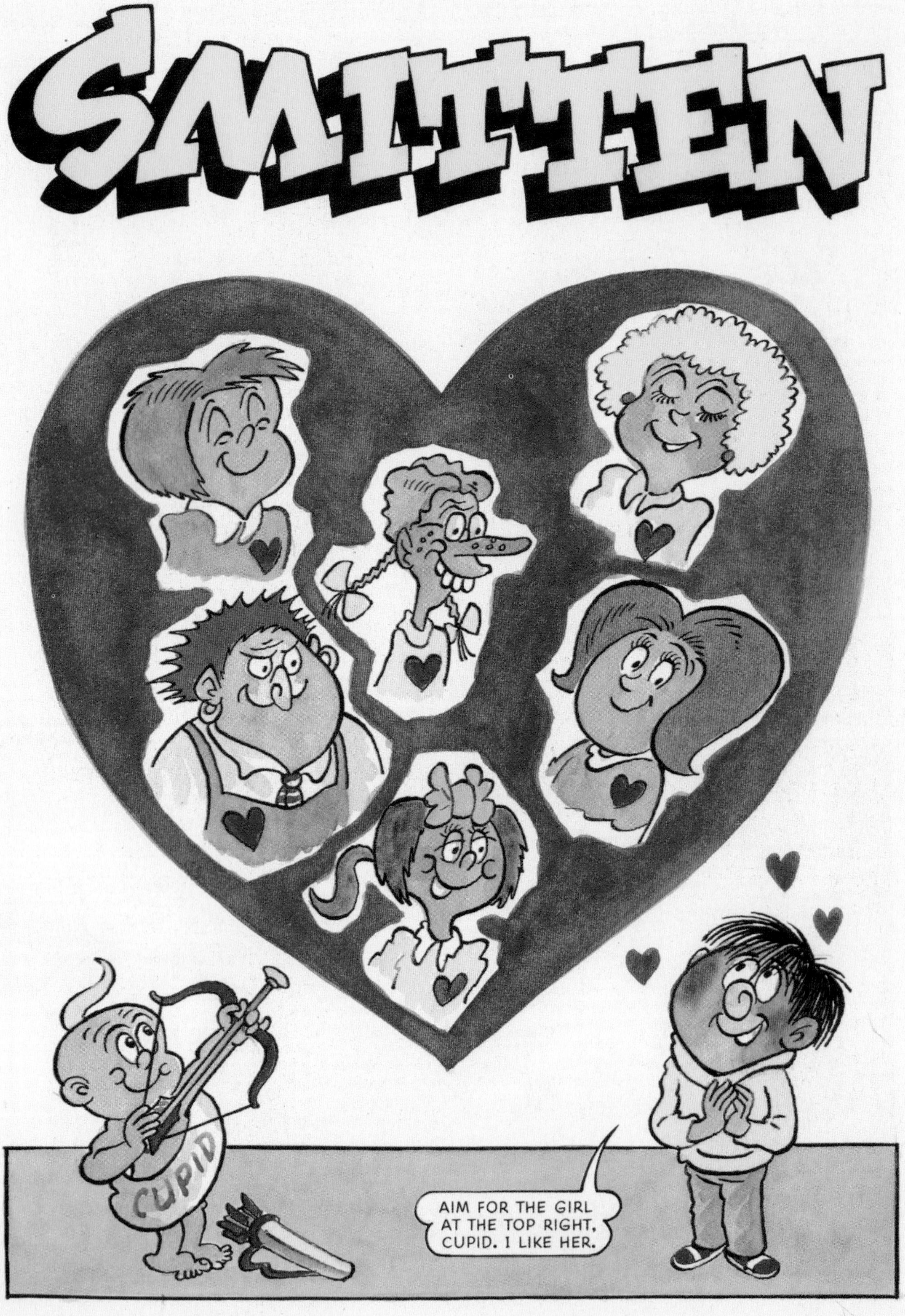
SMITTEN
CUPID
AIM FOR THE GIRL AT THE TOP RIGHT, CUPID. I LIKE HER.

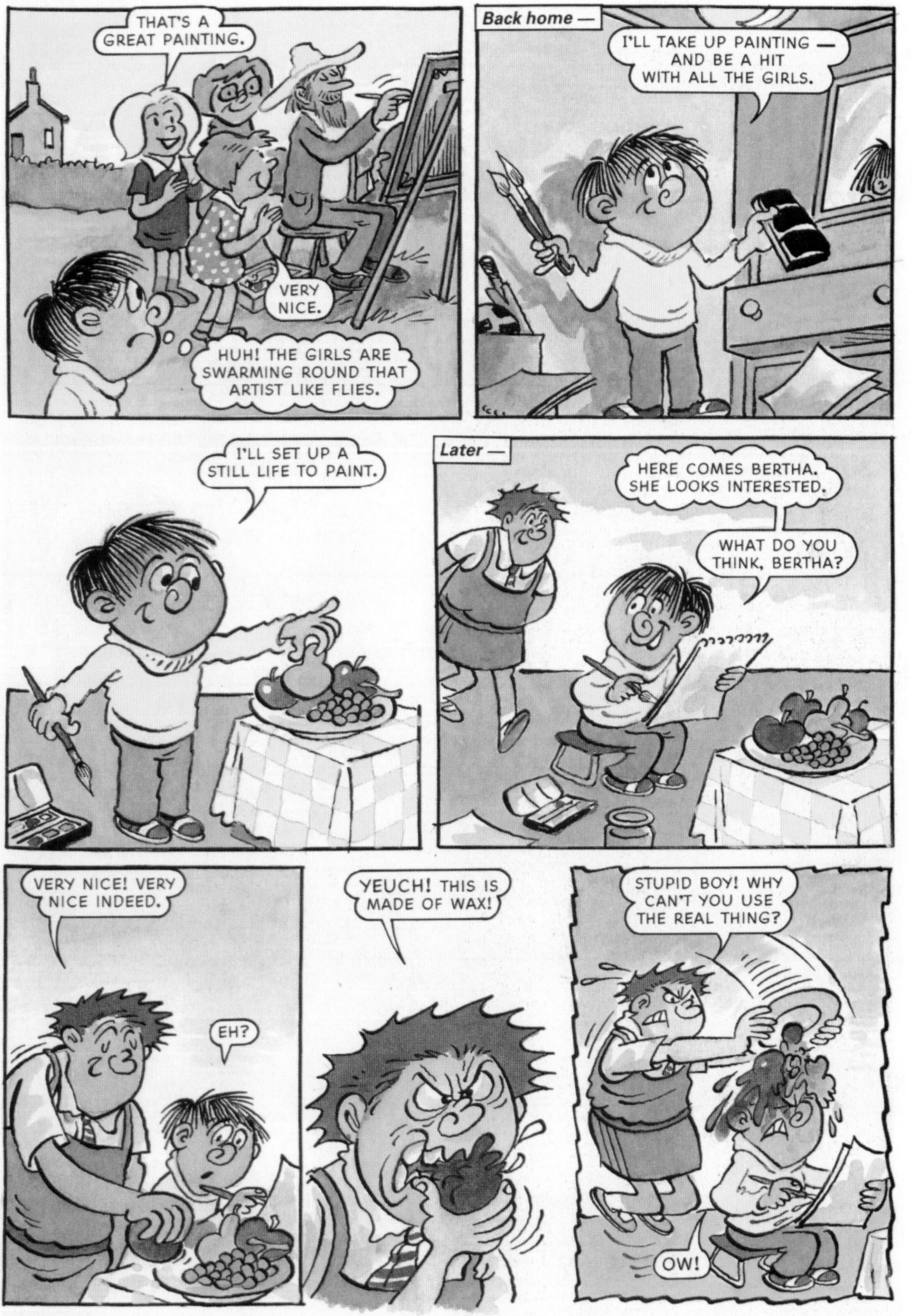
THAT'S A GREAT PAINTING.
VERY NICE.
HUH! THE GIRLS ARE SWARMING ROUND THAT ARTIST LIKE FLIES.
Back home —
I'LL TAKE UP PAINTING — AND BE A HIT WITH ALL THE GIRLS.
I'LL SET UP A STILL LIFE TO PAINT.
Later —
HERE COMES BERTHA. SHE LOOKS INTERESTED.
WHAT DO YOU THINK, BERTHA?
VERY NICE! VERY NICE INDEED.
EH?
YEUCH! THIS IS MADE OF WAX!
STUPID BOY! WHY CAN'T YOU USE THE REAL THING?
OW!

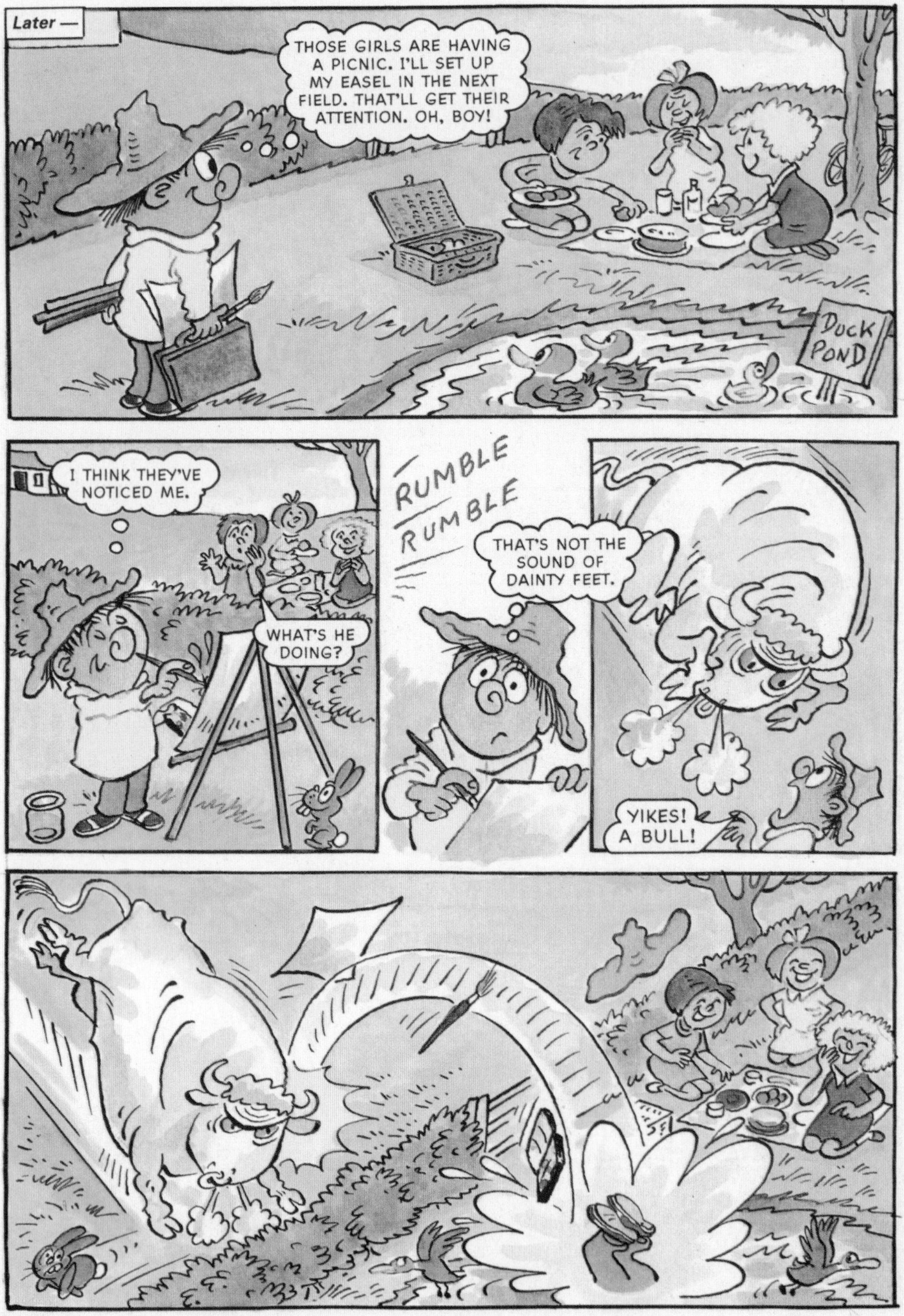
Later —
THOSE GIRLS ARE HAVING A PICNIC. I'LL SET UP MY EASEL IN THE NEXT FIELD. THAT'LL GET THEIR ATTENTION. OH, BOY!
DUCK POND
I THINK THEY'VE NOTICED ME.
WHAT'S HE DOING?
RUMBLE
RUMBLE
THAT'S NOT THE SOUND OF DAINTY FEET.
YIKES! A BULL!

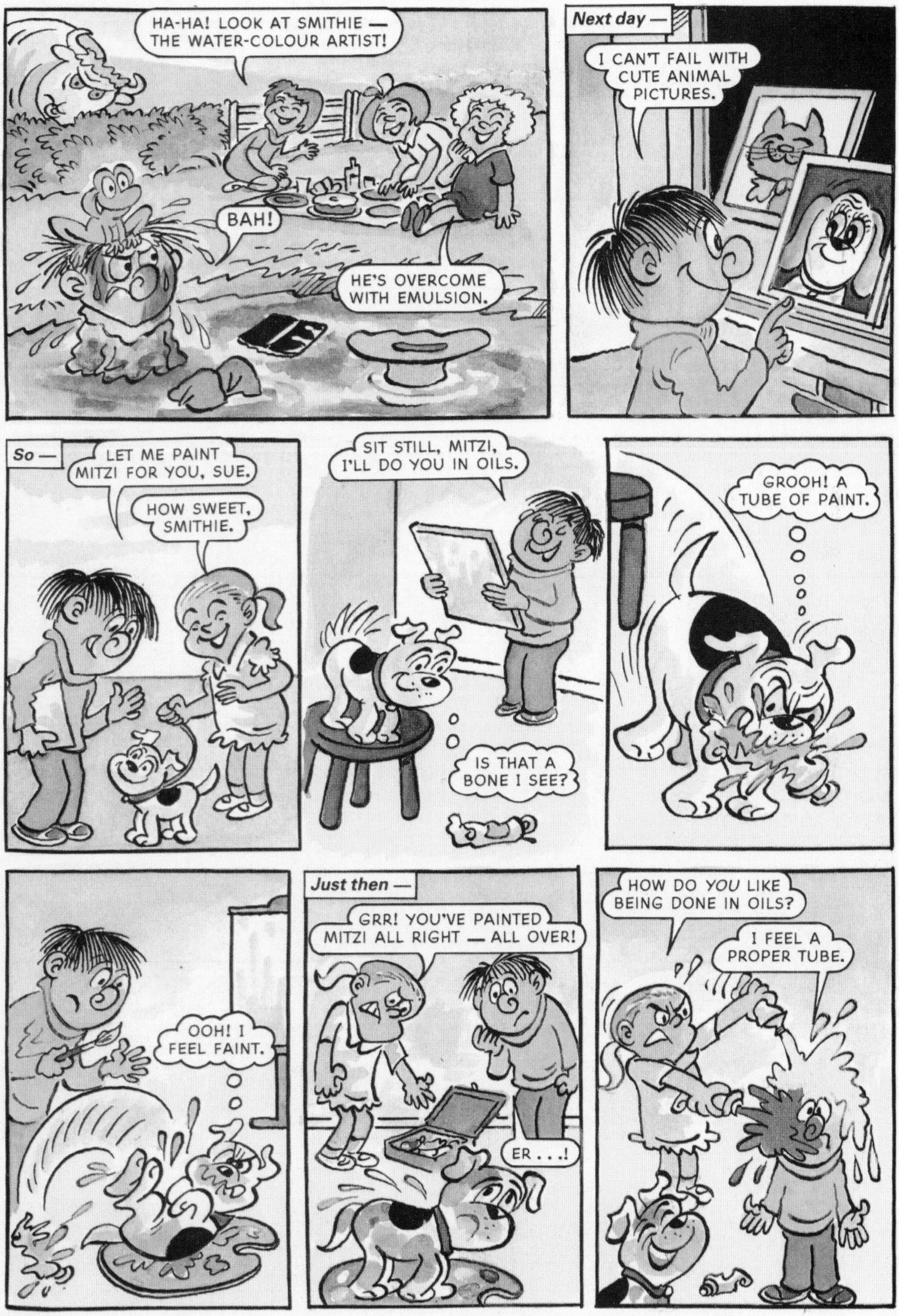
HA-HA! LOOK AT SMITHIE — THE WATER-COLOUR ARTIST!
BAH!
HE'S OVERCOME WITH EMULSION.
Next day —
I CAN'T FAIL WITH CUTE ANIMAL PICTURES.
So —
LET ME PAINT MITZI FOR YOU, SUE.
HOW SWEET, SMITHIE.
SIT STILL, MITZI, I'LL DO YOU IN OILS.
IS THAT A BONE I SEE?
GROOH! A TUBE OF PAINT.
OOH! I FEEL FAINT.
Just then —
GRR! YOU'VE PAINTED MITZI ALL RIGHT — ALL OVER!
ER . . .!
HOW DO *YOU* LIKE BEING DONE IN OILS?
I FEEL A PROPER TUBE.

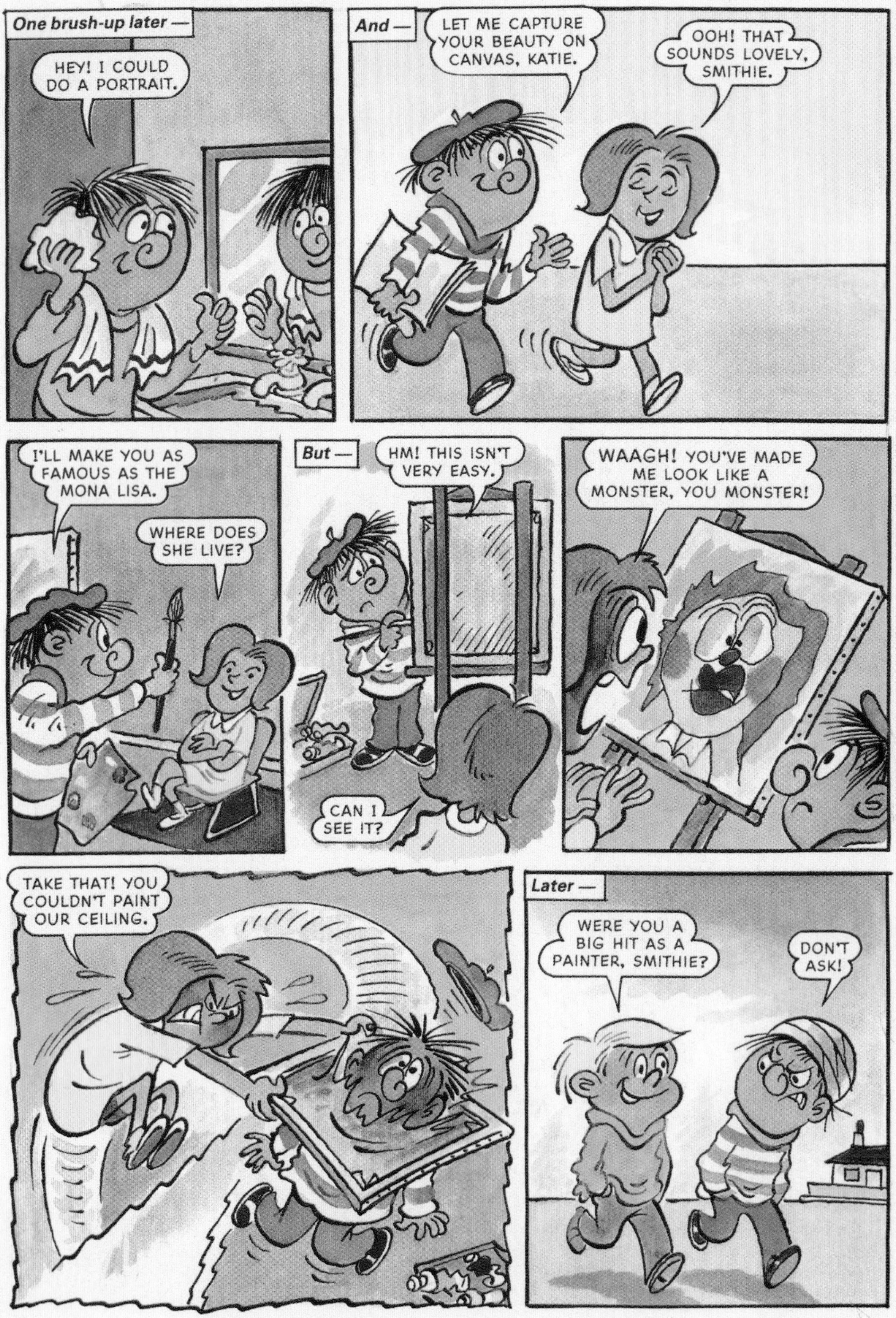
One brush-up later —
HEY! I COULD DO A PORTRAIT.
And —
LET ME CAPTURE YOUR BEAUTY ON CANVAS, KATIE.
OOH! THAT SOUNDS LOVELY, SMITHIE.
I'LL MAKE YOU AS FAMOUS AS THE MONA LISA.
WHERE DOES SHE LIVE?
But —
HM! THIS ISN'T VERY EASY.
CAN I SEE IT?
WAAGH! YOU'VE MADE ME LOOK LIKE A MONSTER, YOU MONSTER!
TAKE THAT! YOU COULDN'T PAINT OUR CEILING.
Later —
WERE YOU A BIG HIT AS A PAINTER, SMITHIE?
DON'T ASK!

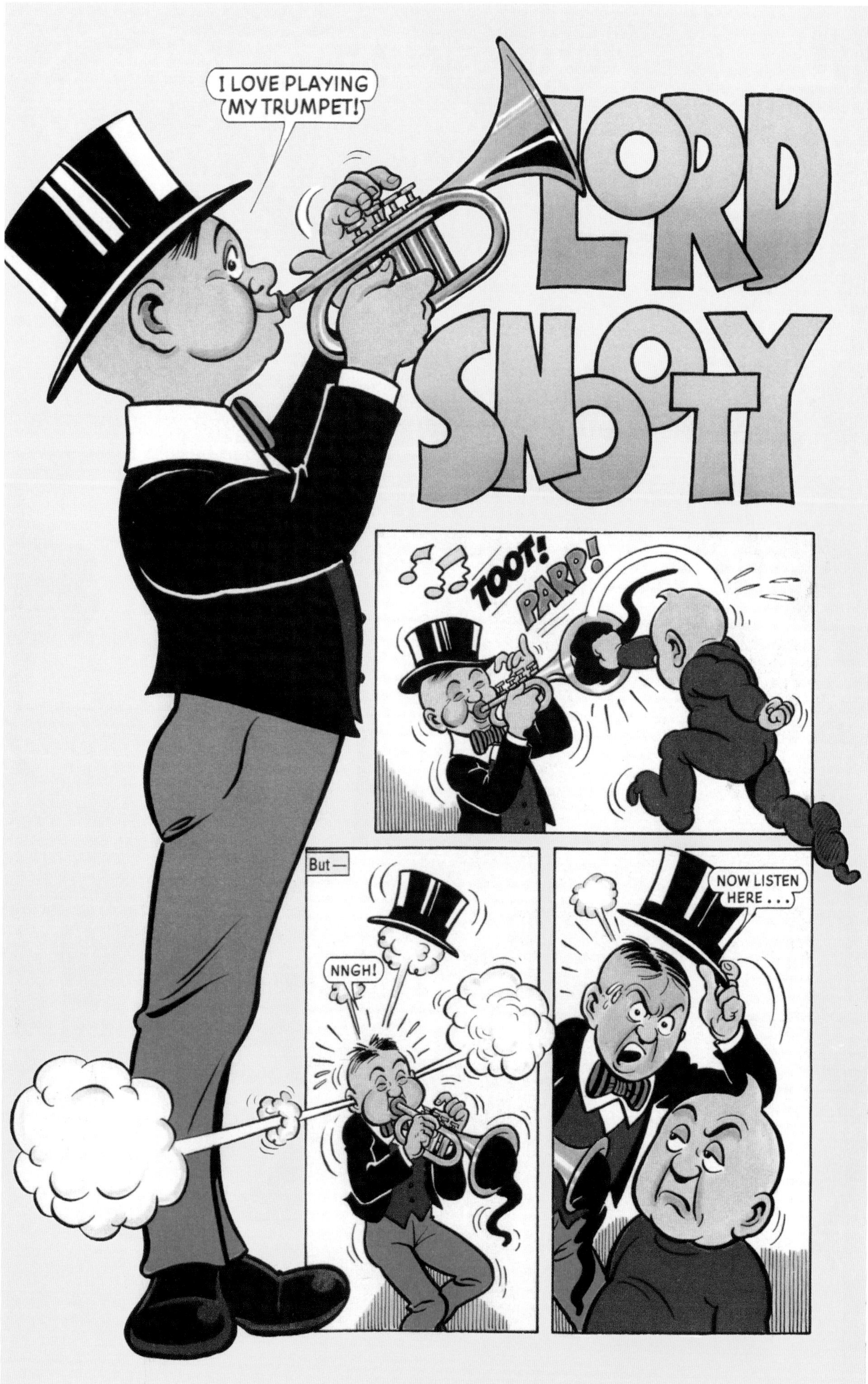
I LOVE PLAYING MY TRUMPET!
LORD SNOOTY
TOOT!
PARP!
But—
NNGH!
NOW LISTEN HERE . . .

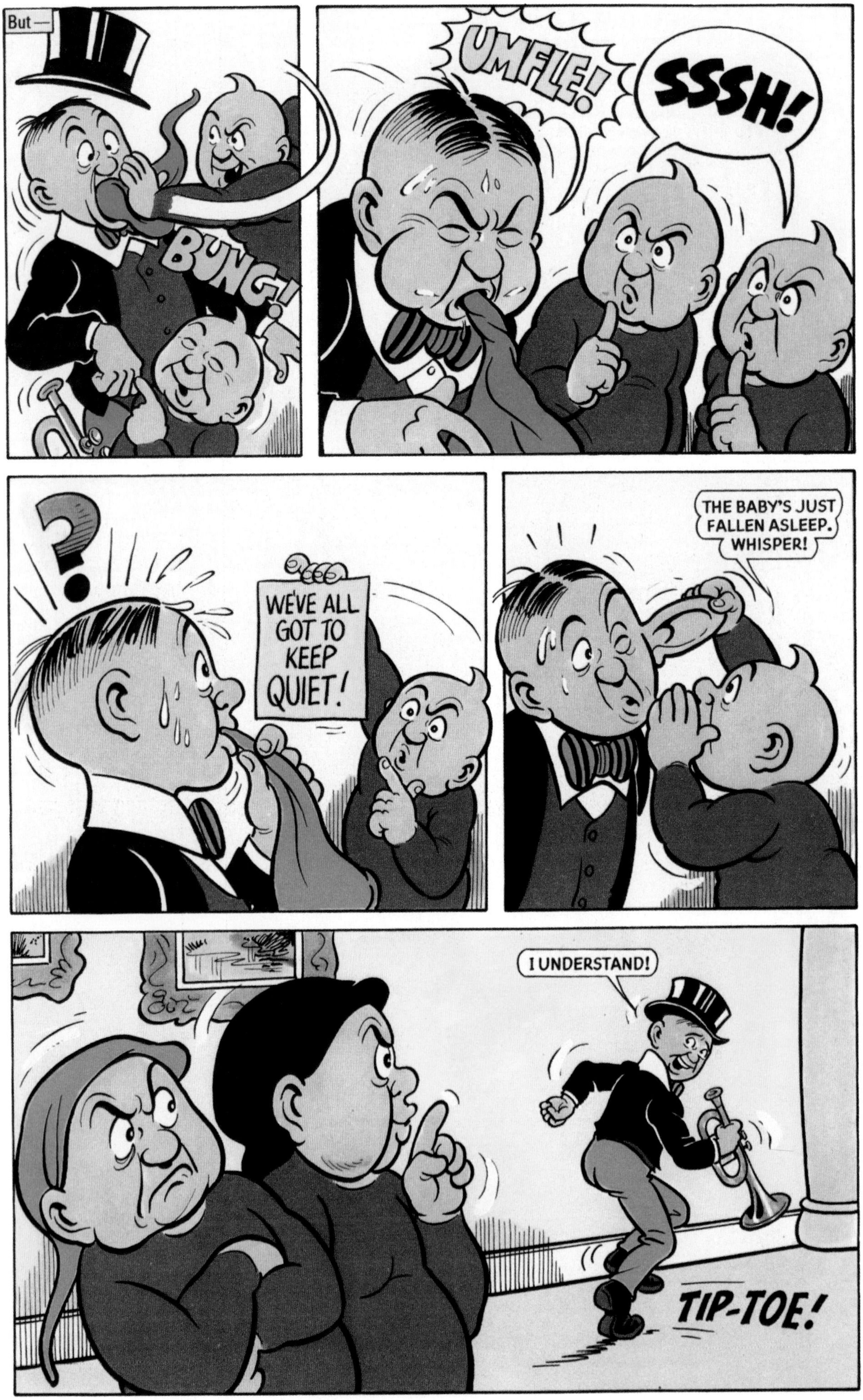
But —
BUNG!
UMFLE!
SSSH!
WE'VE ALL GOT TO KEEP QUIET!
THE BABY'S JUST FALLEN ASLEEP. WHISPER!
I UNDERSTAND!
TIP-TOE!

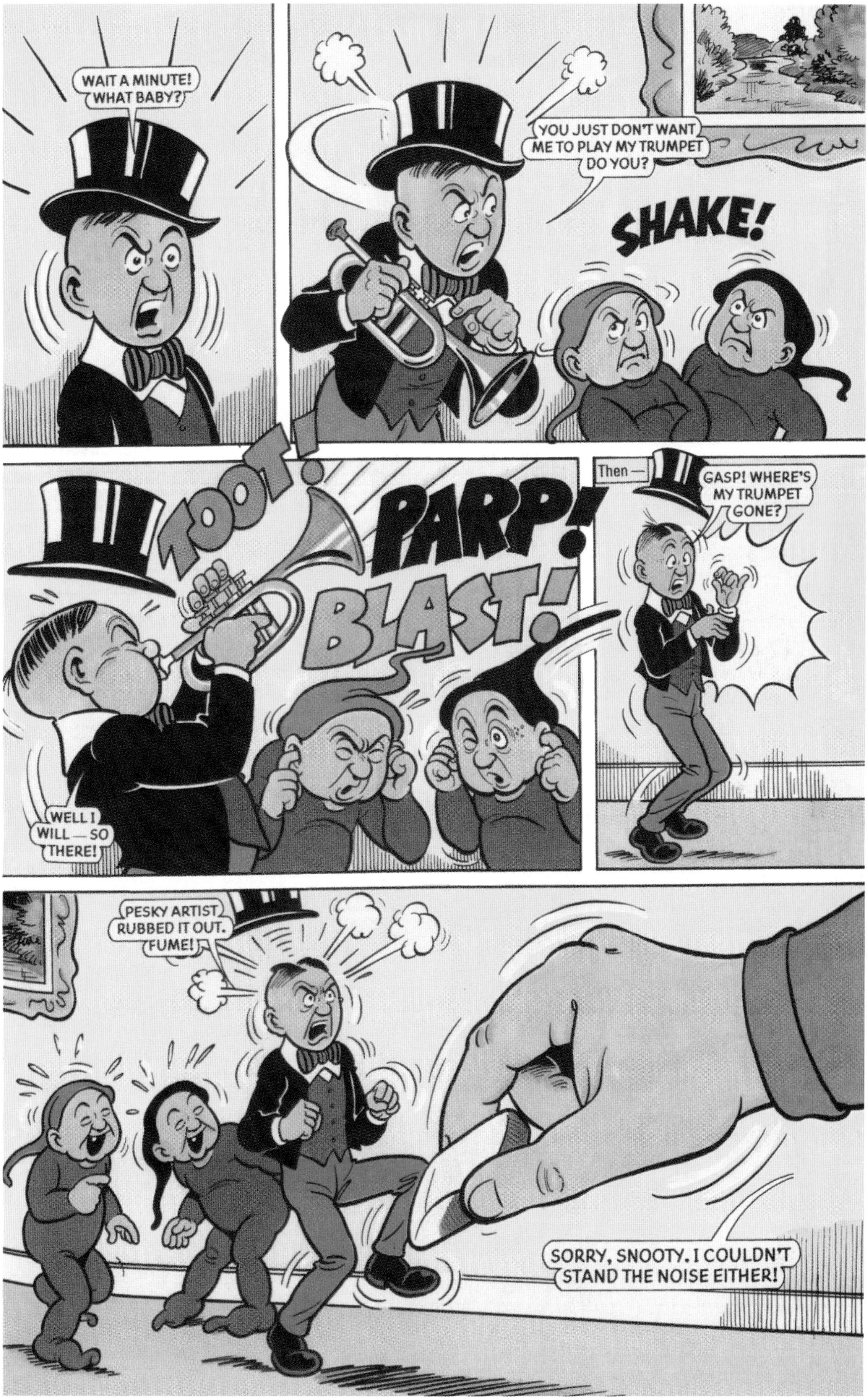
WAIT A MINUTE! WHAT BABY?
YOU JUST DON'T WANT ME TO PLAY MY TRUMPET DO YOU?
SHAKE!
TOOT!
PARP!
BLAST!
WELL I WILL — SO THERE!
Then —
GASP! WHERE'S MY TRUMPET GONE?
PESKY ARTIST RUBBED IT OUT. FUME!
SORRY, SNOOTY. I COULDN'T STAND THE NOISE EITHER!

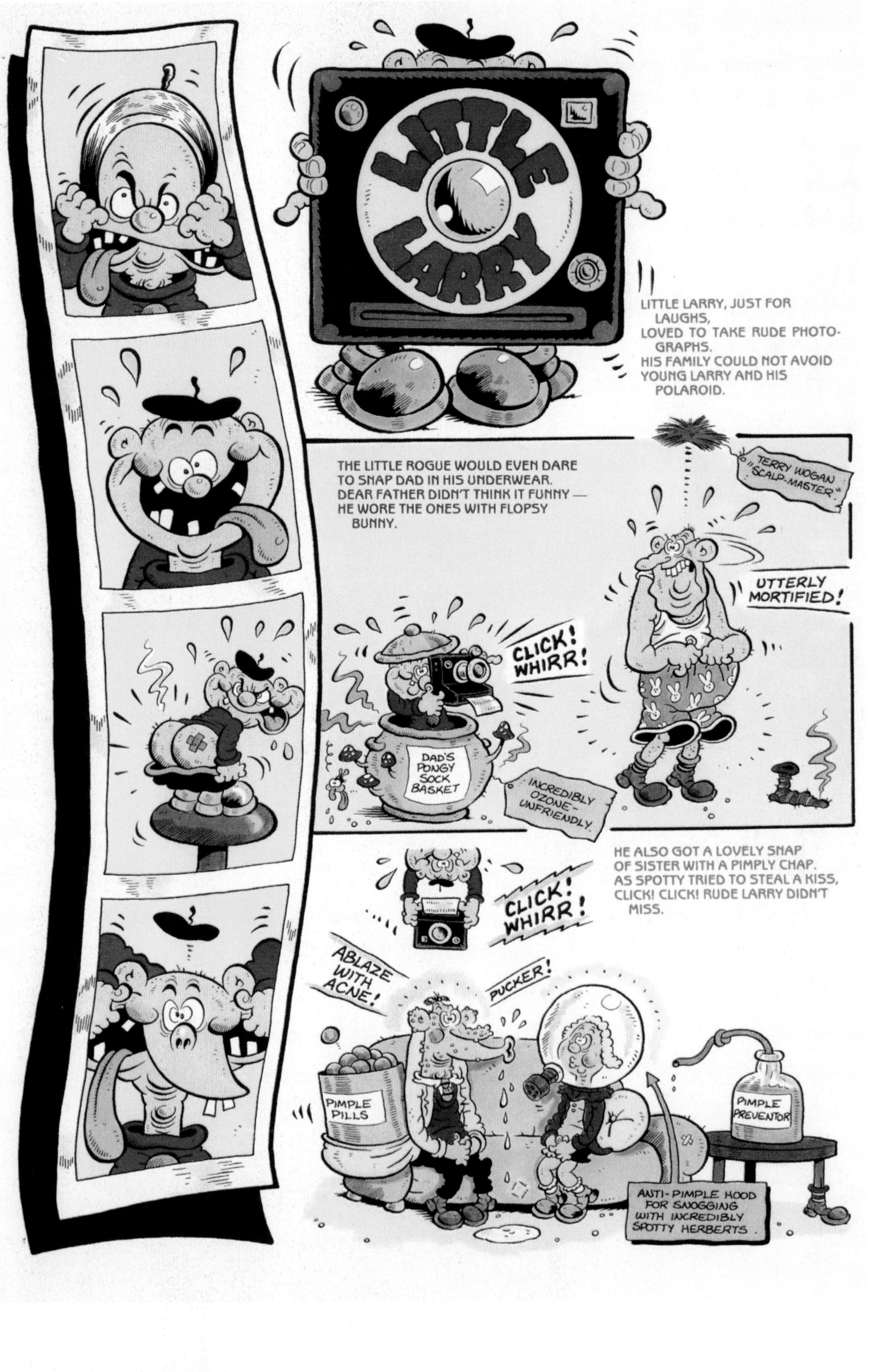
LITTLE LARRY
LITTLE LARRY, JUST FOR LAUGHS,
LOVED TO TAKE RUDE PHOTOGRAPHS.
HIS FAMILY COULD NOT AVOID
YOUNG LARRY AND HIS POLAROID.
THE LITTLE ROGUE WOULD EVEN DARE
TO SNAP DAD IN HIS UNDERWEAR.
DEAR FATHER DIDN'T THINK IT FUNNY —
HE WORE THE ONES WITH FLOPSY BUNNY.
TERRY WOGAN "SCALP-MASTER"
UTTERLY MORTIFIED!
CLICK! WHIRR!
DAD'S PONGY SOCK BASKET
INCREDIBLY OZONE-UNFRIENDLY
HE ALSO GOT A LOVELY SNAP
OF SISTER WITH A PIMPLY CHAP.
AS SPOTTY TRIED TO STEAL A KISS,
CLICK! CLICK! RUDE LARRY DIDN'T MISS.
CLICK! WHIRR!
ABLAZE WITH ACNE!
PUCKER!
PIMPLE PILLS
PIMPLE PREVENTOR
ANTI-PIMPLE HOOD FOR SNOGGING WITH INCREDIBLY SPOTTY HERBERTS.

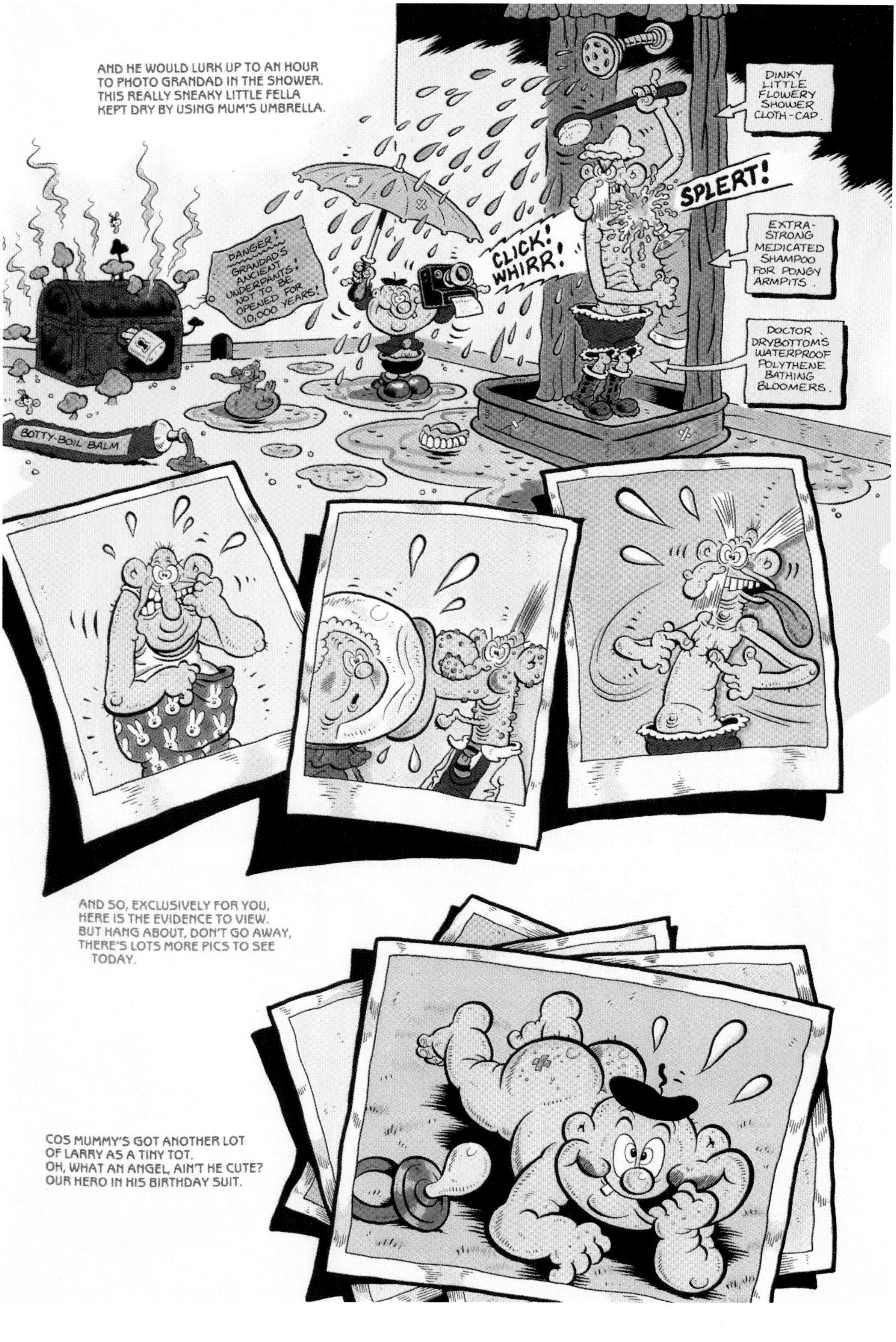
AND HE WOULD LURK UP TO AN HOUR
TO PHOTO GRANDAD IN THE SHOWER.
THIS REALLY SNEAKY LITTLE FELLA
KEPT DRY BY USING MUM'S UMBRELLA.
DINKY LITTLE FLOWERY SHOWER CLOTH-CAP.
SPLERT!
CLICK! WHIRR!
DANGER! GRANDAD'S ANCIENT UNDERPANTS! NOT TO BE OPENED FOR 10,000 YEARS!
EXTRA-STRONG MEDICATED SHAMPOO FOR PONGY ARMPITS.
DOCTOR DRYBOTTOMS WATERPROOF POLYTHENE BATHING BLOOMERS.
BOTTY-BOIL BALM
AND SO, EXCLUSIVELY FOR YOU,
HERE IS THE EVIDENCE TO VIEW.
BUT HANG ABOUT, DON'T GO AWAY,
THERE'S LOTS MORE PICS TO SEE
TODAY.
COS MUMMY'S GOT ANOTHER LOT
OF LARRY AS A TINY TOT.
OH, WHAT AN ANGEL, AIN'T HE CUTE?
OUR HERO IN HIS BIRTHDAY SUIT.

BULLY BEEF and CHIPS

I WOULDN'T STAND THERE, CHIPS.
WHY NOT?
'COS I'M ABOUT TO PAINT IT!
ERK!
SPLOSH!
YOU'RE AN ABSOLUTE ROTTER, BEEFY.
HOO! LOVELY MATCHING SHIRT AND TIE, CHIPS.

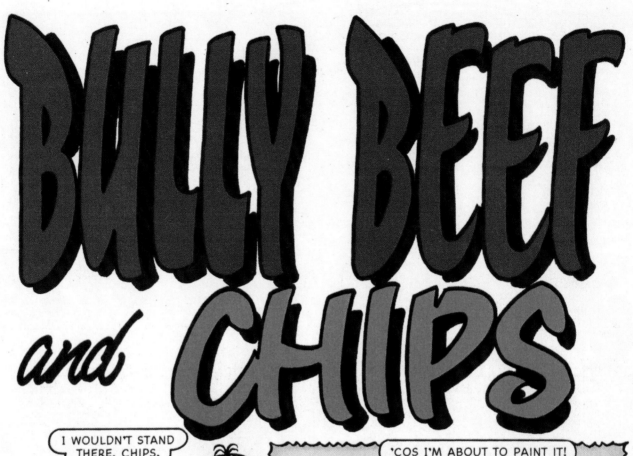

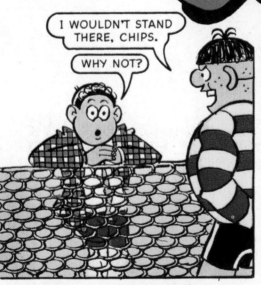

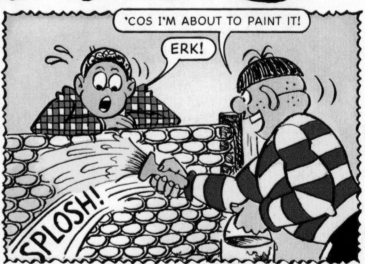

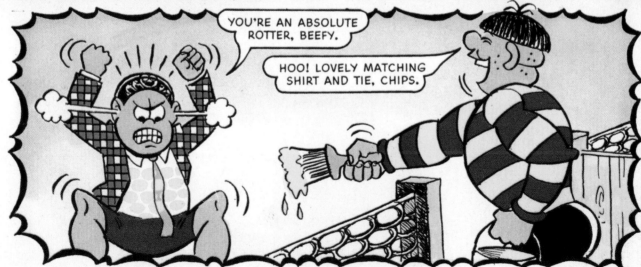

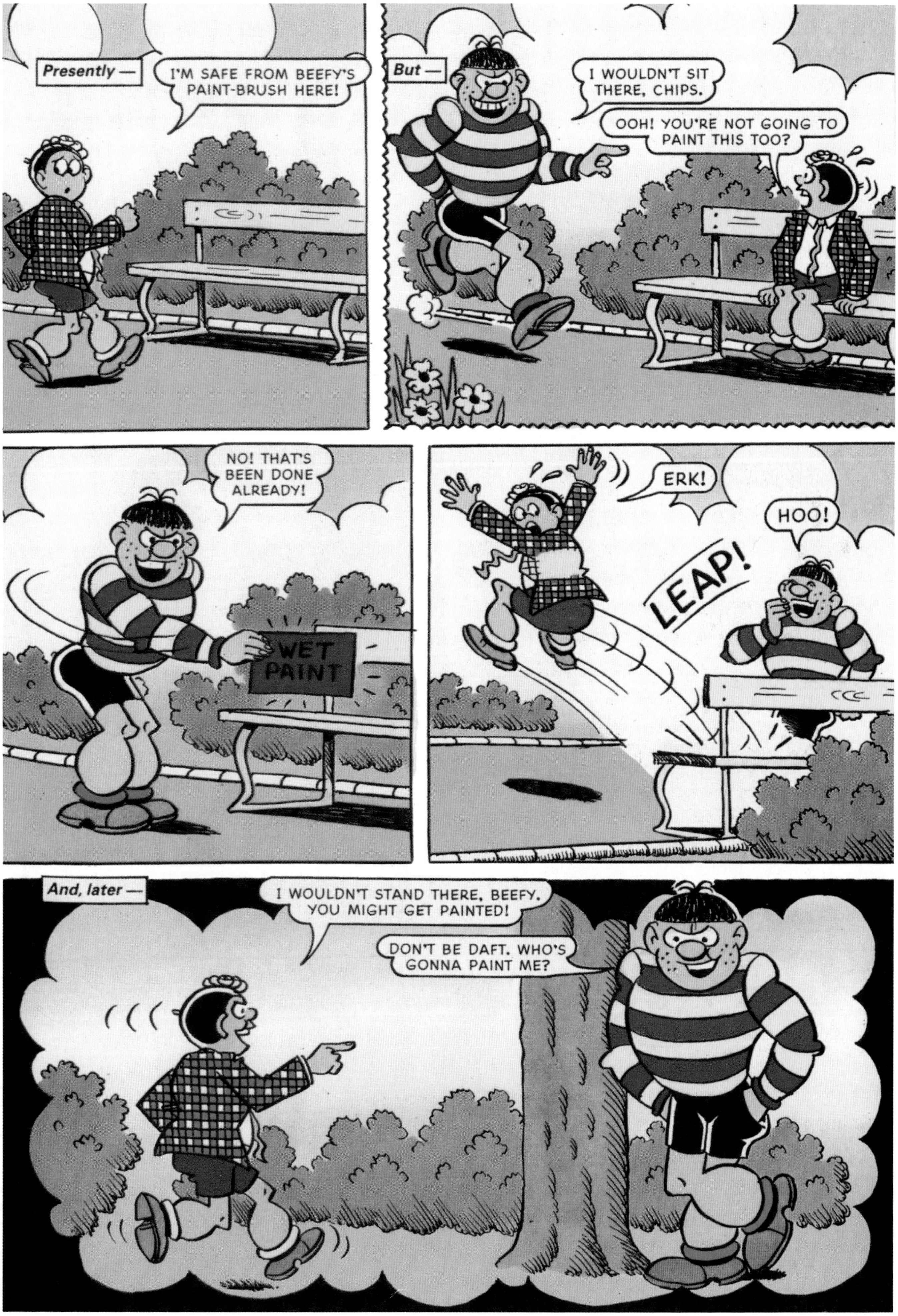
Presently —
I'M SAFE FROM BEEFY'S PAINT-BRUSH HERE!
But —
I WOULDN'T SIT THERE, CHIPS.
OOH! YOU'RE NOT GOING TO PAINT THIS TOO?
NO! THAT'S BEEN DONE ALREADY!
WET PAINT
ERK!
HOO!
LEAP!
And, later —
I WOULDN'T STAND THERE, BEEFY. YOU MIGHT GET PAINTED!
DON'T BE DAFT. WHO'S GONNA PAINT ME?

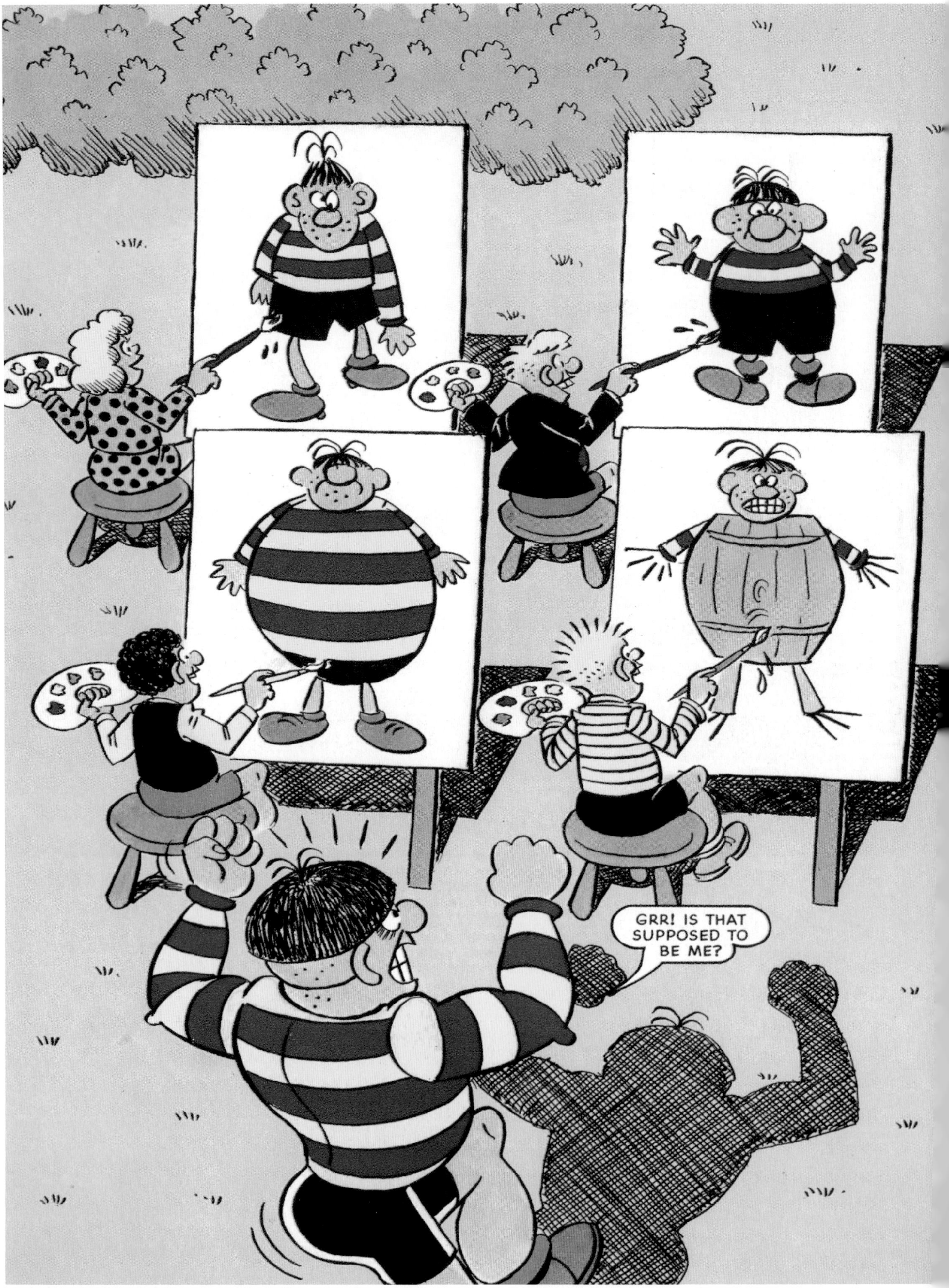
GRR! IS THAT SUPPOSED TO BE ME?

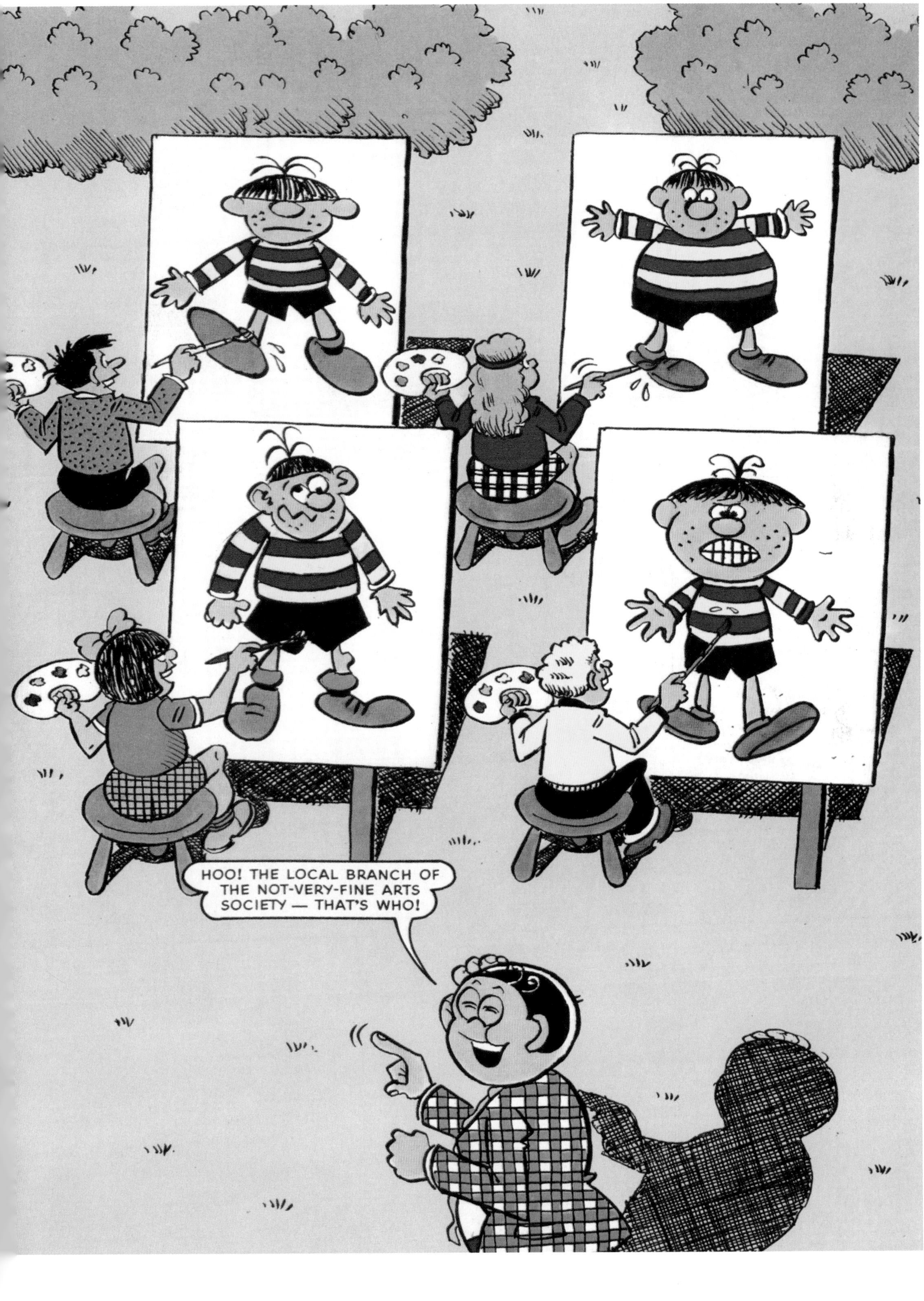
HOO! THE LOCAL BRANCH OF THE NOT-VERY-FINE ARTS SOCIETY — THAT'S WHO!

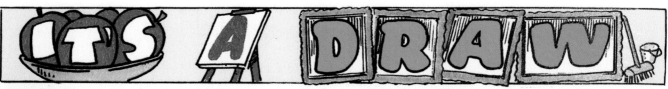

IT'S A DRAW

DAILY SPLURGE

AMERICAN GRANDMOTHER'S PAINTINGS SELL FOR LARGE SUMS OF MONEY.

See this, Granny. This old lady started painting as a hobby and now her pictures sell for thousands of dollars!

Pots of money, eh? I'll have a go at that! I've got plenty of artistic talent!

"A boy and his dog." That'll be my first masterpiece!

BUT — Sit at peace. You're ruining my masterpiece!

Aw, Granny! It's hard to hold that pose!

I'll try a "still-life" instead! Apples can't move!

THEN — What's that I hear?

A BOWL OF APPLES BY GRANNY

CHOMP! SLURP! MUNCH!

Bah! Now I'll have to call my picture "A bowl of apple-cores."

LATER — Some posh-looking gents to see you, Granny!

We're from the art gallery—we've a place for you down there.

Chuckle! I told you I had talent, Dennis.

It's your brushwork that we admire the most, Granny.

ART GALLERY

I must tell Mum and Dad about this.

Come and see Granny, the great artist, at the art gallery!

Ho-ho! They just wanted Granny as a cleaner!

Bah!

LOVELY BRUSHWORK

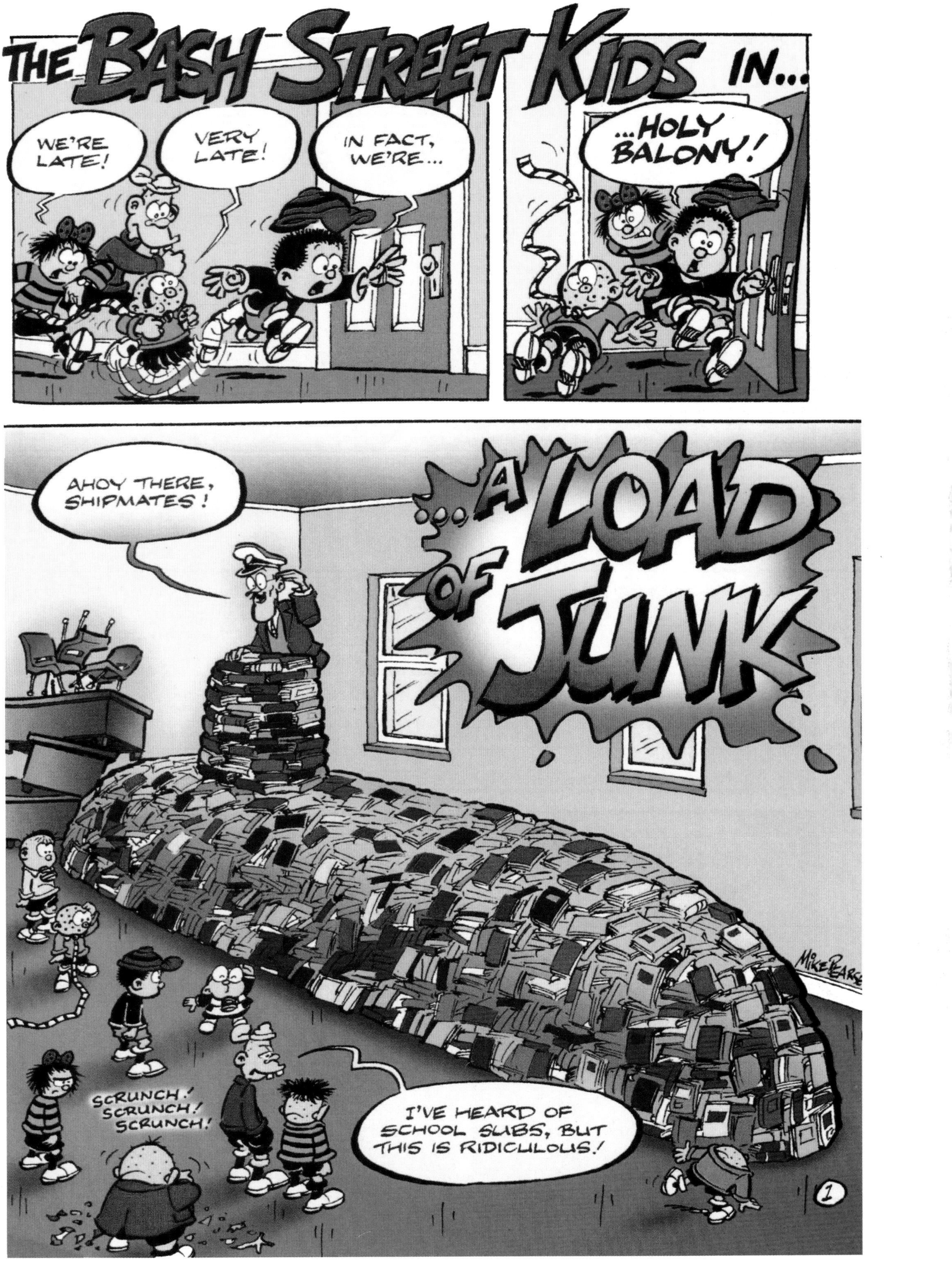
THE BASH STREET KIDS IN...
WE'RE LATE!
VERY LATE!
IN FACT, WE'RE...
...HOLY BALONY!
AHOY THERE, SHIPMATES!
...A LOAD OF JUNK
SCRUNCH! SCRUNCH! SCRUNCH!
I'VE HEARD OF SCHOOL SUBS, BUT THIS IS RIDICULOUS!
MIKE PEARSE
1

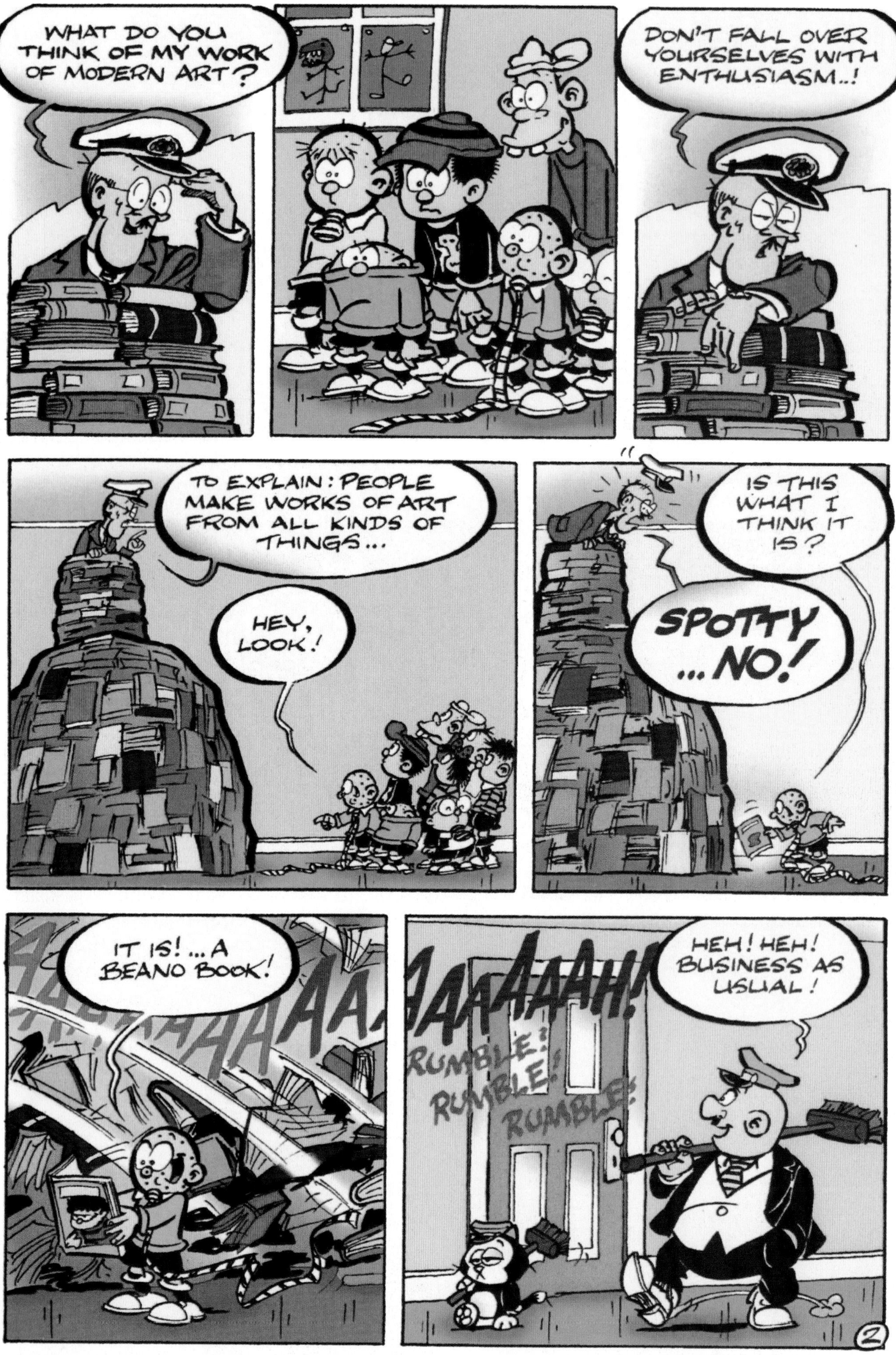
WHAT DO YOU THINK OF MY WORK OF MODERN ART?
DON'T FALL OVER YOURSELVES WITH ENTHUSIASM..!
TO EXPLAIN: PEOPLE MAKE WORKS OF ART FROM ALL KINDS OF THINGS...
HEY, LOOK!
IS THIS WHAT I THINK IT IS?
SPOTTY ...NO!
IT IS! ...A BEANO BOOK!
AAAAAAAAAAAAAAH!
RUMBLE! RUMBLE! RUMBLE!
HEH! HEH! BUSINESS AS USUAL!

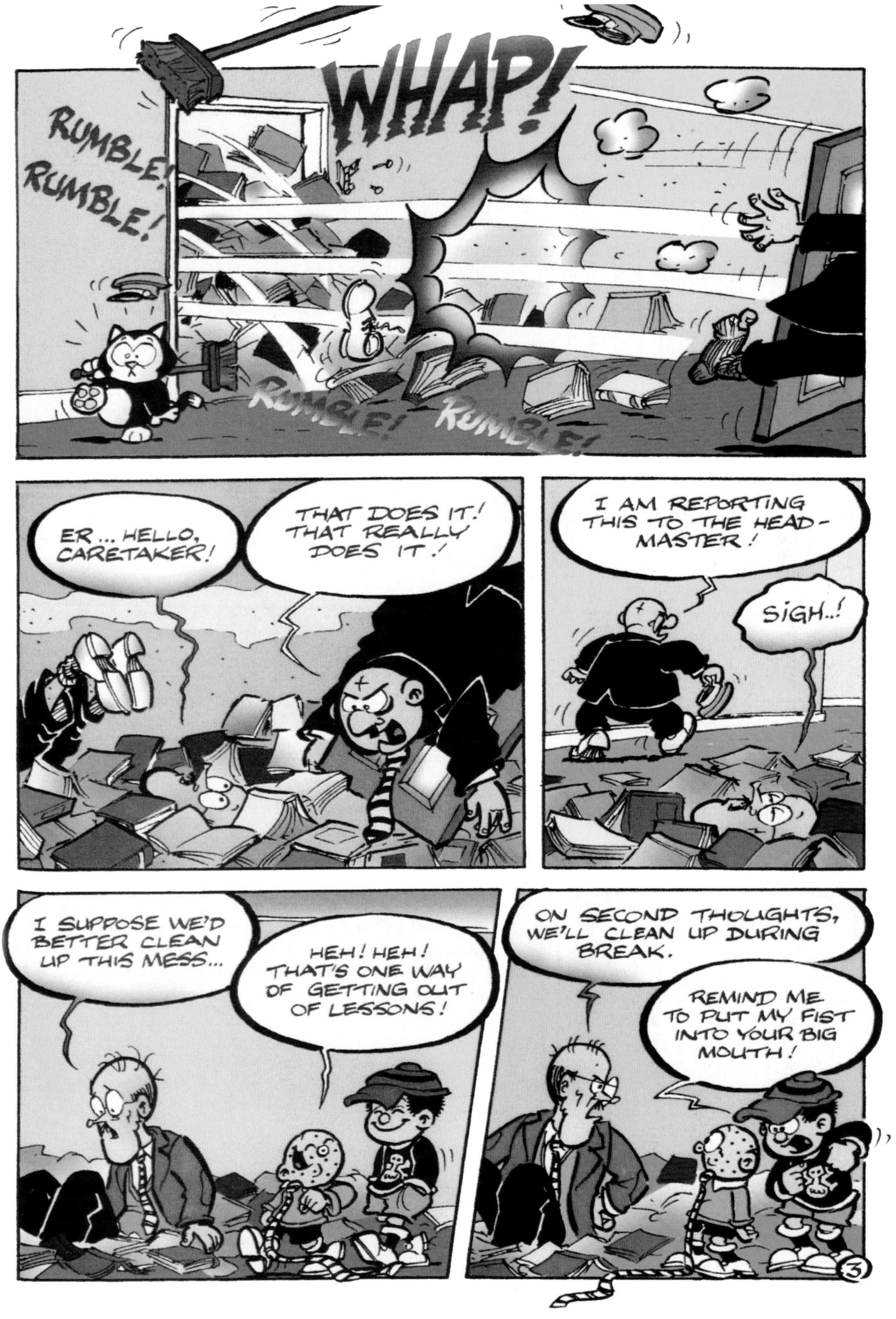
WHAP!
RUMBLE! RUMBLE! RUMBLE!
RUMBLE! RUMBLE!
ER ... HELLO, CARETAKER!
THAT DOES IT! THAT REALLY DOES IT!
I AM REPORTING THIS TO THE HEAD-MASTER!
SIGH..!
I SUPPOSE WE'D BETTER CLEAN UP THIS MESS...
HEH! HEH! THAT'S ONE WAY OF GETTING OUT OF LESSONS!
ON SECOND THOUGHTS, WE'LL CLEAN UP DURING BREAK.
REMIND ME TO PUT MY FIST INTO YOUR BIG MOUTH!
3

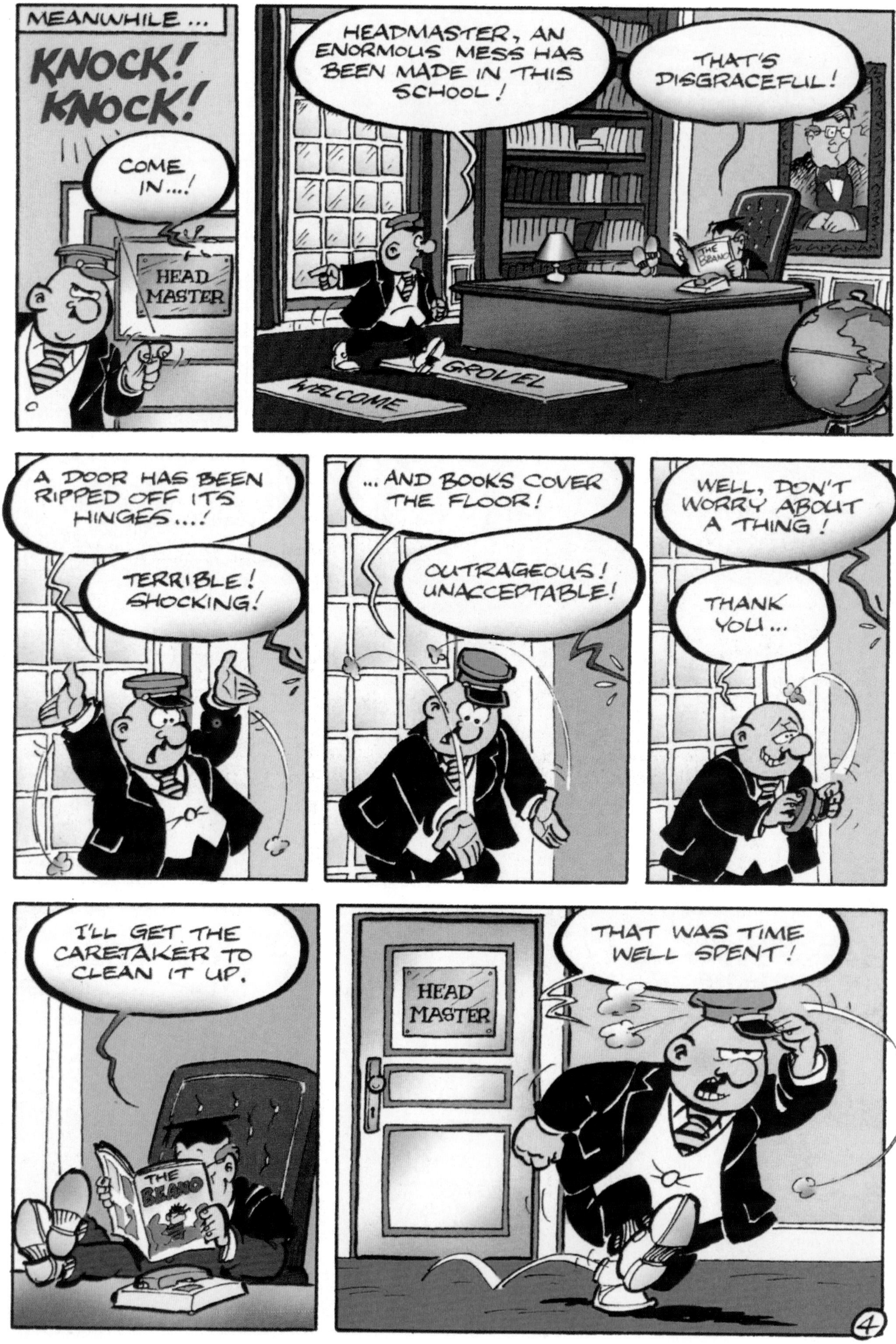
MEANWHILE ...
KNOCK! KNOCK!
COME IN....!
HEAD MASTER
HEADMASTER, AN ENORMOUS MESS HAS BEEN MADE IN THIS SCHOOL!
THAT'S DISGRACEFUL!
THE BEANO
GROVEL
WELCOME
A DOOR HAS BEEN RIPPED OFF ITS HINGES....!
TERRIBLE! SHOCKING!
... AND BOOKS COVER THE FLOOR!
OUTRAGEOUS! UNACCEPTABLE!
WELL, DON'T WORRY ABOUT A THING!
THANK YOU...
I'LL GET THE CARETAKER TO CLEAN IT UP.
THE BEANO
HEAD MASTER
THAT WAS TIME WELL SPENT!

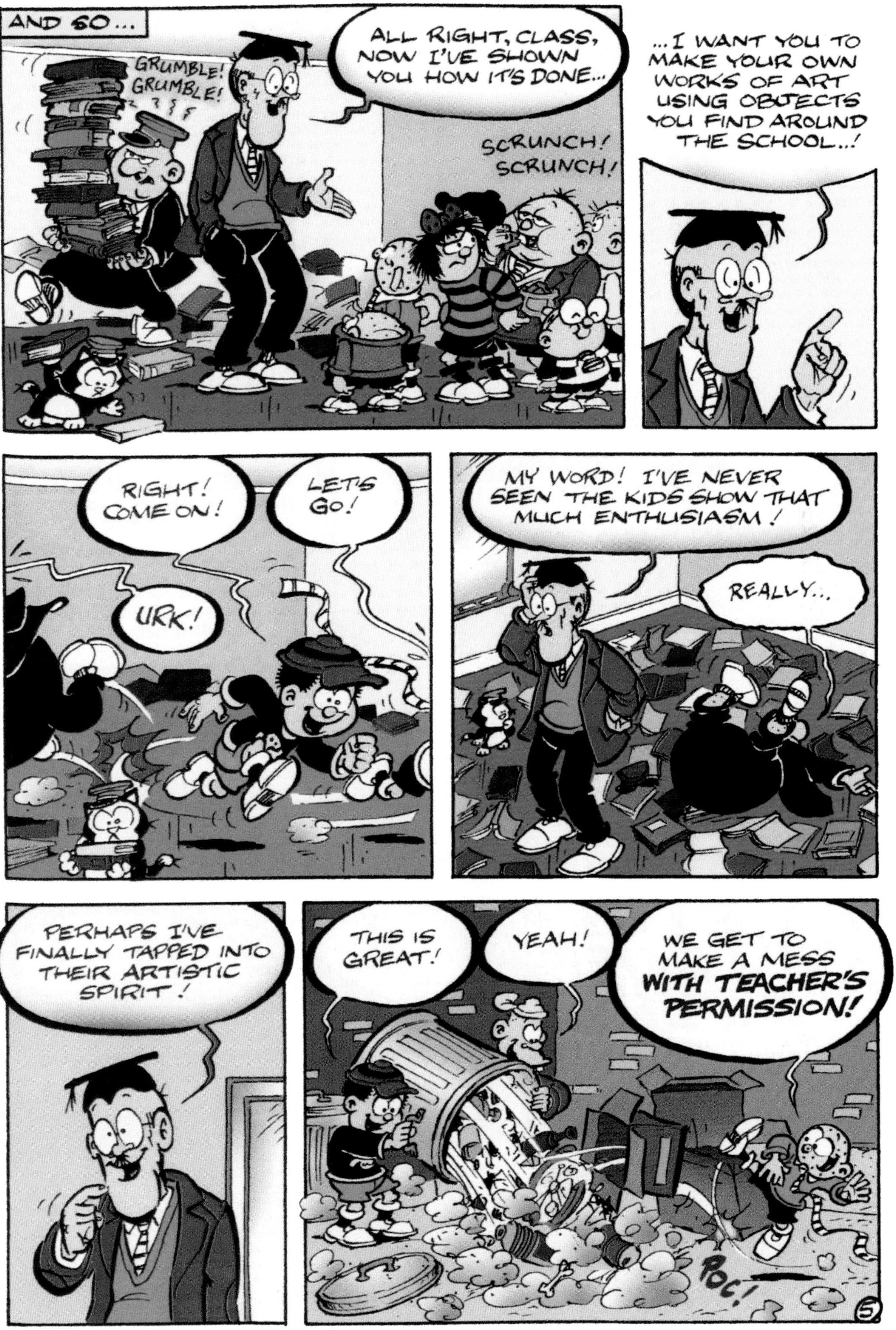
AND SO...
GRUMBLE! GRUMBLE!
ALL RIGHT, CLASS, NOW I'VE SHOWN YOU HOW IT'S DONE...
SCRUNCH! SCRUNCH!
...I WANT YOU TO MAKE YOUR OWN WORKS OF ART USING OBJECTS YOU FIND AROUND THE SCHOOL...!
RIGHT! COME ON!
LET'S GO!
URK!
MY WORD! I'VE NEVER SEEN THE KIDS SHOW THAT MUCH ENTHUSIASM!
REALLY...
PERHAPS I'VE FINALLY TAPPED INTO THEIR ARTISTIC SPIRIT!
THIS IS GREAT!
YEAH!
WE GET TO MAKE A MESS **WITH TEACHER'S PERMISSION!**
POC!
5

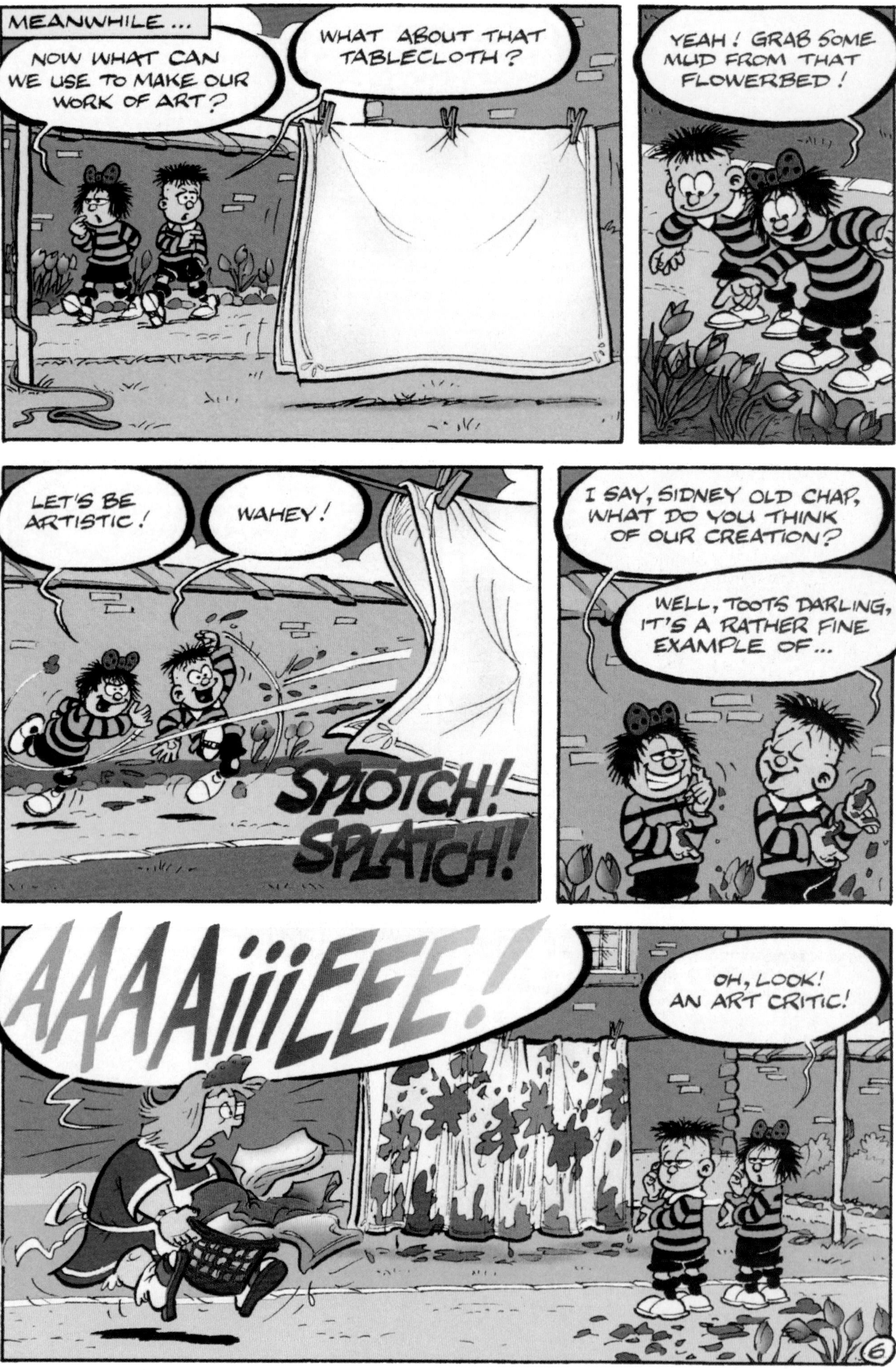
MEANWHILE ...
NOW WHAT CAN WE USE TO MAKE OUR WORK OF ART?
WHAT ABOUT THAT TABLECLOTH?
YEAH! GRAB SOME MUD FROM THAT FLOWERBED!
LET'S BE ARTISTIC!
WAHEY!
SPLOTCH! SPLATCH!
I SAY, SIDNEY OLD CHAP, WHAT DO YOU THINK OF OUR CREATION?
WELL, TOOTS DARLING, IT'S A RATHER FINE EXAMPLE OF...
AAAAiiiEEE!
OH, LOOK! AN ART CRITIC!

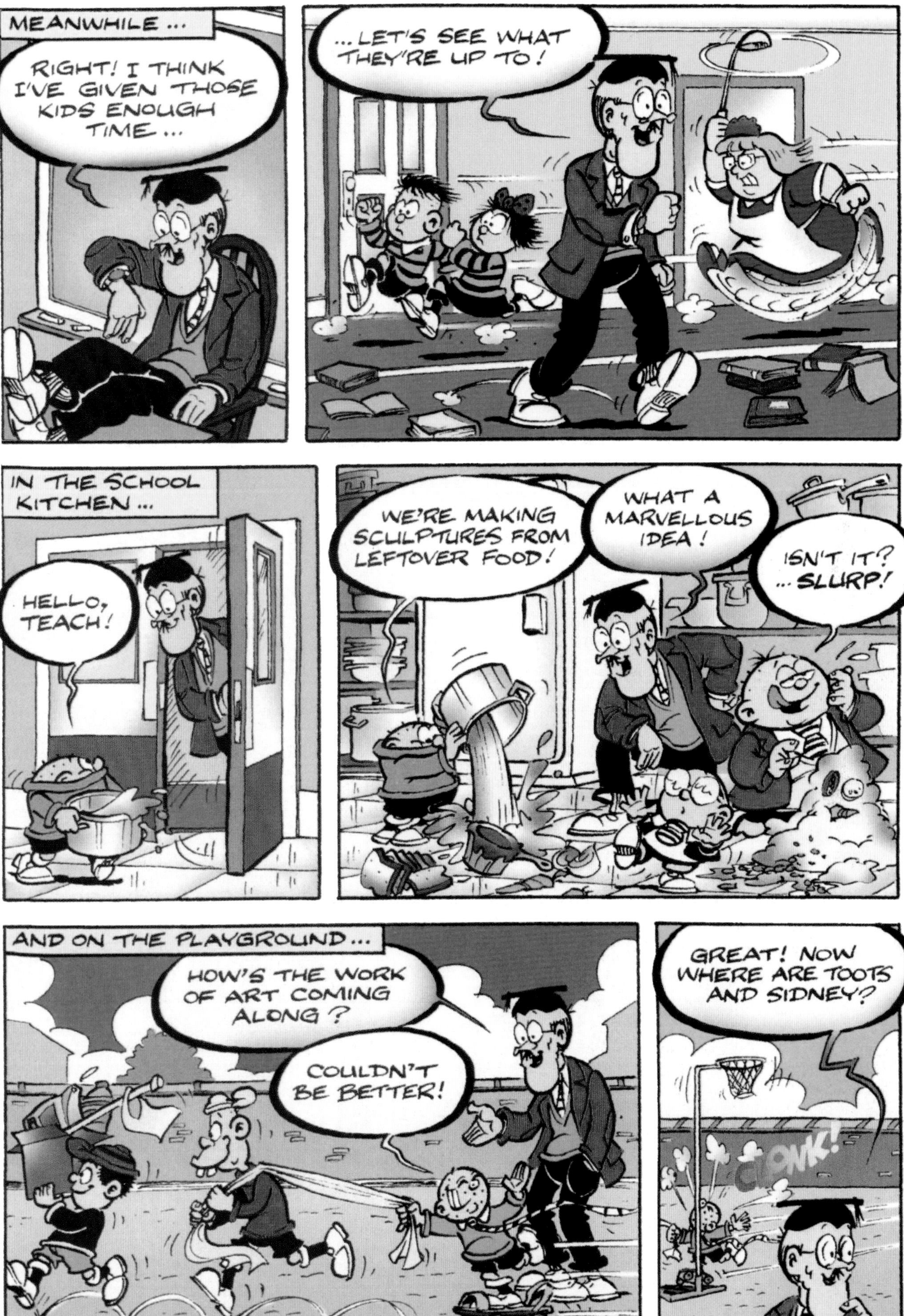
MEANWHILE ...
RIGHT! I THINK I'VE GIVEN THOSE KIDS ENOUGH TIME ...
... LET'S SEE WHAT THEY'RE UP TO!
IN THE SCHOOL KITCHEN ...
HELLO, TEACH!
WE'RE MAKING SCULPTURES FROM LEFTOVER FOOD!
WHAT A MARVELLOUS IDEA!
ISN'T IT? ... SLURP!
AND ON THE PLAYGROUND ...
HOW'S THE WORK OF ART COMING ALONG?
COULDN'T BE BETTER!
GREAT! NOW WHERE ARE TOOTS AND SIDNEY?
CLONK!

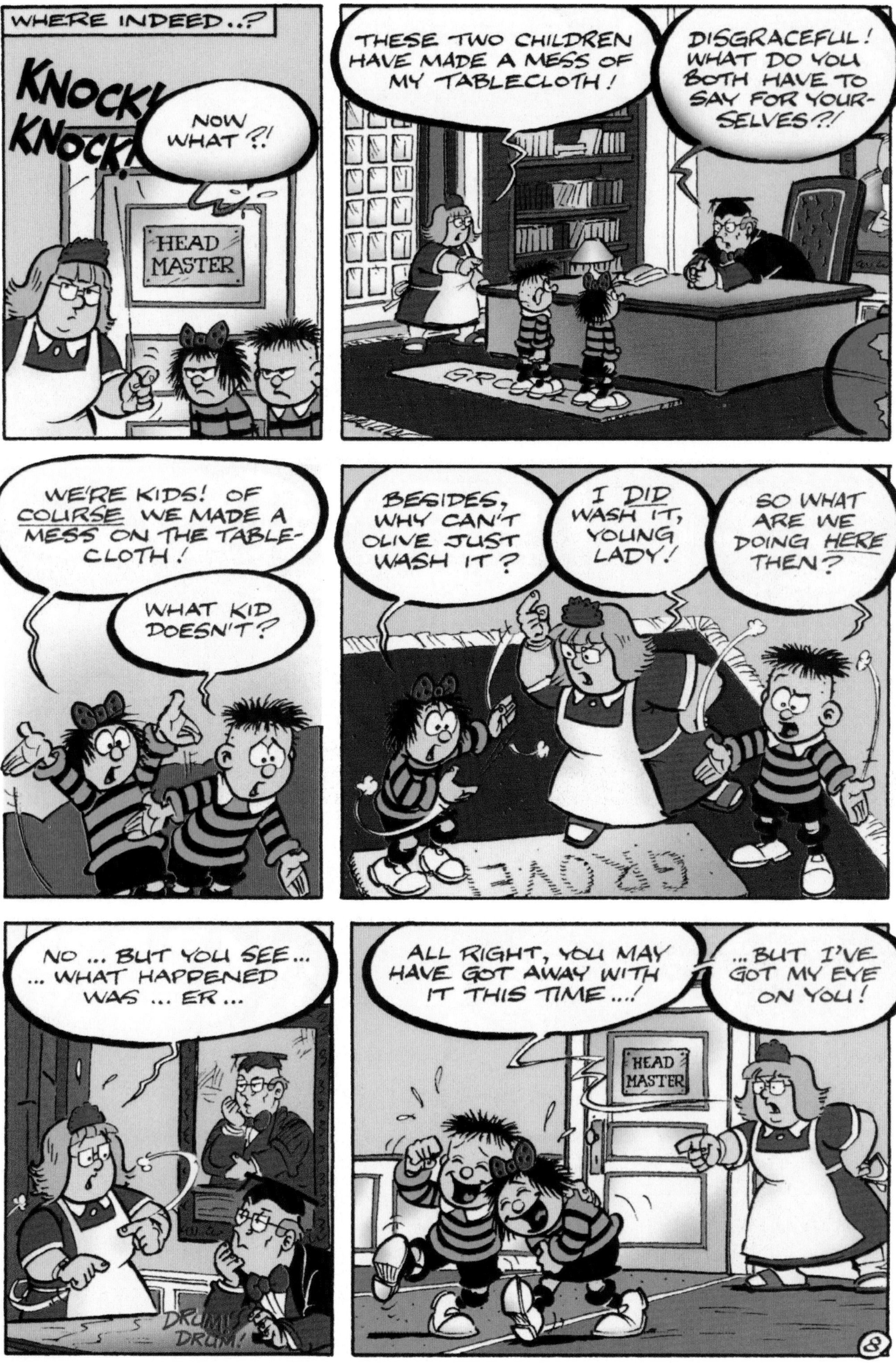

WHERE INDEED ..?
KNOCK! KNOCK!
NOW WHAT ?!
HEAD MASTER
THESE TWO CHILDREN HAVE MADE A MESS OF MY TABLECLOTH!
DISGRACEFUL! WHAT DO YOU BOTH HAVE TO SAY FOR YOURSELVES?!
WE'RE KIDS! OF COURSE WE MADE A MESS ON THE TABLECLOTH!
WHAT KID DOESN'T?
BESIDES, WHY CAN'T OLIVE JUST WASH IT?
I DID WASH IT, YOUNG LADY!
SO WHAT ARE WE DOING HERE THEN?
NO ... BUT YOU SEE... ... WHAT HAPPENED WAS ... ER ...
DRUM! DRUM!
ALL RIGHT, YOU MAY HAVE GOT AWAY WITH IT THIS TIME ...!
... BUT I'VE GOT MY EYE ON YOU!
HEAD MASTER
8

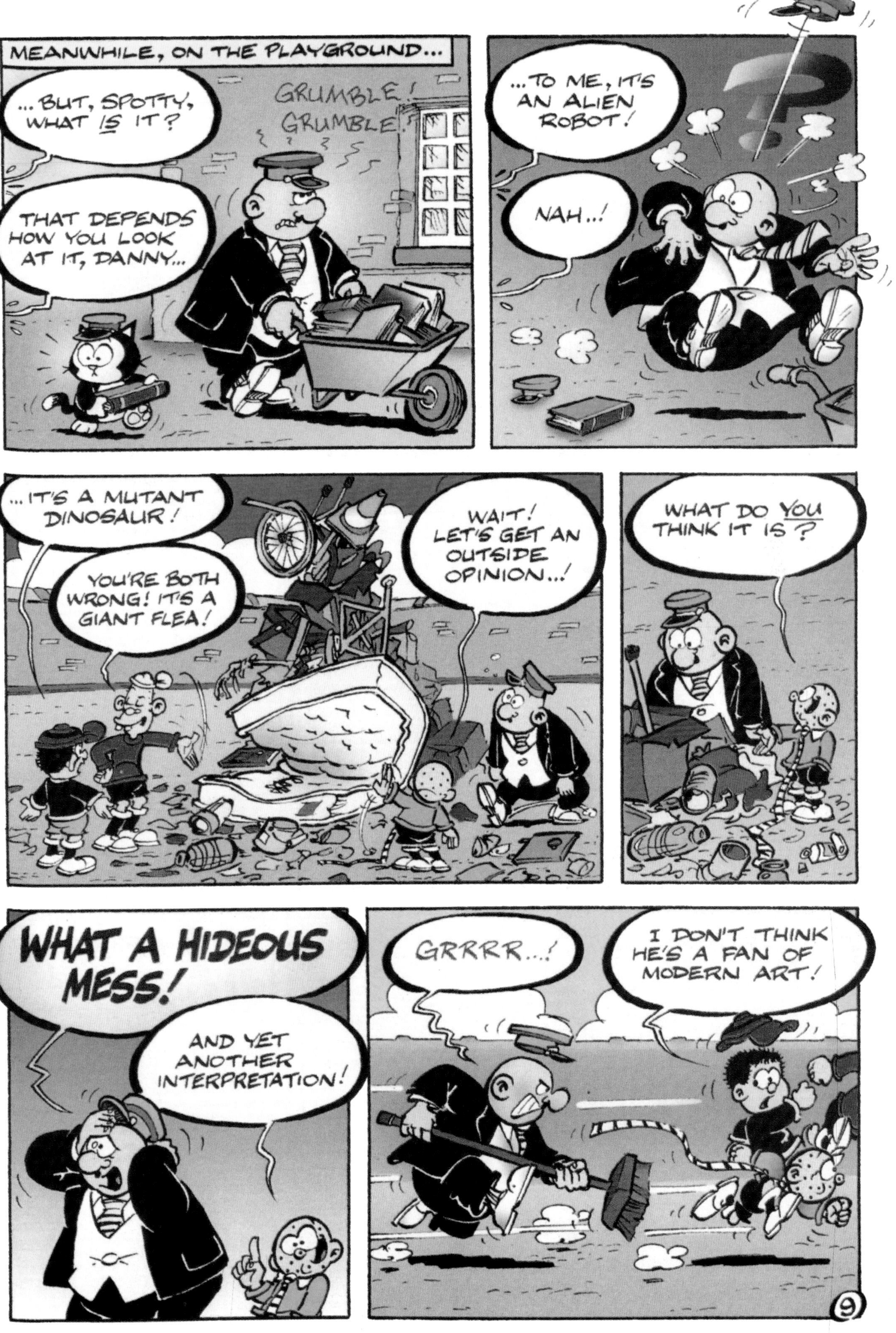

MEANWHILE, ON THE PLAYGROUND...
...BUT, SPOTTY, WHAT IS IT?
GRUMBLE! GRUMBLE!
THAT DEPENDS HOW YOU LOOK AT IT, DANNY...
...TO ME, IT'S AN ALIEN ROBOT!
NAH...!
...IT'S A MUTANT DINOSAUR!
YOU'RE BOTH WRONG! IT'S A GIANT FLEA!
WAIT! LET'S GET AN OUTSIDE OPINION...!
WHAT DO YOU THINK IT IS?
WHAT A HIDEOUS MESS!
AND YET ANOTHER INTERPRETATION!
GRRRR...!
I DON'T THINK HE'S A FAN OF MODERN ART!

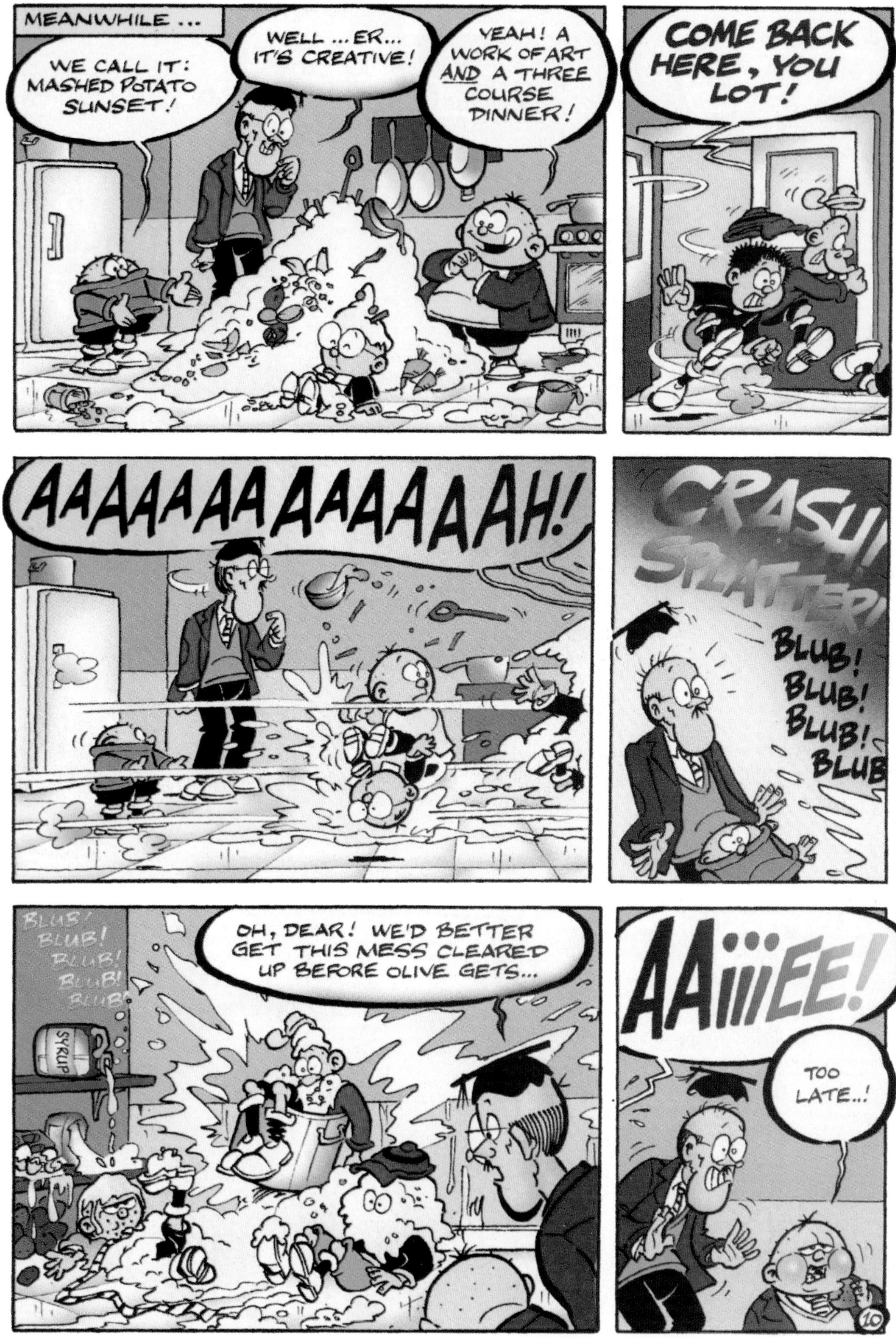
MEANWHILE ...
WE CALL IT: MASHED POTATO SUNSET!
WELL ... ER... IT'S CREATIVE!
YEAH! A WORK OF ART AND A THREE COURSE DINNER!
COME BACK HERE, YOU LOT!
AAAAAAAAAAAAAH!
CRASH! SPLATTER!
BLUB! BLUB! BLUB! BLUB
BLUB! BLUB! BLUB! BLUB! BLUB!
OH, DEAR! WE'D BETTER GET THIS MESS CLEARED UP BEFORE OLIVE GETS...
SYRUP
AAiiiiEE!
TOO LATE..!
10

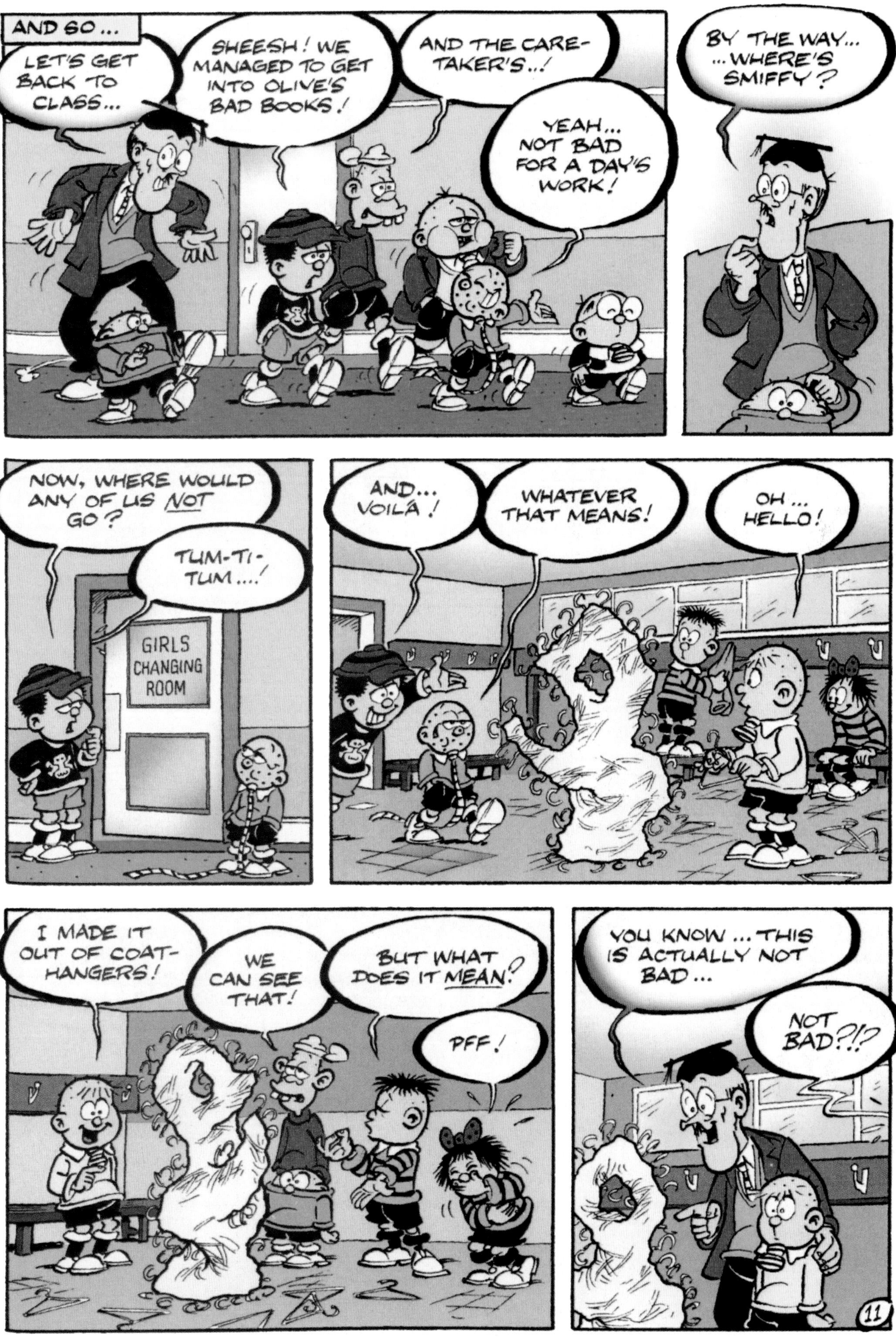
AND SO...
LET'S GET BACK TO CLASS...
SHEESH! WE MANAGED TO GET INTO OLIVE'S BAD BOOKS!
AND THE CARE-TAKER'S...!
YEAH... NOT BAD FOR A DAY'S WORK!
BY THE WAY... ...WHERE'S SMIFFY?
NOW, WHERE WOULD ANY OF US NOT GO?
TUM-TI-TUM....!
GIRLS CHANGING ROOM
AND... VOILÀ!
WHATEVER THAT MEANS!
OH... HELLO!
I MADE IT OUT OF COAT-HANGERS!
WE CAN SEE THAT!
BUT WHAT DOES IT MEAN?
PFF!
YOU KNOW... THIS IS ACTUALLY NOT BAD...
NOT BAD?!?

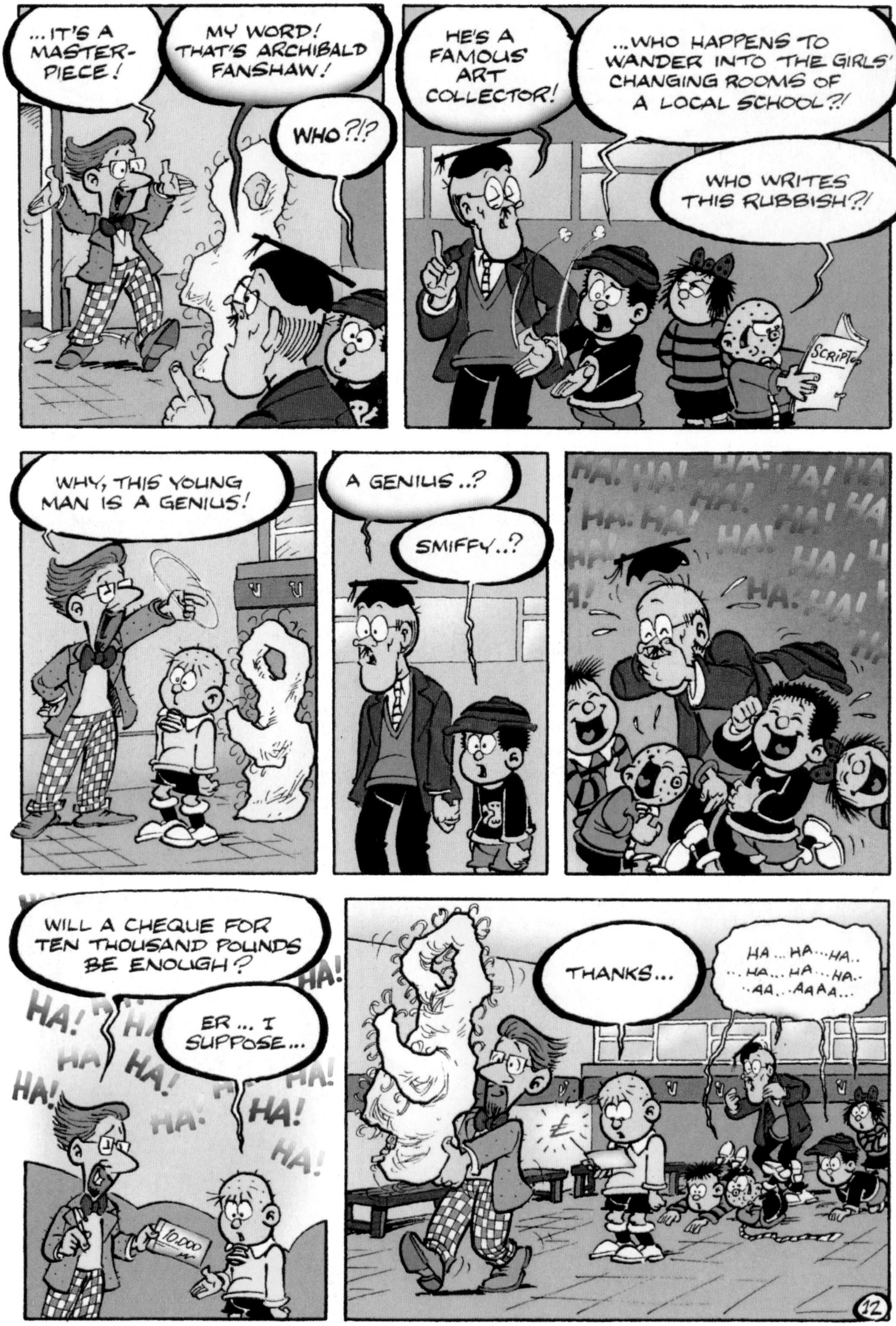
...IT'S A MASTER-PIECE!
MY WORD! THAT'S ARCHIBALD FANSHAW!
WHO?!?
HE'S A FAMOUS ART COLLECTOR!
...WHO HAPPENS TO WANDER INTO THE GIRLS' CHANGING ROOMS OF A LOCAL SCHOOL?!
WHO WRITES THIS RUBBISH?!
SCRIPT
WHY, THIS YOUNG MAN IS A GENIUS!
A GENIUS..?
SMIFFY..?
HA! HA! HA! HA! HA! HA! HA! HA! HA!
WILL A CHEQUE FOR TEN THOUSAND POUNDS BE ENOUGH?
ER ... I SUPPOSE...
HA! HA! HA! HA! HA! HA! HA! HA!
10,000
THANKS...
HA ... HA ... HA.. .. HA... HA... HA.. ..AA...AAAA...

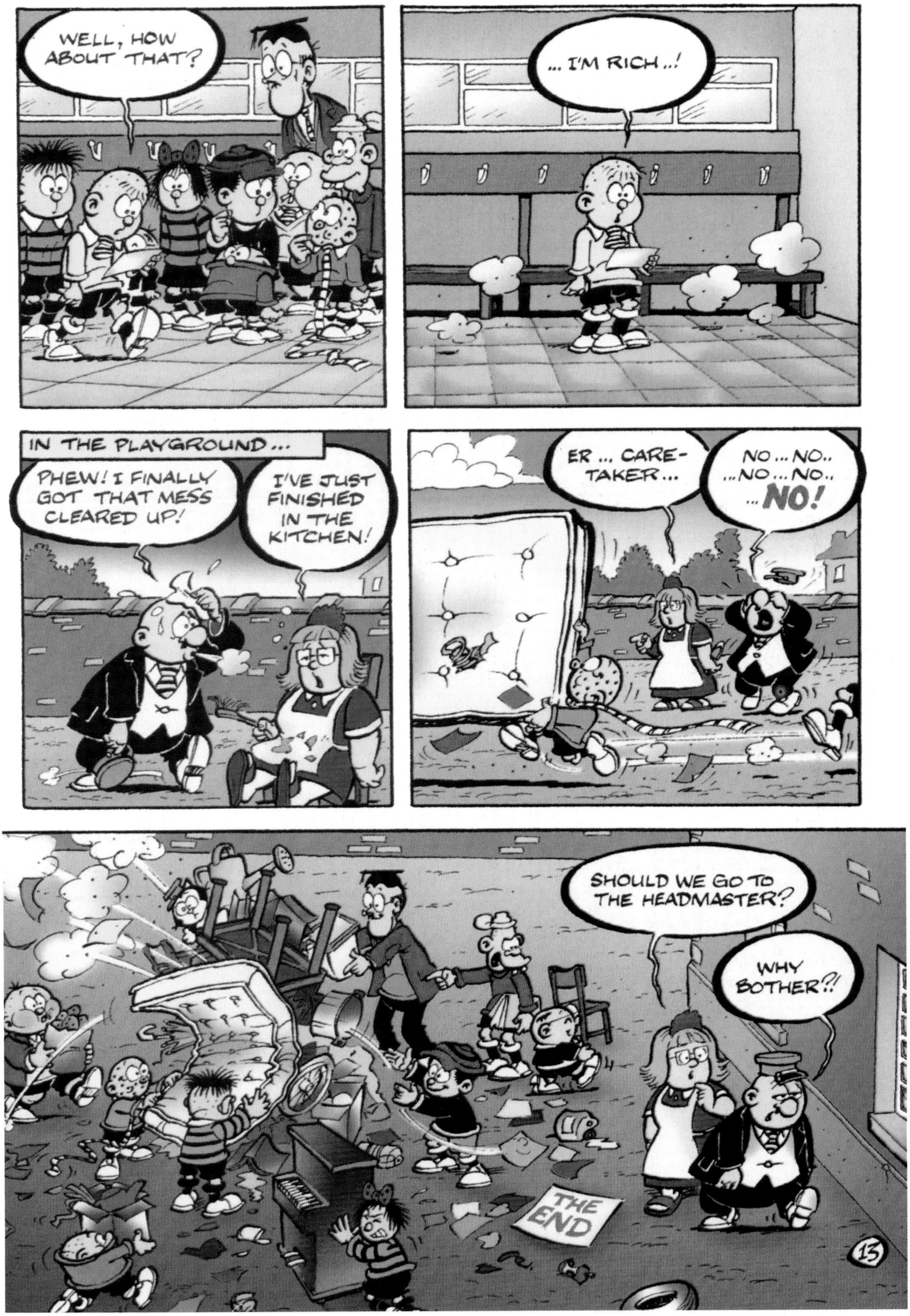
WELL, HOW ABOUT THAT?
... I'M RICH ...!
IN THE PLAYGROUND ...
PHEW! I FINALLY GOT THAT MESS CLEARED UP!
I'VE JUST FINISHED IN THE KITCHEN!
ER ... CARE-TAKER ...
NO ... NO.. ..NO ... NO.. ... NO!
SHOULD WE GO TO THE HEADMASTER?
WHY BOTHER?!
THE END
13

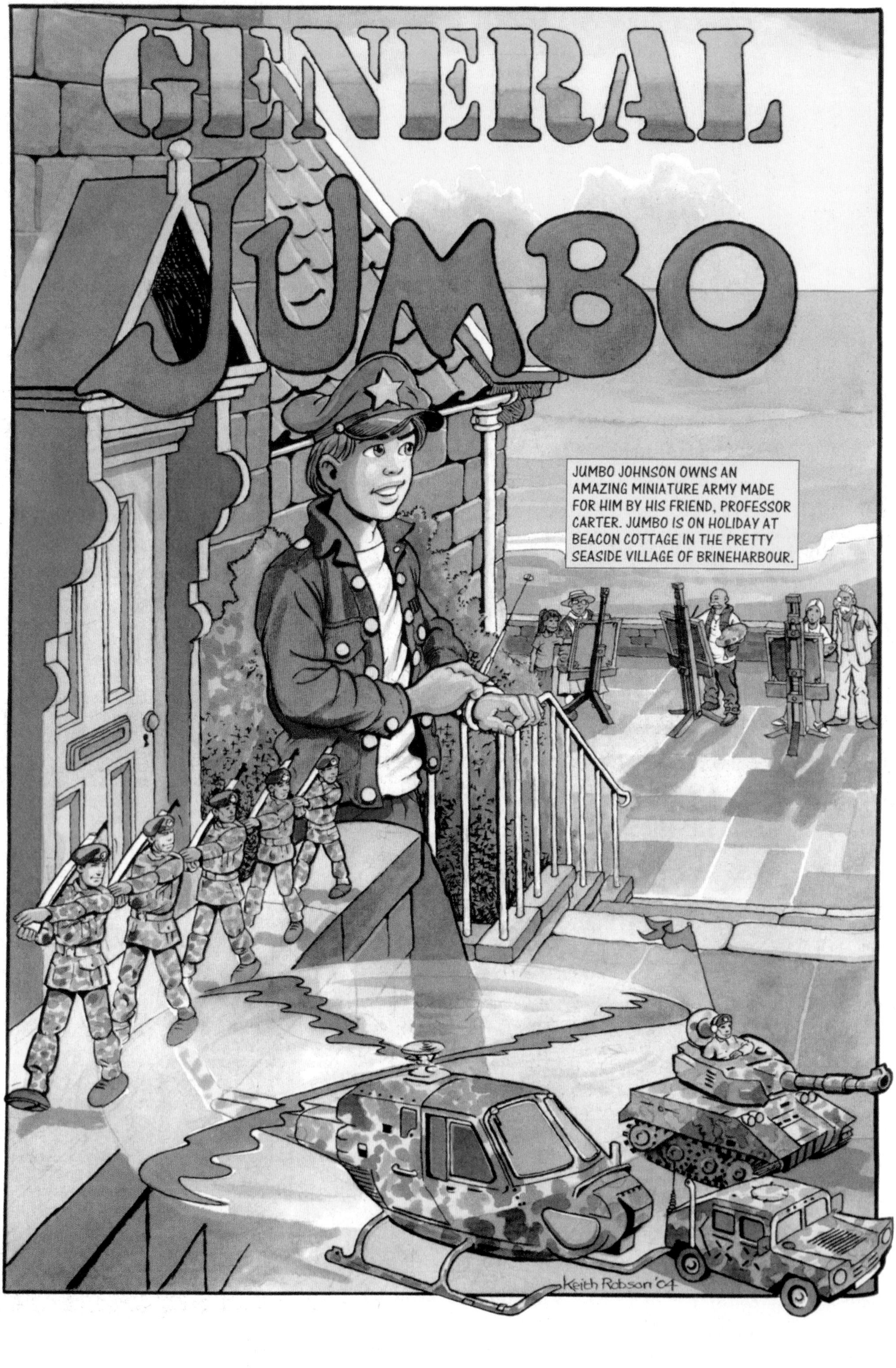
GENERAL
JUMBO
JUMBO JOHNSON OWNS AN AMAZING MINIATURE ARMY MADE FOR HIM BY HIS FRIEND, PROFESSOR CARTER. JUMBO IS ON HOLIDAY AT BEACON COTTAGE IN THE PRETTY SEASIDE VILLAGE OF BRINEHARBOUR.
Keith Robson '04

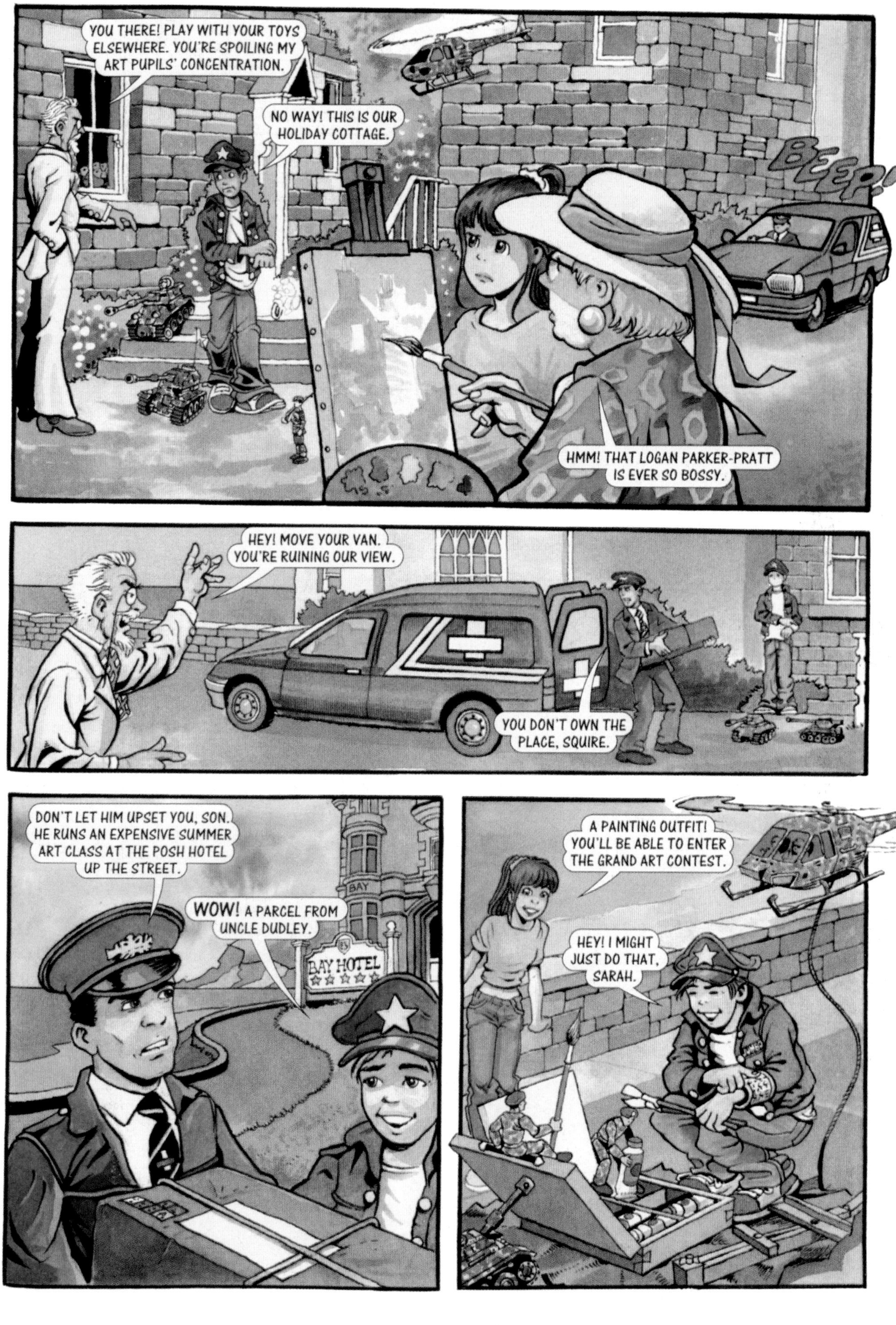
YOU THERE! PLAY WITH YOUR TOYS ELSEWHERE. YOU'RE SPOILING MY ART PUPILS' CONCENTRATION.
NO WAY! THIS IS OUR HOLIDAY COTTAGE.
BEEP!
HMM! THAT LOGAN PARKER-PRATT IS EVER SO BOSSY.
HEY! MOVE YOUR VAN. YOU'RE RUINING OUR VIEW.
YOU DON'T OWN THE PLACE, SQUIRE.
DON'T LET HIM UPSET YOU, SON. HE RUNS AN EXPENSIVE SUMMER ART CLASS AT THE POSH HOTEL UP THE STREET.
WOW! A PARCEL FROM UNCLE DUDLEY.
BAY HOTEL
A PAINTING OUTFIT! YOU'LL BE ABLE TO ENTER THE GRAND ART CONTEST.
HEY! I MIGHT JUST DO THAT, SARAH.

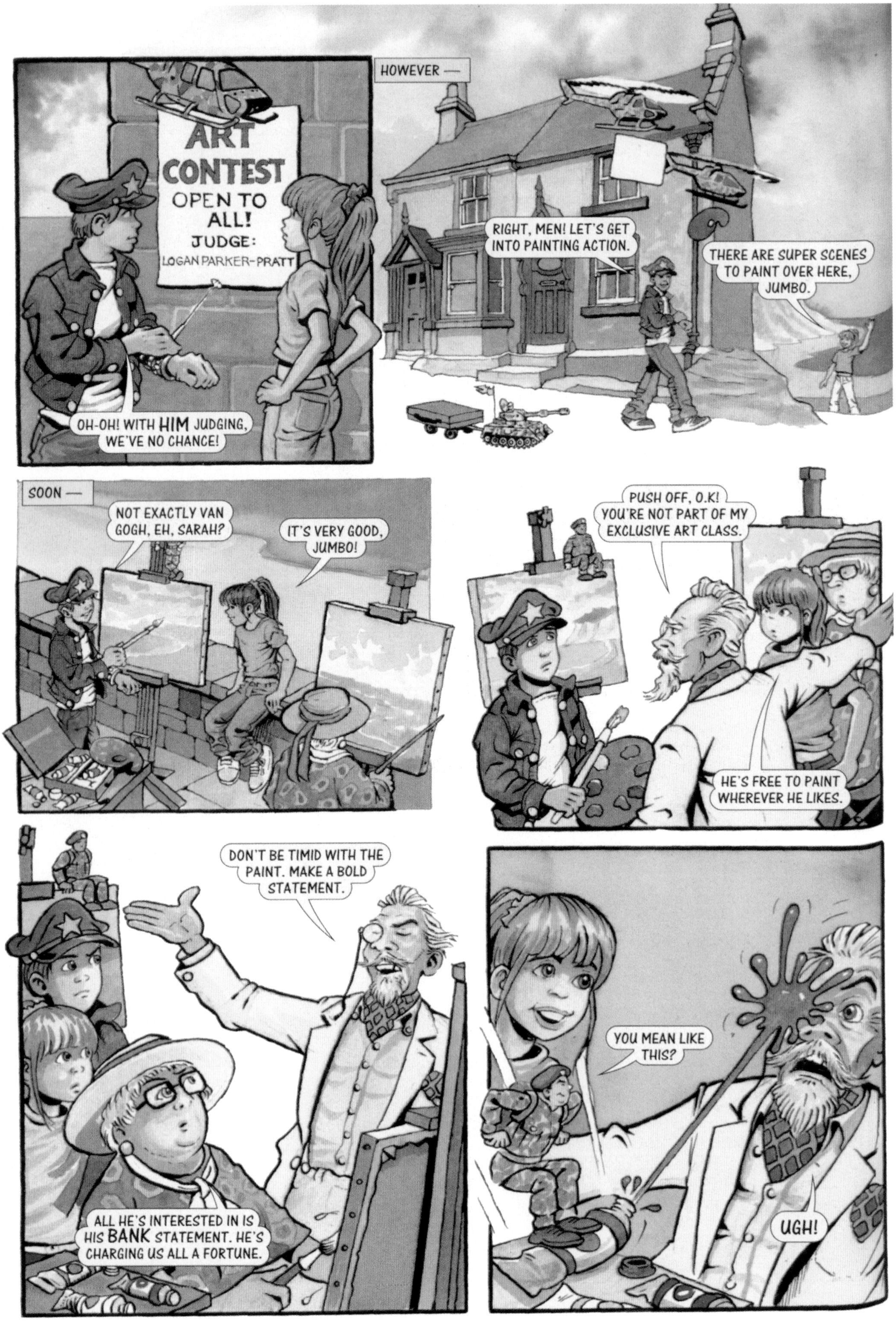
ART CONTEST
OPEN TO ALL!
JUDGE: LOGAN PARKER-PRATT
OH-OH! WITH HIM JUDGING, WE'VE NO CHANCE!
HOWEVER —
RIGHT, MEN! LET'S GET INTO PAINTING ACTION.
THERE ARE SUPER SCENES TO PAINT OVER HERE, JUMBO.
SOON —
NOT EXACTLY VAN GOGH, EH, SARAH?
IT'S VERY GOOD, JUMBO!
PUSH OFF, O.K! YOU'RE NOT PART OF MY EXCLUSIVE ART CLASS.
HE'S FREE TO PAINT WHEREVER HE LIKES.
DON'T BE TIMID WITH THE PAINT. MAKE A BOLD STATEMENT.
ALL HE'S INTERESTED IN IS HIS BANK STATEMENT. HE'S CHARGING US ALL A FORTUNE.
YOU MEAN LIKE THIS?
UGH!

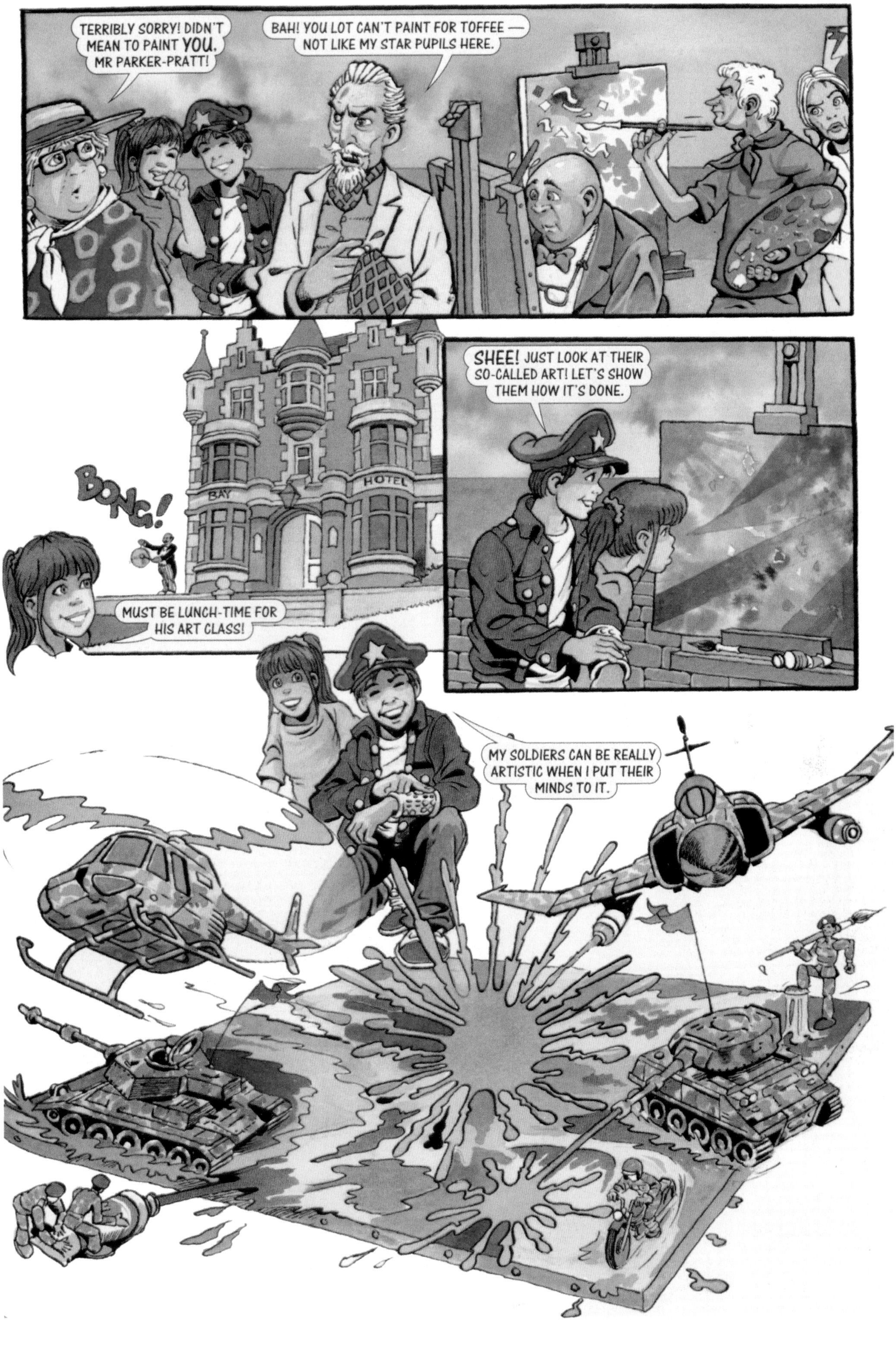
TERRIBLY SORRY! DIDN'T MEAN TO PAINT YOU, MR PARKER-PRATT!
BAH! YOU LOT CAN'T PAINT FOR TOFFEE — NOT LIKE MY STAR PUPILS HERE.
BAY HOTEL
BONG!
MUST BE LUNCH-TIME FOR HIS ART CLASS!
SHEE! JUST LOOK AT THEIR SO-CALLED ART! LET'S SHOW THEM HOW IT'S DONE.
MY SOLDIERS CAN BE REALLY ARTISTIC WHEN I PUT THEIR MINDS TO IT.

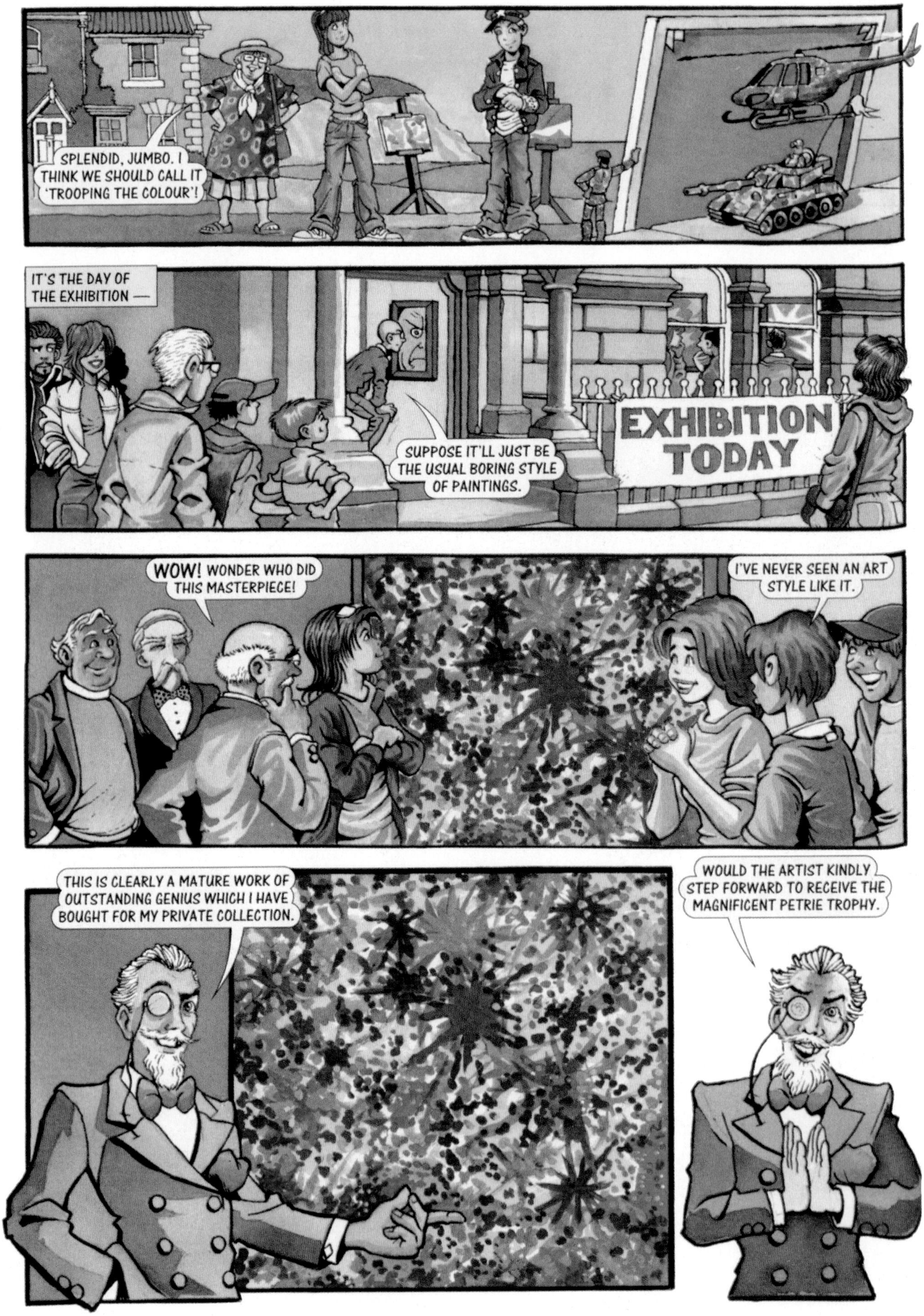
SPLENDID, JUMBO. I THINK WE SHOULD CALL IT 'TROOPING THE COLOUR'!
IT'S THE DAY OF THE EXHIBITION —
EXHIBITION TODAY
SUPPOSE IT'LL JUST BE THE USUAL BORING STYLE OF PAINTINGS.
WOW! WONDER WHO DID THIS MASTERPIECE!
I'VE NEVER SEEN AN ART STYLE LIKE IT.
THIS IS CLEARLY A MATURE WORK OF OUTSTANDING GENIUS WHICH I HAVE BOUGHT FOR MY PRIVATE COLLECTION.
WOULD THE ARTIST KINDLY STEP FORWARD TO RECEIVE THE MAGNIFICENT PETRIE TROPHY.

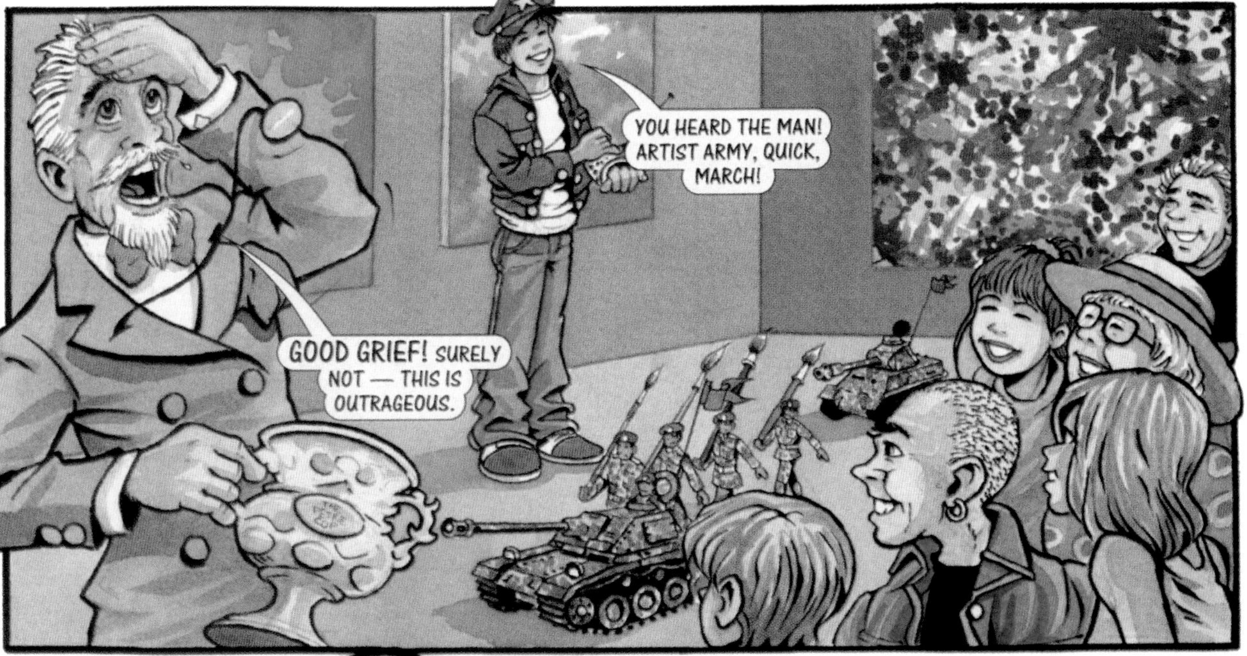
YOU HEARD THE MAN! ARTIST ARMY, QUICK, MARCH!
GOOD GRIEF! SURELY NOT — THIS IS OUTRAGEOUS.

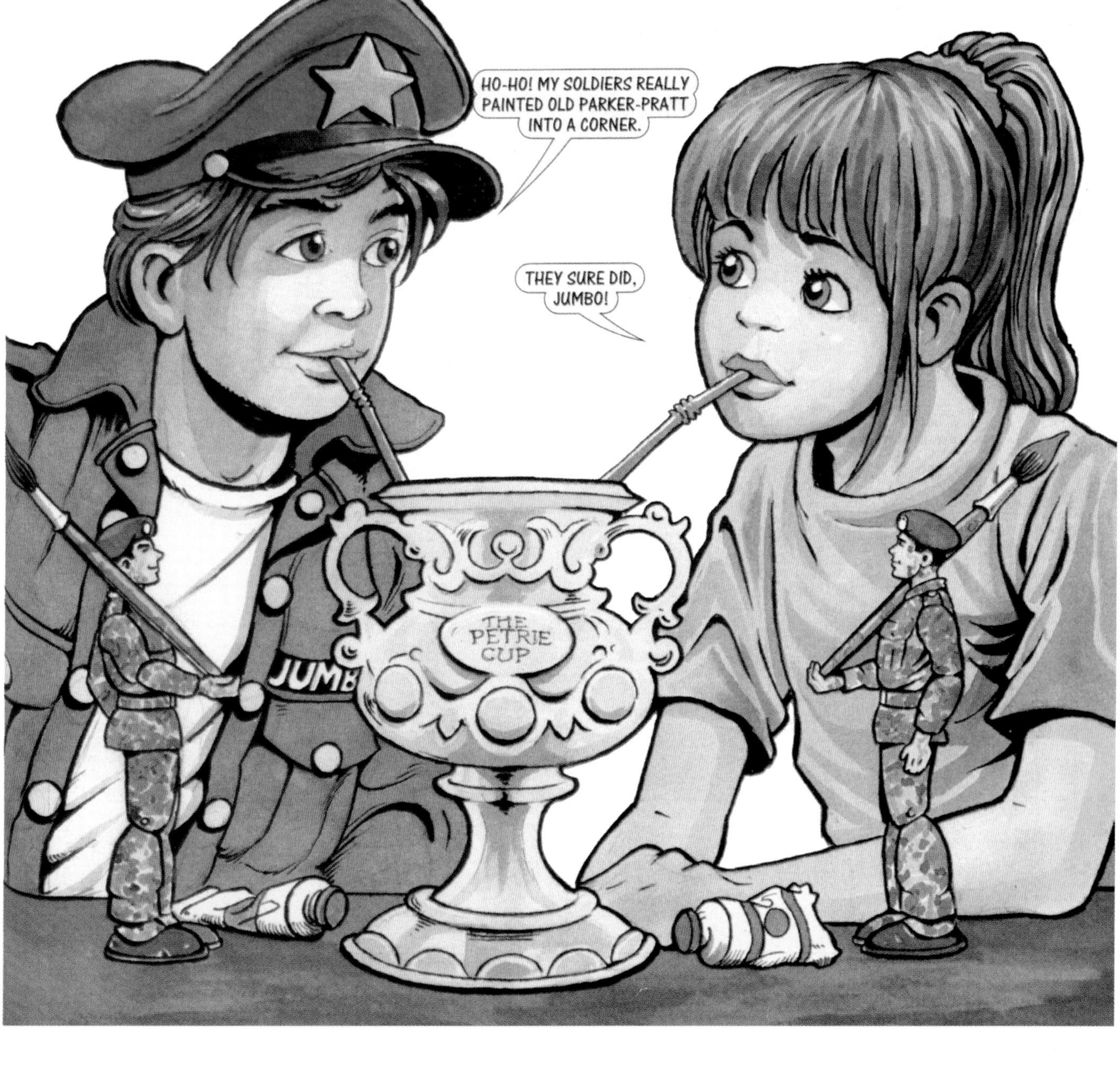
HO-HO! MY SOLDIERS REALLY PAINTED OLD PARKER-PRATT INTO A CORNER.
THEY SURE DID, JUMBO!
THE PETRIE CUP
JUMB

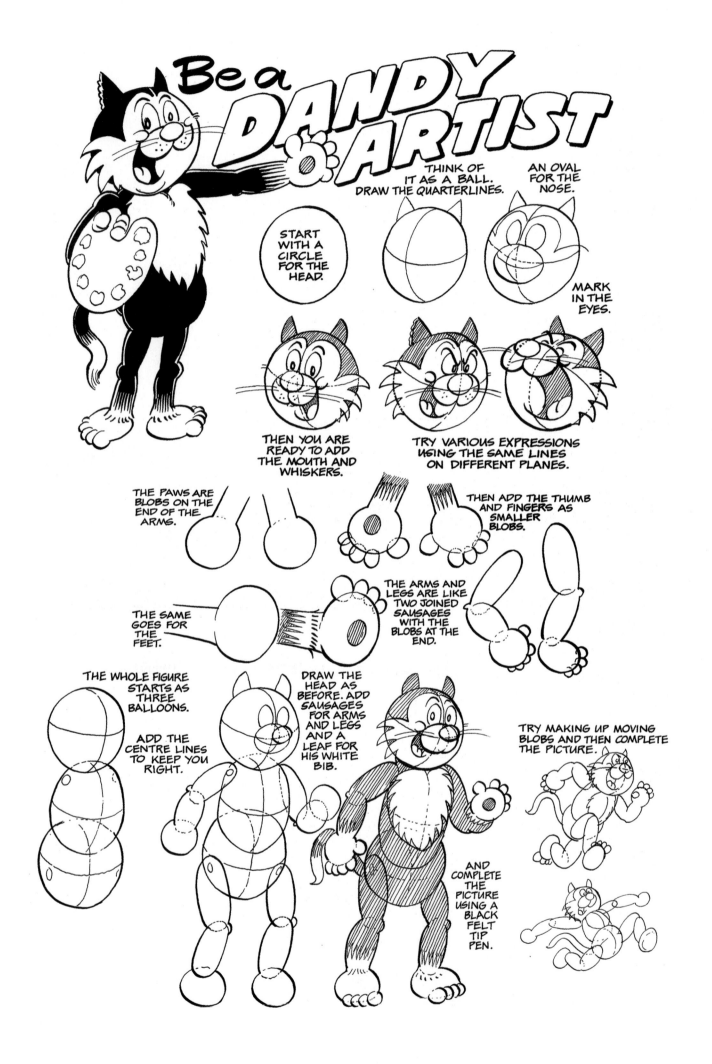

Be a DANDY ARTIST

START WITH A CIRCLE FOR THE HEAD.

THINK OF IT AS A BALL. DRAW THE QUARTERLINES.

AN OVAL FOR THE NOSE.

MARK IN THE EYES.

THEN YOU ARE READY TO ADD THE MOUTH AND WHISKERS.

TRY VARIOUS EXPRESSIONS USING THE SAME LINES ON DIFFERENT PLANES.

THE PAWS ARE BLOBS ON THE END OF THE ARMS.

THEN ADD THE THUMB AND FINGERS AS SMALLER BLOBS.

THE SAME GOES FOR THE FEET.

THE ARMS AND LEGS ARE LIKE TWO JOINED SAUSAGES WITH THE BLOBS AT THE END.

THE WHOLE FIGURE STARTS AS THREE BALLOONS.

ADD THE CENTRE LINES TO KEEP YOU RIGHT.

DRAW THE HEAD AS BEFORE. ADD SAUSAGES FOR ARMS AND LEGS AND A LEAF FOR HIS WHITE BIB.

TRY MAKING UP MOVING BLOBS AND THEN COMPLETE THE PICTURE.

AND COMPLETE THE PICTURE USING A BLACK FELT TIP PEN.

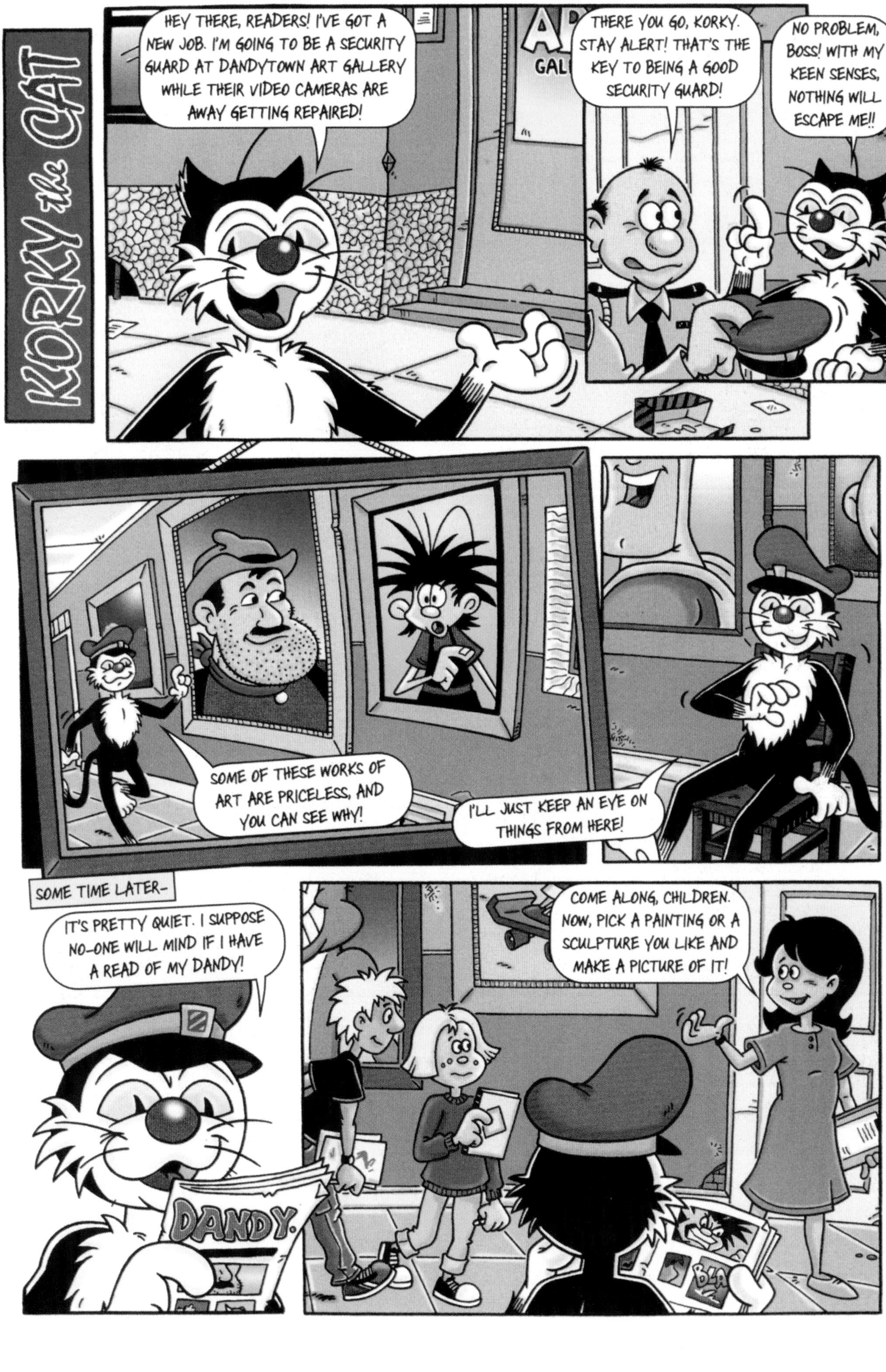
KORKY the CAT
HEY THERE, READERS! I'VE GOT A NEW JOB. I'M GOING TO BE A SECURITY GUARD AT DANDYTOWN ART GALLERY WHILE THEIR VIDEO CAMERAS ARE AWAY GETTING REPAIRED!
THERE YOU GO, KORKY. STAY ALERT! THAT'S THE KEY TO BEING A GOOD SECURITY GUARD!
NO PROBLEM, BOSS! WITH MY KEEN SENSES, NOTHING WILL ESCAPE ME!!
SOME OF THESE WORKS OF ART ARE PRICELESS, AND YOU CAN SEE WHY!
I'LL JUST KEEP AN EYE ON THINGS FROM HERE!
SOME TIME LATER-
IT'S PRETTY QUIET. I SUPPOSE NO-ONE WILL MIND IF I HAVE A READ OF MY DANDY!
DANDY
COME ALONG, CHILDREN. NOW, PICK A PAINTING OR A SCULPTURE YOU LIKE AND MAKE A PICTURE OF IT!

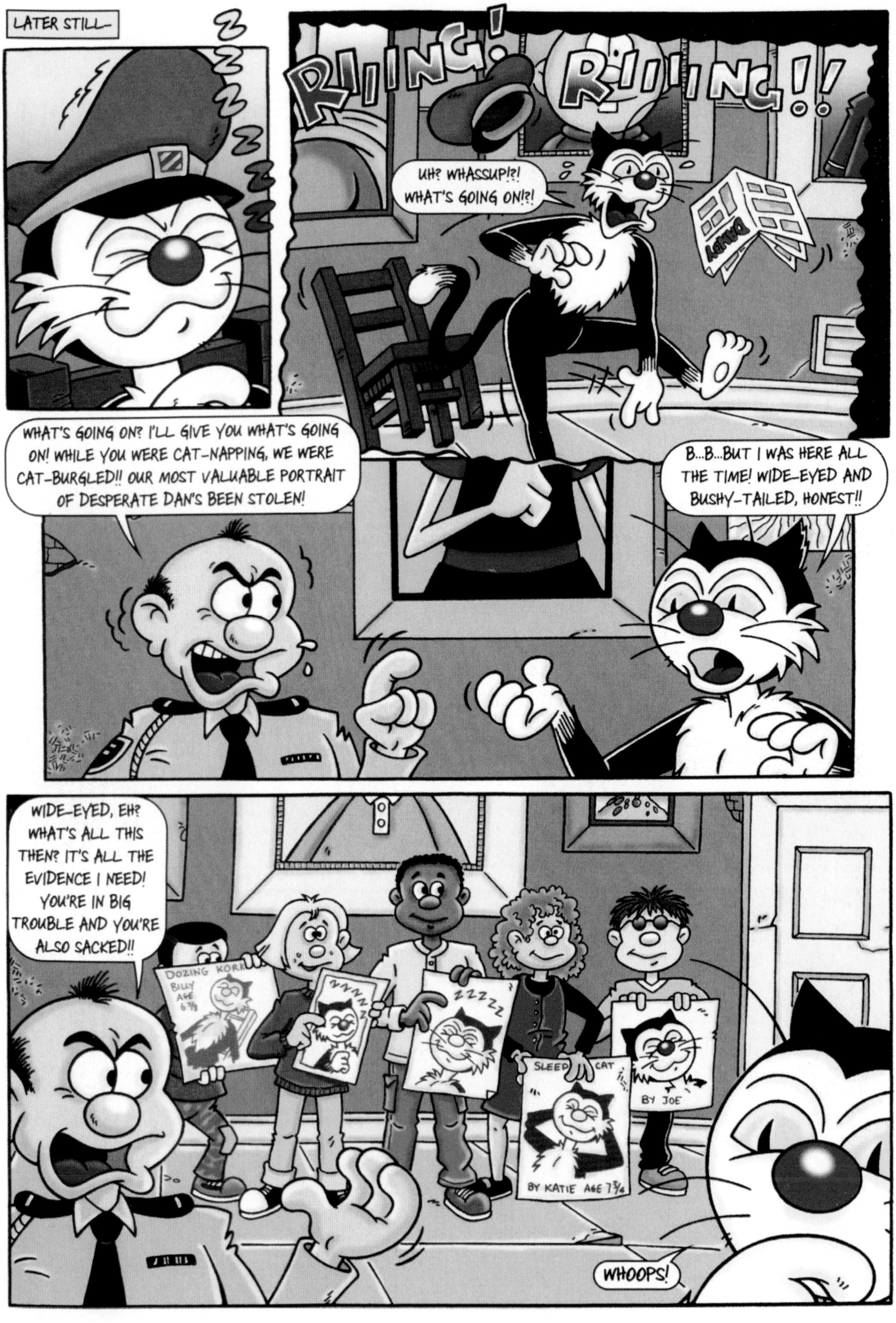
LATER STILL–
Z Z Z Z Z Z Z
RIIING! RIIIING!!
UH? WHASSUP!?! WHAT'S GOING ON!?!
DANDY
WHAT'S GOING ON? I'LL GIVE YOU WHAT'S GOING ON! WHILE YOU WERE CAT-NAPPING, WE WERE CAT-BURGLED!! OUR MOST VALUABLE PORTRAIT OF DESPERATE DAN'S BEEN STOLEN!
B...B...BUT I WAS HERE ALL THE TIME! WIDE-EYED AND BUSHY-TAILED, HONEST!!
WIDE-EYED, EH? WHAT'S ALL THIS THEN? IT'S ALL THE EVIDENCE I NEED! YOU'RE IN BIG TROUBLE AND YOU'RE ALSO SACKED!!
DOZING KORK BILLY AGE 6 7/8
ZZZZ
SLEEP CAT BY KATIE AGE 7 3/4
BY JOE
WHOOPS!

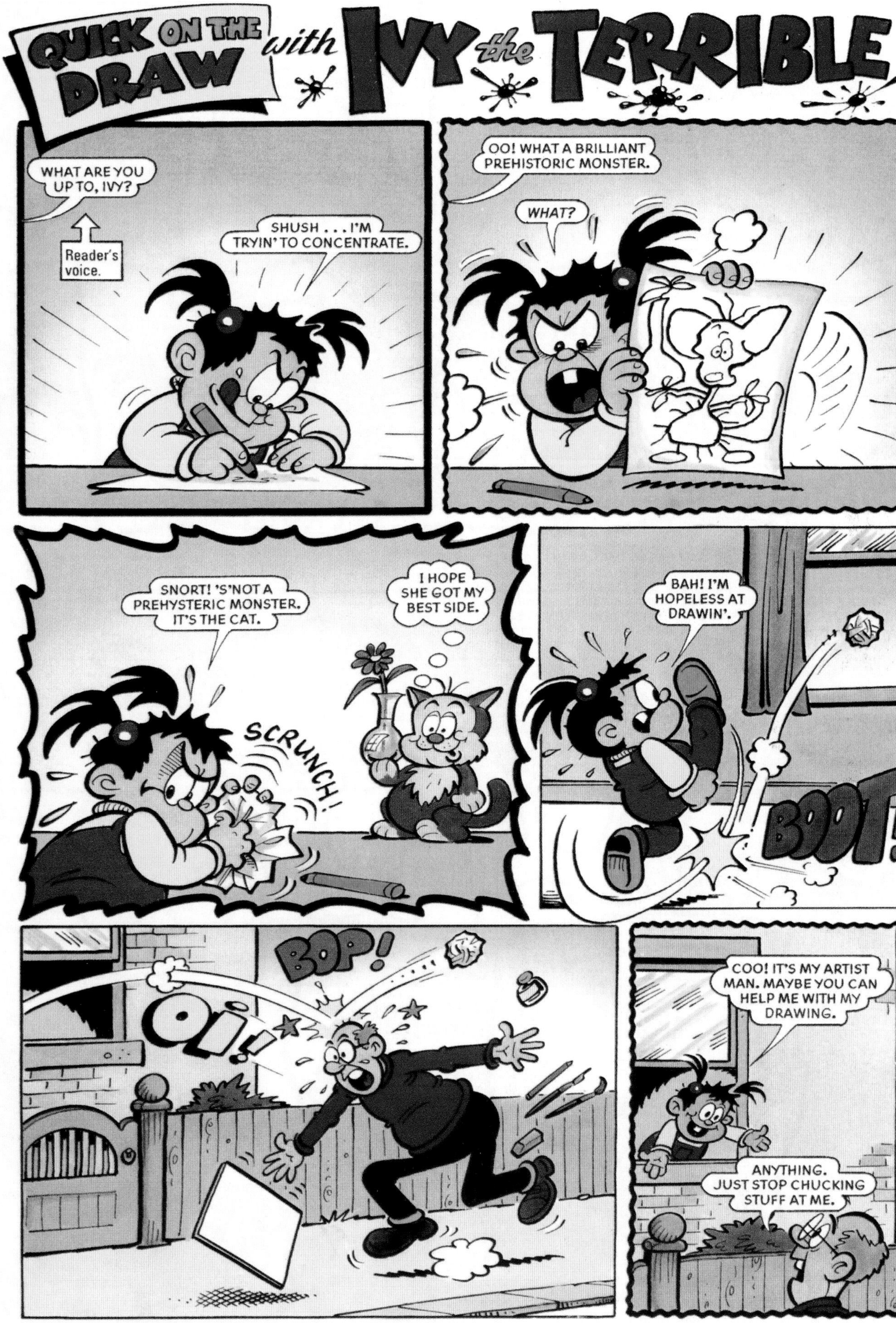
QUICK ON THE DRAW with IVY the TERRIBLE
WHAT ARE YOU UP TO, IVY?
Reader's voice.
SHUSH . . . I'M TRYIN' TO CONCENTRATE.
OO! WHAT A BRILLIANT PREHISTORIC MONSTER.
WHAT?
SNORT! 'S'NOT A PREHYSTERIC MONSTER. IT'S THE CAT.
I HOPE SHE GOT MY BEST SIDE.
SCRUNCH!
BAH! I'M HOPELESS AT DRAWIN'.
BOOT!
BOP!
OI!
COO! IT'S MY ARTIST MAN. MAYBE YOU CAN HELP ME WITH MY DRAWING.
ANYTHING. JUST STOP CHUCKING STUFF AT ME.

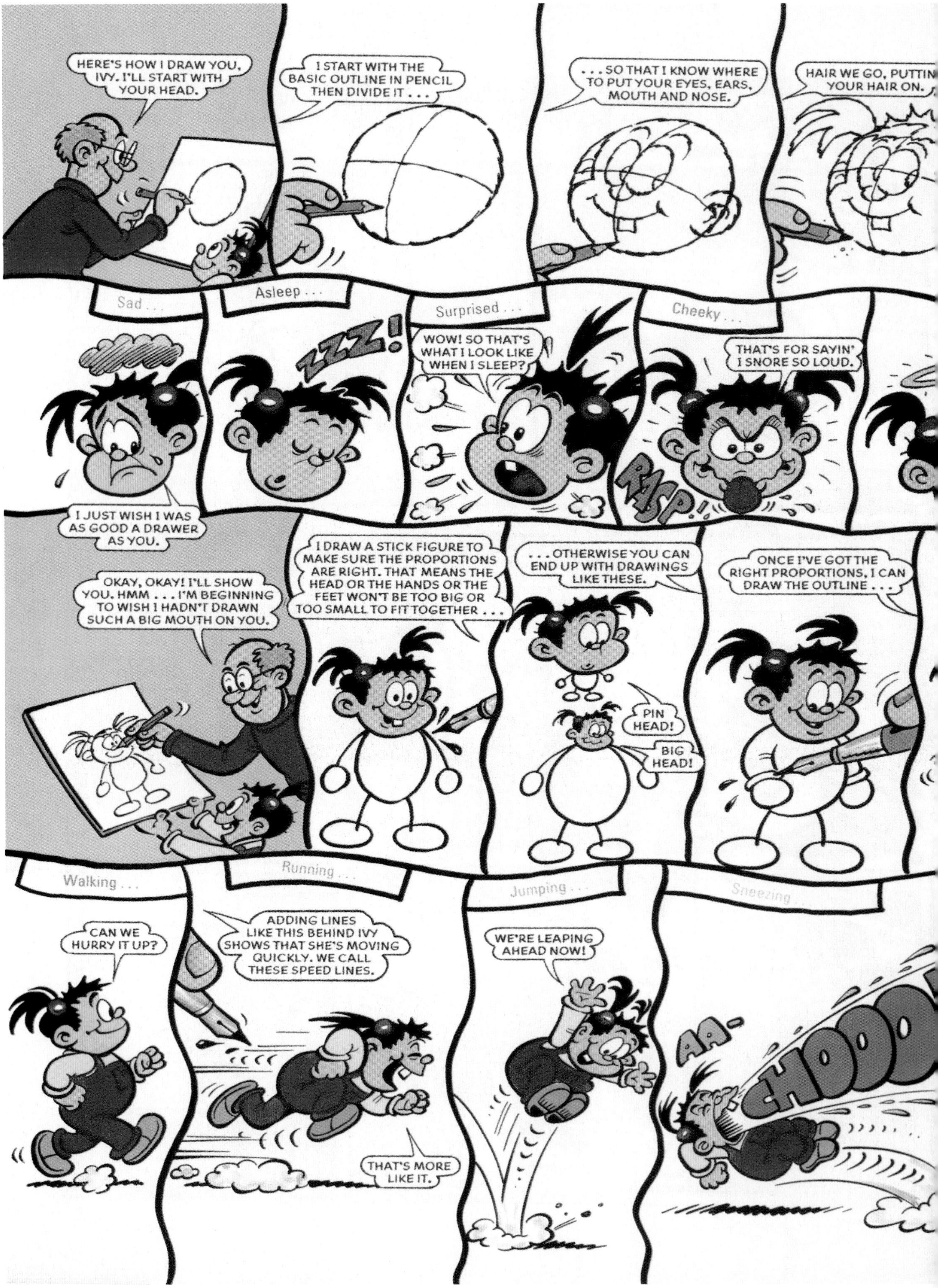
HERE'S HOW I DRAW YOU, IVY. I'LL START WITH YOUR HEAD.
I START WITH THE BASIC OUTLINE IN PENCIL THEN DIVIDE IT . . .
. . . SO THAT I KNOW WHERE TO PUT YOUR EYES, EARS, MOUTH AND NOSE.
HAIR WE GO, PUTTIN YOUR HAIR ON.
Sad . . .
Asleep . . .
ZZZ!
Surprised . . .
WOW! SO THAT'S WHAT I LOOK LIKE WHEN I SLEEP?
Cheeky . . .
THAT'S FOR SAYIN' I SNORE SO LOUD.
RASP!!
I JUST WISH I WAS AS GOOD A DRAWER AS YOU.
OKAY, OKAY! I'LL SHOW YOU. HMM . . . I'M BEGINNING TO WISH I HADN'T DRAWN SUCH A BIG MOUTH ON YOU.
I DRAW A STICK FIGURE TO MAKE SURE THE PROPORTIONS ARE RIGHT. THAT MEANS THE HEAD OR THE HANDS OR THE FEET WON'T BE TOO BIG OR TOO SMALL TO FIT TOGETHER . . .
. . . OTHERWISE YOU CAN END UP WITH DRAWINGS LIKE THESE.
PIN HEAD!
BIG HEAD!
ONCE I'VE GOT THE RIGHT PROPORTIONS, I CAN DRAW THE OUTLINE . . .
Walking . . .
CAN WE HURRY IT UP?
Running . . .
ADDING LINES LIKE THIS BEHIND IVY SHOWS THAT SHE'S MOVING QUICKLY. WE CALL THESE SPEED LINES.
THAT'S MORE LIKE IT.
Jumping . . .
WE'RE LEAPING AHEAD NOW!
Sneezing . . .
AA-
CHOOO

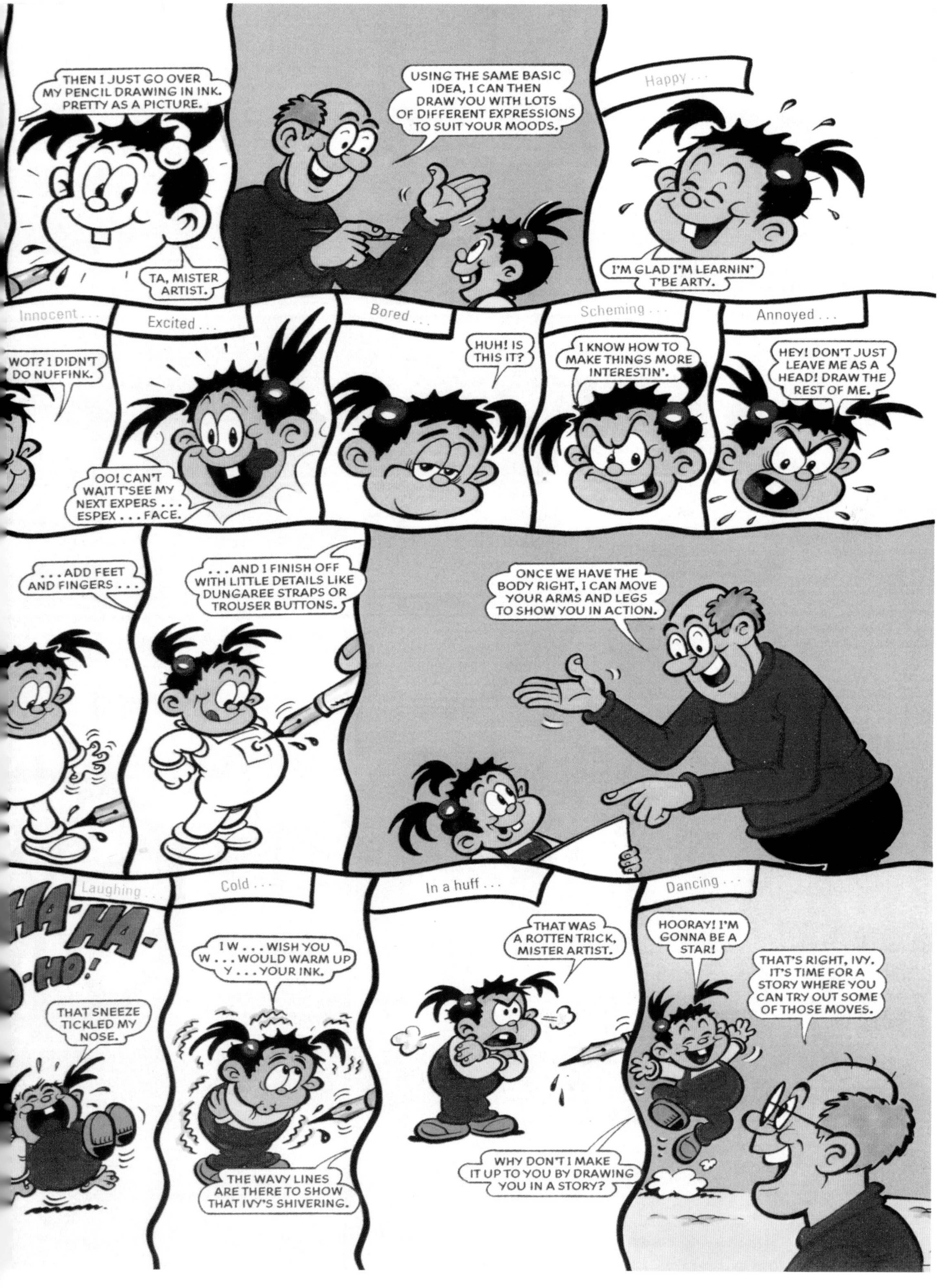
THEN I JUST GO OVER MY PENCIL DRAWING IN INK. PRETTY AS A PICTURE.
TA, MISTER ARTIST.
USING THE SAME BASIC IDEA, I CAN THEN DRAW YOU WITH LOTS OF DIFFERENT EXPRESSIONS TO SUIT YOUR MOODS.
Happy . . .
I'M GLAD I'M LEARNIN' T'BE ARTY.
Innocent . . .
WOT? I DIDN'T DO NUFFINK.
Excited . . .
OO! CAN'T WAIT T'SEE MY NEXT EXPERS . . . ESPEX . . . FACE.
Bored . . .
HUH! IS THIS IT?
Scheming . . .
I KNOW HOW TO MAKE THINGS MORE INTERESTIN'.
Annoyed . . .
HEY! DON'T JUST LEAVE ME AS A HEAD! DRAW THE REST OF ME.
. . . ADD FEET AND FINGERS . . .
. . . AND I FINISH OFF WITH LITTLE DETAILS LIKE DUNGAREE STRAPS OR TROUSER BUTTONS.
ONCE WE HAVE THE BODY RIGHT, I CAN MOVE YOUR ARMS AND LEGS TO SHOW YOU IN ACTION.
Laughing . . .
HA-HA-HO-HO!
THAT SNEEZE TICKLED MY NOSE.
Cold . . .
I W . . . WISH YOU W . . . WOULD WARM UP Y . . . YOUR INK.
THE WAVY LINES ARE THERE TO SHOW THAT IVY'S SHIVERING.
In a huff . . .
THAT WAS A ROTTEN TRICK, MISTER ARTIST.
WHY DON'T I MAKE IT UP TO YOU BY DRAWING YOU IN A STORY?
Dancing . . .
HOORAY! I'M GONNA BE A STAR!
THAT'S RIGHT, IVY. IT'S TIME FOR A STORY WHERE YOU CAN TRY OUT SOME OF THOSE MOVES.

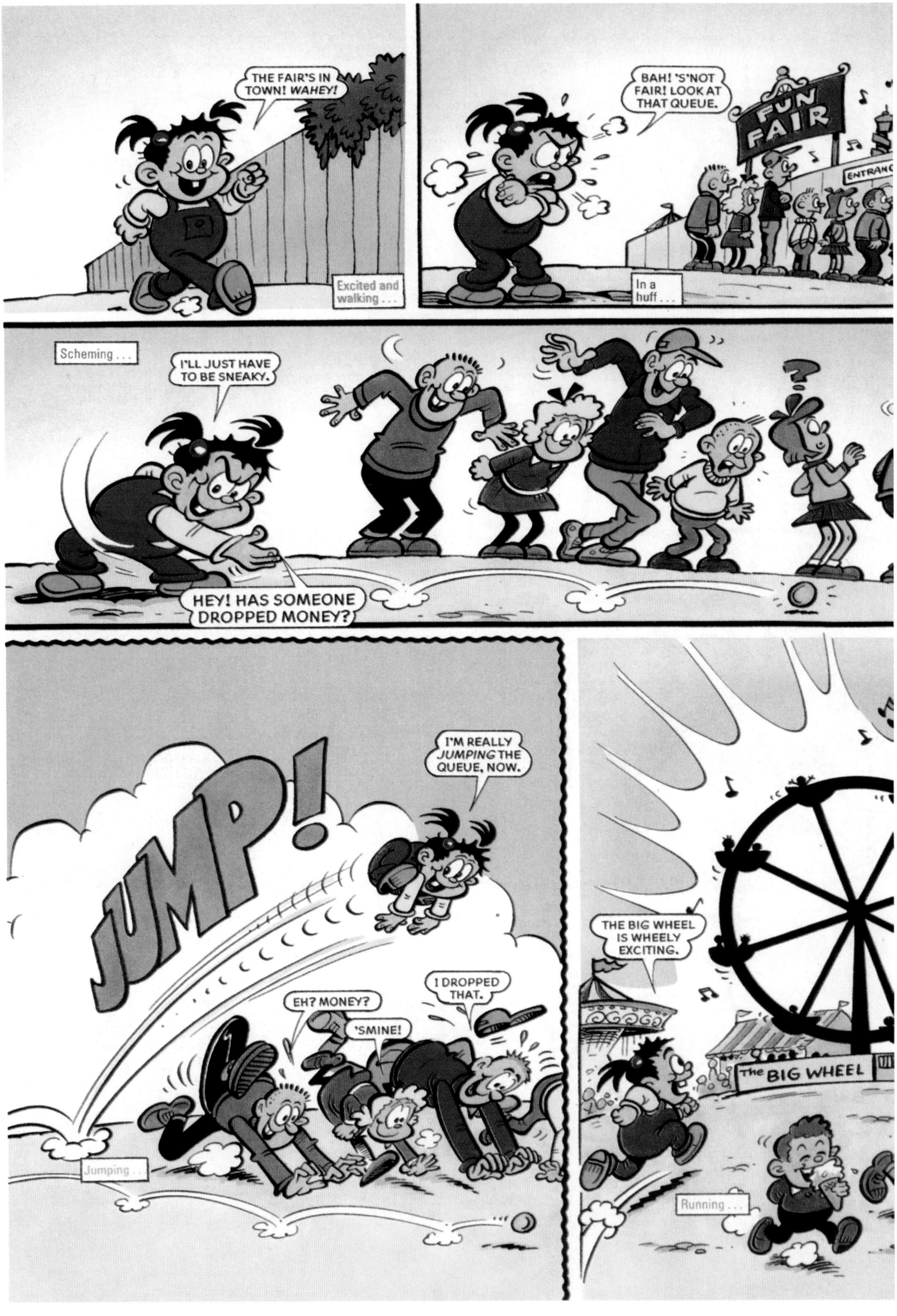
THE FAIR'S IN TOWN! WAHEY!
Excited and walking . . .
BAH! 'S'NOT FAIR! LOOK AT THAT QUEUE.
FUN FAIR
ENTRANC
In a huff . . .
Scheming . . .
I'LL JUST HAVE TO BE SNEAKY.
HEY! HAS SOMEONE DROPPED MONEY?
JUMP!
I'M REALLY JUMPING THE QUEUE, NOW.
EH? MONEY?
'SMINE!
I DROPPED THAT.
Jumping . . .
THE BIG WHEEL IS WHEELY EXCITING.
The BIG WHEEL
Running . . .

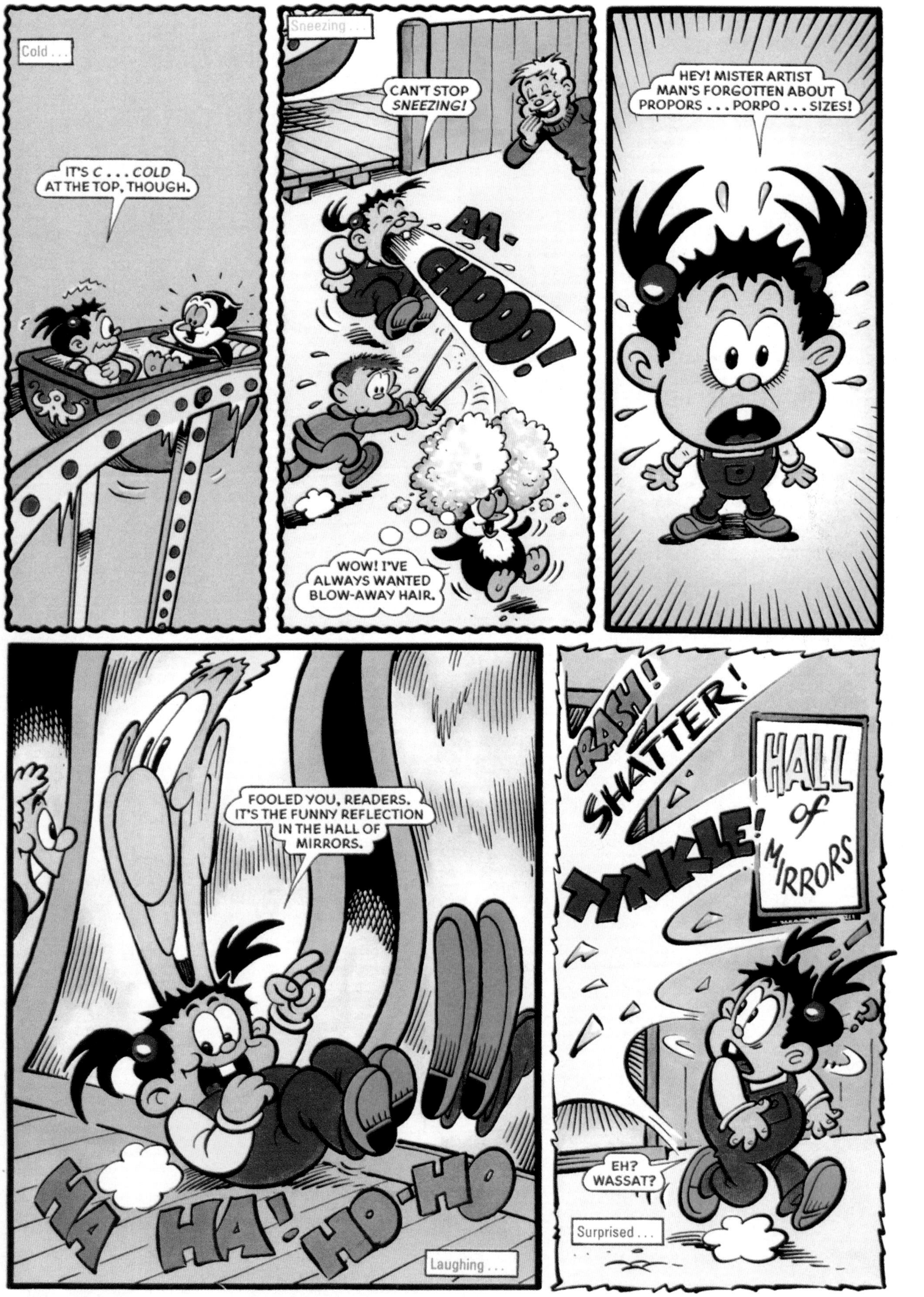
Cold . . .
IT'S C . . . COLD AT THE TOP, THOUGH.
Sneezing . . .
CAN'T STOP SNEEZING!
AA-CHOOO!
WOW! I'VE ALWAYS WANTED BLOW-AWAY HAIR.
HEY! MISTER ARTIST MAN'S FORGOTTEN ABOUT PROPORS . . . PORPO . . . SIZES!
FOOLED YOU, READERS. IT'S THE FUNNY REFLECTION IN THE HALL OF MIRRORS.
HA HA! HO-HO
Laughing . . .
CRASH! SHATTER! TYNKLE!
HALL of MIRRORS
EH? WASSAT?
Surprised . . .

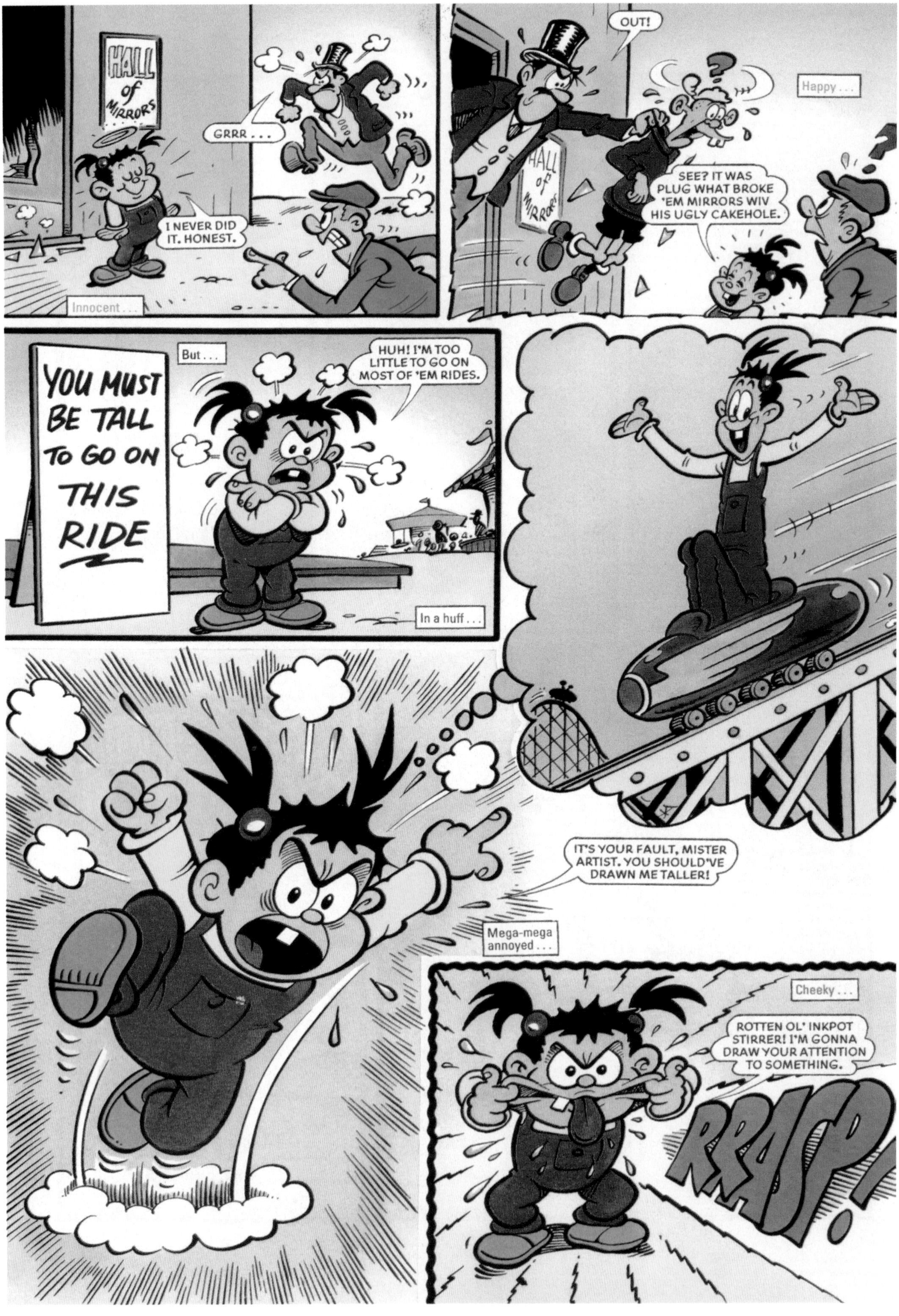

HALL of MIRRORS
GRRR . . .
I NEVER DID IT. HONEST.
Innocent . . .
OUT!
HALL of MIRRORS
SEE? IT WAS PLUG WHAT BROKE 'EM MIRRORS WIV HIS UGLY CAKEHOLE.
Happy . . .
YOU MUST BE TALL TO GO ON THIS RIDE
But . . .
HUH! I'M TOO LITTLE TO GO ON MOST OF 'EM RIDES.
In a huff . . .
IT'S YOUR FAULT, MISTER ARTIST. YOU SHOULD'VE DRAWN ME TALLER!
Mega-mega annoyed . . .
Cheeky . . .
ROTTEN OL' INKPOT STIRRER! I'M GONNA DRAW YOUR ATTENTION TO SOMETHING.
RRASP!

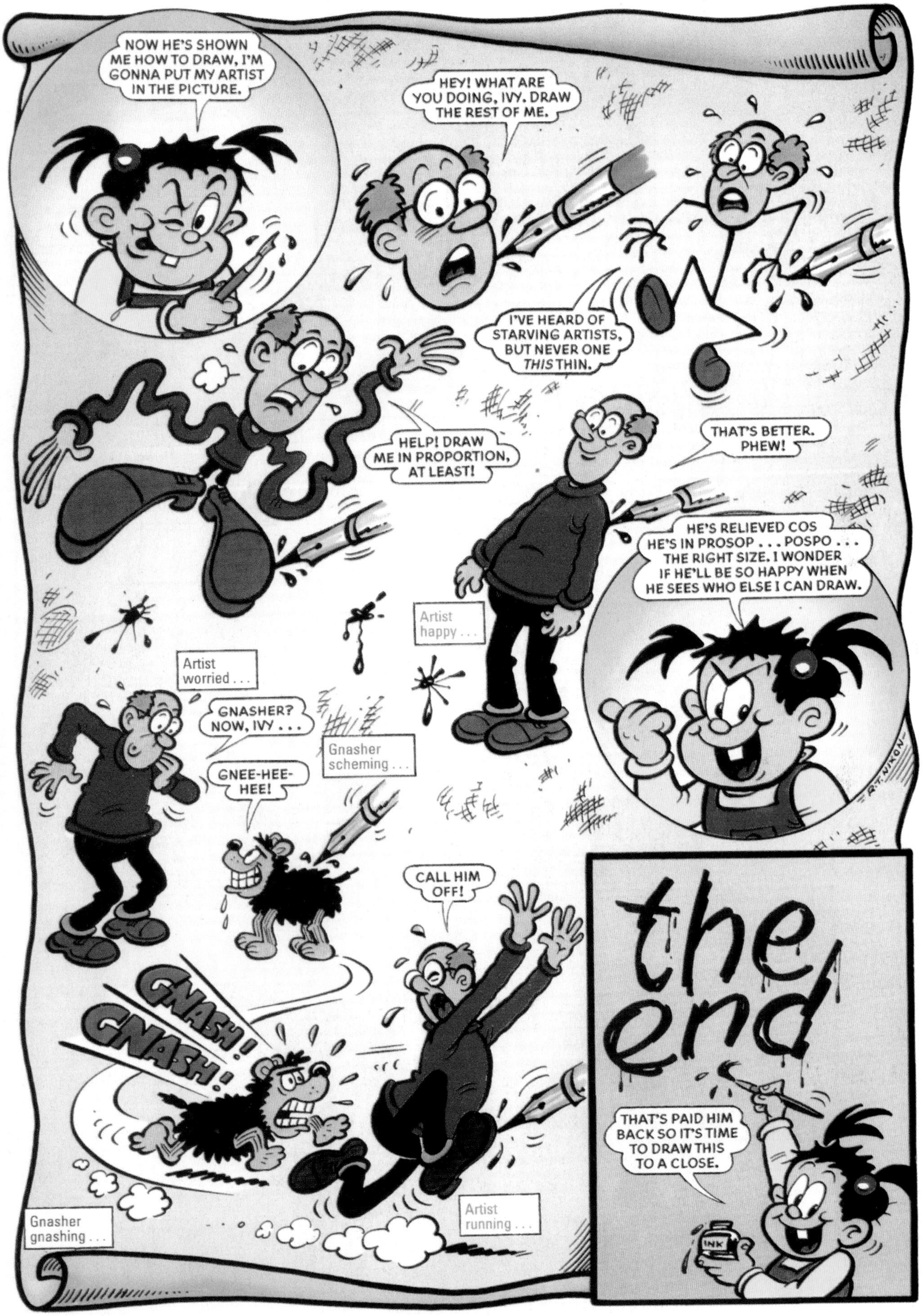
NOW HE'S SHOWN ME HOW TO DRAW, I'M GONNA PUT MY ARTIST IN THE PICTURE.
HEY! WHAT ARE YOU DOING, IVY. DRAW THE REST OF ME.
I'VE HEARD OF STARVING ARTISTS, BUT NEVER ONE *THIS* THIN.
HELP! DRAW ME IN PROPORTION, AT LEAST!
THAT'S BETTER. PHEW!
HE'S RELIEVED COS HE'S IN PROSOP . . . POSPO . . . THE RIGHT SIZE. I WONDER IF HE'LL BE SO HAPPY WHEN HE SEES WHO ELSE I CAN DRAW.
Artist happy . . .
Artist worried . . .
GNASHER? NOW, IVY . . .
Gnasher scheming . . .
GNEE-HEE-HEE!
CALL HIM OFF!
GNASH! GNASH!
Gnasher gnashing . . .
Artist running . . .
the end
THAT'S PAID HIM BACK SO IT'S TIME TO DRAW THIS TO A CLOSE.
INK
R.T. NIXON

the End

And there you have it! We hope you've enjoyed your tour of The Dandy and Beano's mirthful and magnificent masterworks. You'll have noticed our crafty characters have no issues making an exhibition of themselves, their nearest and dearest, or any other hapless individual who happens to cross their paint-splattered path. We hope they never change.

Please exit via the giftshop.

PEFC Certified
This product is from sustainably managed forests and controlled sources
PEFC
PEFC/16-31-107
www.pefc.co.uk

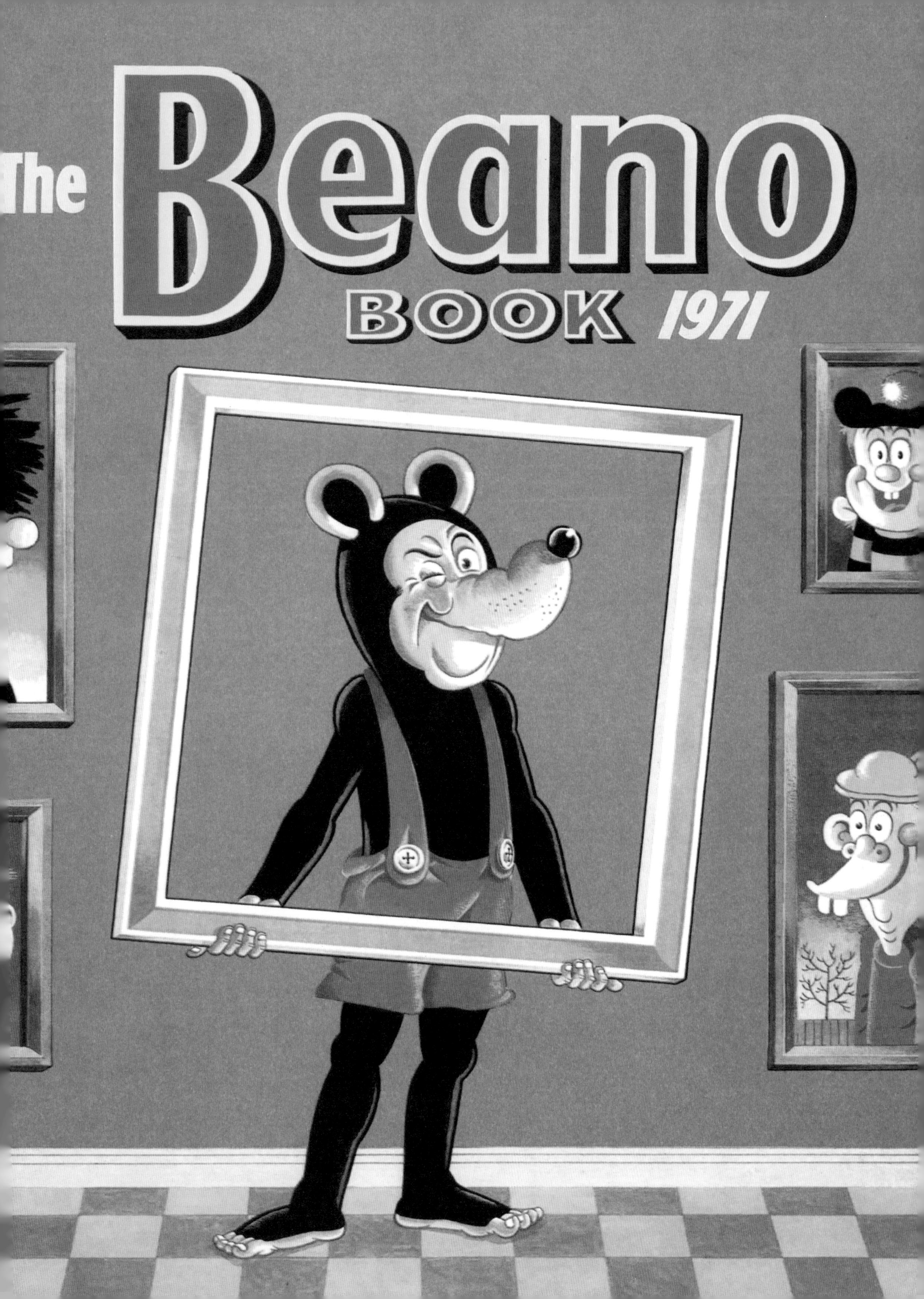
The Beano
BOOK 1971

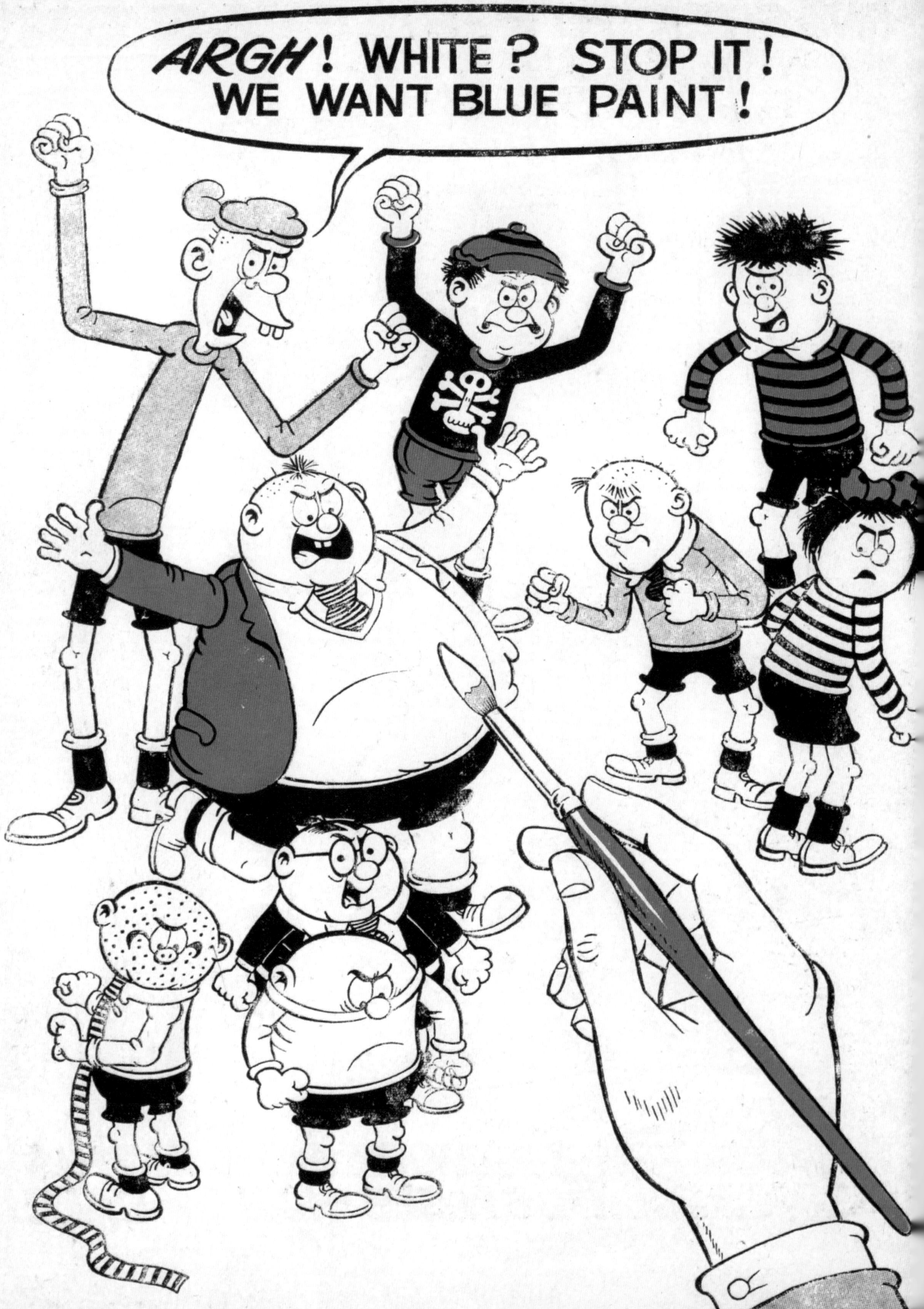
ARGH! WHITE? STOP IT! WE WANT BLUE PAINT!